Joel Best is Professor of Sociology and Criminal Justice at the University of Delaware and author of *Damned Lies and Statistics, Stat-Spotting*, and *Everyone's a Winner*, all from UC Press. **Eric Best** is Assistant Professor of Emergency Management at Jacksonville State University.

An Atkinson Book in Higher Education

Jacket design: Sandy Drooker. Jacket illustration: Chris Hall. Jacket images: iStock. Author photo: Kathy Atkinson, University of Delaware Photo Services.

D0593453

THE ATKINSON FAMILY

IMPRINT IN HIGHER EDUCATION

The Atkinson Family Foundation has endowed this imprint to

illuminate the role of higher education in contemporary society.

The publisher gratefully acknowledges the generous support of the Atkinson Family Imprint in Higher Education of the University of California Press Foundation, which was established by a major gift from the Atkinson Family Foundation.

The Student Loan Mess

The Student Loan Mess

How Good Intentions Created
a Trillion-Dollar Problem

Joel Best

Eric Best

UNIVERSITY OF CALIFORNIA PRESS

Berkeley   Los Angeles   London

University of California Press, one of the most distinguished university presses in the United States, enriches lives around the world by advancing scholarship in the humanities, social sciences, and natural sciences. Its activities are supported by the UC Press Foundation and by philanthropic contributions from individuals and institutions. For more information, visit www.ucpress.edu.

University of California Press
Berkeley and Los Angeles, California

University of California Press, Ltd.
London, England

"Awake at last." Editorial cartoon by Edwin Marcus, *New York Times* (October 13, 1957). Used by permission of the Marcus Family.

"Does this mean we have to sell the Porsche?" Editorial cartoon by Kate Salley Palmer, *Greenville [SC] News* (December 14, 1982). Used by permission of the Kate Salley Palmer Collection, The Ohio State University Cartoon Library and Museum.

"We are moving back into my old room." Editorial cartoon by John Darkow, *Columbia [MO] Daily Tribune* (October 28, 2011). Used by permission of Cagle Cartoons.

"Stylized Flow of Student Loan Processing." Reprinted from Edmiston, Brooks, and Shelpelwich, "Student Loans: Overview and Issues (Update)." *Federal Reserve Bank of Kansas City Research Working Papers,* April 2013. Used by permission.

"Aren't you tired of the rankings?" Doonesbury comic strip © by Garry B. Trudeau (August 7, 2012). Used by permission of Universal Uclick. All rights reserved.

"The True Size of the Student Debt Crisis." Dēmos.org (2013). Used by permission.

Library of Congress Cataloging-in-Publication Data

Best, Joel.
    The student loan mess : how good intentions created a trillion-dollar problem / Joel Best, Eric Best.
        pages   cm
    Includes bibliographical references and index.
    ISBN 978-0-520-27645-1 (hardback) — ISBN 978-0-520-95844-9 (e-book)
        1. Student loans—United States.   2. Student loans—Government policy—United States.
3. College graduates—United States—Finance, Personal.   I. Best, Eric.   II. Title.
    LB2340.2.B48   2014
    378.3'62—dc23

                                                                                    2013043272

Manufactured in the United States of America

23   22   21   20   19   18   17   16   15   14
10   9   8   7   6   5   4   3   2   1

In keeping with a commitment to support environmentally responsible and sustainable printing practices, UC Press has printed this book on Natures Natural, a fiber that contains 30% post-consumer waste and meets the minimum requirements of ANSI/NISO Z39.48–1992 (R 1997) (*Permanence of Paper*).

CONTENTS

FIGURES AND TABLE

FIGURES

TABLE

ACKNOWLEDGMENTS

A lot of people get interested when you tell them you're writing about student loans. We have lost track of all the people who directed our attention to specific topics and sources, and we apologize. However, we do want to thank Joan Best, Richard J. Mahoney, Michele Maughan, Dan Rich, and Leland Ware, who took the time to go through our entire manuscript and give us valuable feedback. Any errors and omissions are our own. We also want to thank the folks at the University of California Press who helped us create this book, especially Naomi Schneider, Dore Brown, Elizabeth Berg, and Christopher Lura.

Introduction

In 2012, when we decided to write this book, student loans had become—really for the first time ever—a hot topic. Protesters in the Occupy Wall Street movement called for forgiving all student loan debt, even as the high unemployment rate encouraged more young people to stay out of the workforce and pursue a college education. There were news reports that total student loan debt had reached a trillion dollars, that Americans now owed more on student loans than on their credit cards. Young people leaving school were finding that their student loan debt made it vastly harder to launch careers, start families, or buy homes. Some critics warned about an expanding student loan bubble that would inevitably pop and drive the economy into another severe recession, while others challenged the established wisdom that going to college was the most promising route to fulfilling the American Dream.

How, you might ask, did we get into this mess?

This book tries to answer that question. But it doesn't concentrate solely on *this mess* (that is, today's complaints about that trillion-dollar debt, the frustrations of young people trying to deal with massive student loan debt on top of all the other challenges they face, or potential consequences should the bubble burst). Instead, we adopt a broader perspective. Our goal is to understand how we *got into* this mess. And that turns out to be a really interesting story.

It is a story of good intentions gone awry. (Recall the proverb, more than three hundred years old: "The road to hell is paved with good intentions.") Federal student loan programs started as a way to help young Americans get ahead during the Cold War years of the 1950s and 1960s: student loans seemed to offer a solution to what was then considered a social problem—too many bright kids couldn't afford to go to college, causing America to waste precious brainpower. We'll call that the *first student loan mess*.

The earliest student loan programs were inspired by idealism, but we're telling an ironic story. Policies designed to solve social problems don't always work as planned; they can create new, unexpected difficulties. Thus, while we might like to imagine that there is only a single student loan mess, our story is about a series of student loan *messes,* each a reaction to how people understood and tried to resolve an earlier mess. For example, solving the first student loan mess by creating loan programs that would give every promising young person access to college had an unexpected consequence: too many borrowers failed to repay their student loans, and that problem—deadbeat students—became what we'll call the *second student loan mess.* This cycle—the solution to one mess creating the conditions that came to be understood as the next, even bigger mess—has repeated itself several times and continues today. So the short answer to our question is that we got into our current student loan mess by trying to solve earlier messes, and our next mess is likely to be shaped by what we do to solve the one we're in right now. This is both a surprising story and an important one. We didn't wind up in our current mess by accident; we got there by creating well-intentioned policies without thinking through the likely consequences of our actions. And if we want to avoid setting the stage for an even bigger mess, we ought to ask ourselves what we can learn from the tangled history of student loans.

This book is the product of an intergenerational collaboration: Joel and Eric are father and son. We approach our topic from different orientations. Joel is a sociologist who studies social problems; he has been planning to write about student loans for years. Eric majored in economics, then worked in the corporate loan department of a major investment bank before returning to graduate school to earn a master's degree in economics and a PhD in disaster science and management. While working on his dissertation, Eric became interested in student loans and started publishing pieces on the topic.[1] Recognizing that the topic interested both of us but appreciating that we saw it from different angles, we decided to join forces.

OUR STORIES: FOUR GENERATIONS OF OLDEST SONS

Eric is Joel's oldest son. Joel, in turn, was the oldest son of Gordon Best (1919–1986), and Gordon was the oldest son of George Best (1882–1970). The four of us had very different experiences with higher education, and our stories say a lot about how education has changed in the United States.

George grew up on his father's farm, outside Walhalla, in the northeastern corner of North Dakota, just a few miles south of the Canadian border. After he retired from farming, George wrote and self-published a memoir.[2] As a boy, he finished normal school (eighth grade), and then went to work on the family farm. By 1902, when he was twenty, he had saved enough money to afford spending the winter months in town to further his education. The following year, he hoped to begin studying at "the A.C." (the agricultural college, North Dakota's land-grant college located in distant Fargo, today called North Dakota State University), but that summer brought a bad harvest. In his memoir, George recalled: "That was a black day in my life. With Father at that age, Mother and five minors needing a roof over their heads and something to eat, I was mentally shackled there." He would go on to marry Nellie Storey, herself a normal-school graduate who'd started teaching school when she was fifteen, and they had four children: "Nellie, who wanted to see them all through college, drove them relentlessly."

George reports that "Gordon, being the rebellious type, finally jumped school" after graduating from Walhalla's high school. Gordon went to work in town but was soon drafted in the run-up to World War II. He saw combat in the Pacific and became seriously ill; he spent much of the war in military hospitals. As soon as the war ended, he married Beth Greene, who was a college graduate and a schoolteacher. She encouraged Gordon to take advantage of the GI Bill. They held down expenses by living with her parents in Lincoln, Nebraska, while Gordon attended the state university and worked part-time. Gordon became one of the World War II veterans who graduated from college thanks to the support of the GI Bill.[3] His degree in business administration qualified him for a job at Minneapolis Honeywell, where he would have a thirty-year career in middle management.

Joel was a first-year baby boomer, born in 1946.[4] His family moved into a brand-new housing development in Roseville, a suburb just north of Saint Paul, Minnesota, filled with the young families being started by veterans, who were able to buy homes with low-interest veterans' loans. Roseville's schools had to expand to deal with all those boomers; most years, Joel was taught in a brand-new classroom. When he entered the University of Minnesota in 1964, tuition and fees totaled about $75 per quarter. Obviously, the state of Minnesota subsidized much of the cost of his education. In early 1967, tuition and fees were raised to $125 per quarter (about $875 in 2013 dollars), which inspired an outcry. Joel lived at home and commuted to the university; he also received a small scholarship ($125 per year) from Honeywell, and he worked a couple of summers and part-time while he was a student to earn a little money. Joel started graduate school with a fellowship from the National Institute of Mental Health; this amounted to a federal scholarship for graduate study that covered his tuition and fees, and paid a stipend of $1,800 during his first year of study. At the end of the year, he had more money in his savings account than he did at the start (possible because he did not own a car at the time). His out-of-pocket costs for his undergraduate and graduate educations, including tuition and fees, books, and supplies, probably totaled under $1,000; when he received his PhD in 1971, he had no debt.

When Eric started college in 2001, the educational landscape had changed. Anticipating that educating their two sons might be expensive, Eric's parents, Joel and Joan, had set aside what seemed like a fair amount of money. By the time Eric earned his bachelor's degree in economics, most of his share of that money had been spent; although he received his degree from the University of Delaware (where Joel taught and which charged children of faculty very little to attend), he'd had to pay for computing equipment, books, rent in off-campus apartments, and so on. After graduation, Eric worked for a couple of years in the corporate loan office of a major bank, where he handled syndicated loans, essentially large blocks of corporate debt.

Even before the Great Recession began, Eric began to find his job unfulfilling, and he decided to return to graduate school. Eric did not qualify for financial aid, nor was he offered an assistantship during his first year in grad school. Eric's bill for the first year was about $20,000 before fees, books, and other expenses. Eric chose to apply for a federal student loan to cover the cost of that first year of grad school, because he figured that retaining some savings was better than avoiding all debt. Without consulting with his parents, and applying for the loan on a website, Eric had his entire tuition paid by the U.S. government, in addition to receiving a one-time check for living expenses "related to school." After the first year, Eric received research assistantships that paid his tuition and provided a small stipend.

Eric took a tenure-track job at a university immediately after completing his PhD and does not expect paying back student loans to be more than a mild financial inconvenience. However, he was lucky to find a stable, relatively high-earning job immediately after graduation, something that is far from a given for current graduates. Although he is in a good position financially, something like a year of unemployment after school (a realistic possibility in the recent job climate) would have been disastrous.

Those are four stories from four generations of our family. It should be clear that our individual lives were shaped by what was happening in the larger society: George had to choose between furthering his education and fulfilling his responsibility to keep the family farm going. The draft and the GI Bill propelled Gordon from that same farm to a corporate career in a metropolis, while Joel rode the wave of the baby boom, and the global recession affected what happened to Eric. The sorts of education the four of us received and the ways we paid for it—what we could afford, and what we chose to buy—reflected big historical changes: what was happening in the world and what sorts of government policies were in place. We can't but wonder how social changes might affect the educational prospects of our family's next generation. Understanding these intersections between personal experiences and societal changes is what the sociologist C. Wright Mills called the *sociological imagination*.[5] Our goal is to show how big societal changes—and good intentions—led to a series of student loan messes.

OUR APPROACH

Our collaboration is interdisciplinary, as well as intergenerational. As a sociologist, Joel studies the processes by which social problems come to public attention. In this view, social problems are best thought of not as conditions that simply exist in society but as processes by which people come to recognize and try to arouse concern about particular topics; those efforts may lead policymakers to address what they now understand to be a troubling condition, and their policies in turn inspire different reactions.[6] This is a perspective that focuses on language, on what people *say*, on the words they choose when describing what's wrong and prescribing what ought to be done to fix it.

This book traces the shifting ways people have talked about student loans. The history of federal student loans is a story of successive redefinitions of the problem, each identifying a challenging aspect of the larger student loan problem—what we'll call a *student loan mess*. While lots of people have recognized that student loans pose a problem, they haven't all defined that problem in the same ways. Rather, at different periods, people's attention focused on particular aspects of the problem—on a particular mess. Our point is not that these various understandings were wrong, but rather that each mess drew attention to particular features of student loans, much the way a magnifying glass helps us better see part of a larger whole. But just as what isn't magnified tends to be out of focus or lost from view, focusing on a particular mess allowed people to ignore other aspects of student loans. As each successive mess attracted attention, social policies were invented, reformed, or replaced to address the current vision of the student loan problem. Often these policies had unexpected, ironic consequences, in that the ways people reacted to the new policies led to people discovering a new mess, as different aspects of the student loan problem now became the focus of attention. Joel has been thinking about this process, about the way the student loan problem keeps being redefined, for a long time. He's talked about writing a book on the changing definitions of the student loan problem for at least twenty-five years.

Eric studies how regulation (or lack of regulation) changes market behavior—that is, how economic theory relates to public policy. Most of his day-to-day work involves complex computer models and quantitative analysis, but while this book will show that the numbers related to student loans are important, the messes were not the result of creative accounting (although some interesting interpretations about repayment are involved). In Eric's view, the current student lending situation is not an accident or a cause for outrage. It is a story about how Americans incrementally and willingly created our current student loan mess over the last seventy years and what we can do to fix it. His is a perspective that focuses on the intersections of policy, institutional pressures, and individual behavior. The mission of this book is to explain what happened—and what might happen in the future—in a clear manner, free of complicated statistics.

Eric has firsthand experience with the insatiable demand for student loans on both the supply side, in the form of collateral in "student loan asset-backed securities" (SLABS) sold at the bank where he worked, and the demand side, in conversations with college and grad school friends about the costs of financing their educations. He's been badgering Joel to write a book about student loans for the past two years, going as far as publishing about the issue to prove there was interest in this type of research.

Because we come at the topic of student loans from different backgrounds, this book's analysis is rooted in interdisciplinary collaboration. Our conversations, often around holiday dinner tables over groans from the rest of the family, made us realize that we tended to notice different aspects of the topic. Joel emphasizes the social side of student lending and sees the current student loan mess as just the latest way of thinking about a rather old issue. Eric is more interested in the relationship between money and policy, and sees the current student loan policies as a disaster in the making, as much for institutions and the government as for individual students. Neither of us could have or would have written this book as a sole author, but we believe that together we can tell an interesting story and even offer some recommendations.

PLAN OF THE BOOK

This book does not focus on blaming particular people for the student loan messes, nor does it propose a single "solution" to the problem. What it does offer is an overview of student lending and higher education in the United States, as well as suggestions about ways to make future student loan messes—and they are inevitable—more manageable. With more than a trillion dollars of student loan debt in circulation and that total ballooning with each passing year, it is clear that we will not be able to make the problem disappear in a flash. Cleaning up a multigenerational problem is going to be mind-bogglingly expensive, but importantly, it will likely be cheaper than not cleaning it up. Everyone needs to understand that whatever reforms we devise

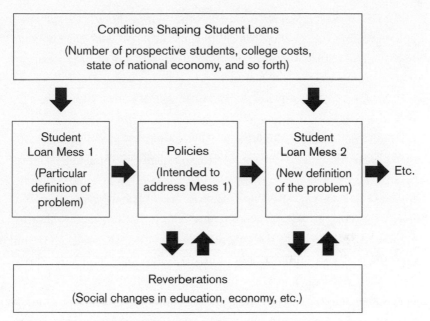

Figure 1. How student loan messes evolve.

are likely to lead to new messes, new discussions, and new policy recommendations.

The history we discuss isn't all that complicated, but it needs to be understood if we are to make sense of our current mess. Unless we acknowledge how our good intentions went awry, we run the risk of creating yet another, even bigger student loan mess as we try to "solve" the problem. Figure 1 illustrates how we conceptualize these processes.

Each chapter, then, examines a particular student loan mess. Each examines how people came to identify particular aspects of student loans as troubling; we then show how they devised social policies to clean up that mess. In addition, each chapter will identify what we call *reverberations*—social changes in the larger society. These changes were not always understood as important—or as directly related to student loans—and they tended to be ignored when people were thinking about devising student loan policies. Nonetheless, these developments, coupled with the unanticipated consequences of whatever policies emerged to address the current mess, helped shape the next student loan mess.

Chapter 1 describes the first student loan mess—the need to establish loan programs that could open access to higher education for all talented young people. This chapter concentrates on the period from 1958 (when the first broad federal student loan program began) until 1972 (when creating Sallie Mae seemed to guarantee stable access to loans). Chapter 2 considers the second student loan mess, when policymakers became alarmed by the unexpectedly high rates of default by borrowers; this topic began to attract attention in the mid-1960s and continued to be a focus of concern until 1998 (when it became nearly impossible for most borrowers to discharge student loan debts by declaring bankruptcy). The third student loan mess, discussed in chapter 3, focuses on growing student loan debt as a crushing burden; this chapter begins in the mid-1990s and ends—somewhat arbitrarily—during Barack Obama's first term. In fact, we are well aware that people continue to talk about crushing debt, that the third student loan mess has not yet ended. However, we also want to draw attention to what we call the fourth student loan mess, which is the subject of chapter 4: the concern that there is a student loan bubble (particularly in for-profit higher education) that threatens to collapse and cause widespread economic damage. This chapter outlines what can happen when market participants actively manipulate well-intentioned policies. People began actively worrying about this bubble shortly after the Great Recession began in 2008.

We argue that each mess was a product of what was ignored in the policies dealing with the preceding mess and of the reverberations in the larger society. Each successive mess has seemed more alarming than its predecessor. This raises the question, What's next? Will there be a fifth student loan mess, and a sixth, and so on? How bad can things get? Chapter 5 tries to imagine where the discussions of student loans are likely to head, by considering what the fourth student loan mess seems to ignore. Finally, chapter 6 offers our suggestions for thinking about and devising policies for student loans.

STUDENT LOANS—WHAT'S THE PROBLEM?

Our thesis, then, is that what might at first glance seem to be a single problem with a single name—student loans—is better understood as a series of problems, or messes. Each of these messes has had advocates who identified particular aspects of student loans as troubling and called for action—and those advocates were successful, in the sense that they changed social policies to address the aspects of student loans that concerned them. However, aspects that get ignored in one mess have a way of becoming central to the next mess.

One reason it has been easy to focus on a series of narrowly defined issues while ignoring the bigger picture is that discussions of student loans have been guided by a set of widely shared assumptions. While not absolutely everyone has shared each of these assumptions, there has been fairly broad consensus about all of them. These shared ideas have provided the foundation for the good intentions that got us here. We outline these assumptions here, and then revisit them later in this book. These key assumptions are:

1. Higher education is a good thing and should be encouraged— the more educated the nation's population, the better.

2. Because individuals who choose to receive more education benefit directly, they should bear most of the costs of that education. A major attraction of student loan programs is that they allow the government to help young people get more education while holding the beneficiaries of those loans responsible for repaying what they borrow.

3. Federal loan policies should not discriminate among educational institutions—young people should be free to choose what and

where they want to study, and they should be eligible for student loans to attend any school that will admit them.

4. Federal loan policies should not discriminate among borrowers. All students should have access to loans on essentially the same terms.

It is easy to nod along while reading over this list of assumptions; they all seem reasonable. But, as we will see, sharing—and not thinking critically about—these assumptions has had serious consequences.

In many ways, America's higher education system has come to resemble our health care system. Both systems are extremely expensive, compared to those in other democracies. Higher education consumes a larger share of our GDP—and costs vastly more per student—than it does in other countries.[7] Yet both systems produce somewhat disappointing results. Where the United States once led the world in the proportion of college graduates among its younger citizens, a number of other countries now boast higher college graduation rates. Perhaps the time has come to ask why we aren't getting a bigger bang from our higher education bucks.

CHAPTER ONE

Good Intentions
and Wasted Brainpower

The First Student Loan Mess

When you were young, you doubtless had this conversation with a parent, a teacher, or some other older person who wanted to help you get ahead:

OLDER PERSON: You need to do well in school.

YOU: Why?

OLDER PERSON: Because you need good grades to get into college.

YOU: Why do I want to go to college?

OLDER PERSON: Because you need a college education to get a good job.

That put things in pretty practical terms. The older person probably didn't talk about a love of learning or some refined sensibility that comes from higher education. Instead, you were encouraged to view college as a ladder, a route toward a better life. When people talk about the American Dream, they often envision something better for the next generation: a more comfortable, secure life made possible by more education. This perspective focuses on what education can do for individuals; it is *individualistic.*

But it is also possible to adopt a loftier viewpoint, to consider what higher education does for an entire nation or society. From this perspective, when more people get more education, we're all better off: we increase our stock of human capital or human resources. Thus when public policy wonks talk about workforce quality, they define it simply in terms of average education. If Country A's people have, on average, one more year of schooling than Country B's population, then Country A is considered to have a higher-quality workforce. A more educated population means more knowledge, more skills, more people who can do more to make things better for all of us. This is a broader *communal* perspective, in that it sees education as benefiting the larger community.

These individualistic and communal perspectives coexist. When parents encourage their kid to do well in school, they are thinking of a college education as something that will be good for their particular child. But imparting individual aspirations to lots of young people results in a communal benefit. The more educated a population, the more productive and prosperous its citizenry. More education reduces all sorts of social problems: on average, educated people live longer, are healthier, have more stable families, are less likely to get into trouble with the law, and so on. More education benefits individuals at the same time that it benefits the community.[1] It is a win-win.

This is why governments invest in education. In colonial America, schooling was a private, individualistic affair; if you wanted your child taught, you paid the schoolmaster for the lessons, all the way through college (Harvard and other early colleges were all private institutions). But as the United States emerged as a great nation, the state and federal governments began supporting education. States passed laws requiring minimal levels of universal education, and communities made that possible by building schools; while you could choose to have your child taught at a private or parochial school, publicly funded schools were available for all children. Over time, states raised their minimum standards for completing schooling. A century ago, many states required only an eighth-grade education; today, most states require that students stay in school until they turn sixteen or seventeen. The logic behind these requirements is that the state benefits if all its citizens are educated. And to ensure that they had enough teachers to teach all those children, as well as enough people trained for engineering and other needed professions, states established their own public colleges and universities.

The federal government also threw its support behind higher education. For instance, the 1862 Morrill Act gave each state federal land to be used to establish a land-grant college that would promote scientific agriculture and engineering. This policy was inspired by a communal vision: by supporting higher education, the federal government would foster a trained workforce that would make farming and industry more productive and, in the process, strengthen the nation. Similarly, at the end of World War II, the GI Bill provided a variety of benefits for returning veterans, including support for those who wanted to attend college. The law was intended to ward off the sorts of protests by angry veterans that had followed World War I, but it also had the communal effect of boosting the nation's stock of human capital.

In other words, Americans have long understood that higher education is a good thing, which brings both individualistic and communal benefits. Parents believe that their children will have brighter prospects if they go to college, even as policymakers understand that a more highly educated population is key to the nation's strength and prosperity. We accept that higher education is important, something that people should want for themselves and for others. Going to college seems interwoven with widely shared, important ideals about equality, opportunity, progress, and the American Dream. There is general agreement: people who aspire to attend college deserve encouragement and assistance.

Like the Morrill Act and the GI Bill, federal student loan policies began as a response to Americans' general approval and endorsement of higher education. This chapter describes the evolution of these policies through 1972, when President Richard Nixon signed legislation establishing the Student Loan Marketing Association (better known as Sallie Mae). It examines the rising demand for higher education and the recognition that college costs posed a key obstacle for many prospective students, and it also describes how specific, federally funded student loan policies emerged to meet these concerns. In addition, it argues that these policies reflected a growing acceptance of credit as a routine, nontroubling feature in the lives of middle- and working-class Americans. It is a story of the ideals, aspirations, and well-intentioned policies that produced the initial student loan mess. But understanding that story requires that we begin by appreciating the dramatic rise in the proportion of Americans seeking higher education during the twentieth century.

THE SPREAD OF HIGHER EDUCATION

Widespread convictions regarding the benefits of higher education led a growing proportion of Americans to complete high school and continue their educations. This was one of the twentieth century's most dramatic social changes. At the century's beginning, college graduates were rare: only about 2–3 percent of adults earned college degrees.[2] A disproportionate percentage of those graduates were white males who had grown up in comfortable circumstances. Males far outnumbered females on campus; women earned less than a fifth of the bachelor's degrees awarded in 1900.[3] No one seems to have kept official records on how many African Americans completed college at the beginning of the twentieth century, but they accounted for less than 1 percent of all graduates; although some historically black colleges and universities (HBCUs) were founded in the nineteenth century, "it was not until the early 1900s that HBCUs began to offer courses and programs at the postsecondary level."[4] In an era when most children who completed their schooling were expected to start work and contribute their earnings to their families, those who entered college were far more likely to have grown up in relatively privileged homes.[5]

By the end of the twentieth century, attending and completing college had become far more common, not only among white men but also

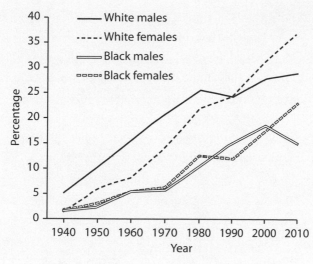

Figure 2. Percentage of whites and blacks ages 25–29
having completed four or more years of college, by sex,
1940–2010. Source: U.S. Census Bureau (2012a).

among women and African Americans. We can see this in figure 2,
which covers the period 1940–2010 and shows the percentages of people
twenty-five to twenty-nine years old with at least four years of college—which we'll treat as equivalent to graduating from college. We've
chosen to examine the age group twenty-five to twenty-nine, rather
than everyone over twenty-five, because the latter category includes
older people (who were much less likely to attend college back in the
day). Although some people graduate from college after leaving their
twenties, most complete college by age twenty-five, so using the
twenty-five to twenty-nine age category tracks the trend in how much
education people have early in their adult careers, at a time in life when
most people who are going to complete college have done so.

The four lines in figure 2 trace the percentages of college graduates
among white males, white females, black males, and black females from
1940 to 2010. All four groups show dramatic increases. In 1940, even the
most educated group, white males, had only about 5 percent college

graduates—not all that much higher than it had been at the beginning of the century. But in 2010, the proportion of white males with four or more years of college was almost 29 percent—more than five times greater than in 1940. The percentage of college graduates within the other three groups grew even faster: more than twenty-five times as many white women, nearly ten times as many black men, and thirteen times more black women twenty-five to twenty-nine had completed college in 2010, compared to 1940.[6]

Of course, demonstrating that a growing proportion of young people are completing college is not all that surprising. After all, young Americans have long been encouraged to pursue higher education for both its individualistic and its communal benefits. But note that figure 2 reveals other, less obvious information. Through 1980, white men maintained their historical lead as the group with the highest percentage of college graduates. But in 1990 white women caught up, and by 2000 they had taken what would become a commanding lead. In 2010, 36.9 percent of white women had completed college, versus only 28.8 percent of white men; the 8.1 percent gap between the two groups was actually greater than it had been at any time when graduation rates for white men were ahead of those for white women. Figure 2 also shows that the college completion rates for African American men and women stayed fairly close through 2000, but in 2010 a large gap appeared, as the percentage of black women completing college continued rising, while the percentage for black men actually fell.

Figure 3 presents comparable information for two other ethnic groups, Hispanics and Asians. The government only began publishing records for these two groups more recently, but figure 3 demonstrates that there are dramatic differences between them.

Asians have a much higher proportion of college graduates than the other three ethnic groups; in both 2000 and 2010, more than half of Asians ages twenty-five to twenty-nine—both men and women—completed college. In contrast, Hispanics had the lowest proportion of college graduates. And in both ethnic groups, a higher percentage of women completed college.

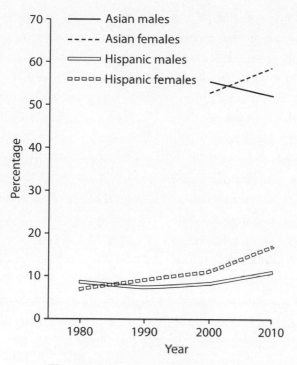

Figure 3. Percentage of Hispanics and Asians ages 25–29 having completed four or more years of college, by sex, 1980–2010. Source: U.S. Census Bureau (2012a).

Although we have been focusing on college graduation, essentially the same patterns can be found at all levels of higher education. Not everyone who begins some sort of post–high school education completes a four-year degree program; some enroll in trade schools or community colleges, while others start college but drop out. But the percentages of people on all these paths have risen in the same way that the percentage of those completing college has increased. Similarly, growing percentages of people continue beyond college graduation to graduate and professional programs. Encouraged to pursue higher education for both its individualistic and its communal benefits, more people continue their schooling.

These aspirations motivate segments of the population formerly blocked from higher education. Women, once a small minority of college students, now outnumber men on most campuses. Ethnic and religious minorities that used to find it difficult to gain admission to many institutions are now attending college in far greater numbers. Increasingly, colleges welcome students who are disabled, and a growing share of these are classified as having learning disabilities; people who once might have had great difficulty completing the work required in college classes now receive accommodations designed to create an educational environment where they can succeed. The spread of higher education reflects the growing participation of not only more people but a broader range of people.

This democratization of higher education is now widely celebrated. Only two generations ago, a minority of young people graduated from high school, and only a fraction of those went on to complete college. But we understand that higher education is the principal ladder for personal advancement in today's world. For inequalities of gender, ethnicity, and class to shrink, categories of children who traditionally found it difficult to attend college need to be encouraged to continue their educations. Americans agree that higher education is good for all individuals and that it will improve their life chances, even as it is good for society, which should experience fewer social problems as educational attainment rises. These assumptions lead to calls for policies that will promote ever more access to higher education.

COST AS AN OBSTACLE

Generations of aspiring college students and their families have faced a basic challenge: going to college costs a lot of money. There are tuition and fees—charges colleges levy for the services they provide. Students must also expect to pay directly related costs: the price of textbooks and other supplies. And there are the costs of the students' food and shelter. Students living in on-campus dormitories must pay dorm fees;

even students who are able to live at home with their parents may have commuting expenses. Finally, there are opportunity costs, as students forgo whatever additional income they might have earned had they chosen not to attend college.

Decades of inflation may make the costs of college in past decades seem trivial. Consider a 1958 magazine article that put the average cost of a year of college at a public institution at $1,500 (nearly $12,100 in 2013 dollars), with a year at a private college averaging $2,000 (about $16,100 in 2013 dollars). These may seem like small sums, but remember that the median family income was only $5,100 in 1958 ($41,140 in 2013 dollars); paying $1,500–$2,000 for college costs would have taken a big bite out of most families' budgets. Meeting the cost of college has always been recognized as a serious challenge. Generations of young people and their parents have been urged to save toward college. All manner of public service organizations and individual benefactors have established scholarships to help students pay for their educations, and a large share of students have found it necessary to work part-time to make ends meet.[7]

The tremendous growth in higher education depicted in figure 2 began in the aftermath of World War II. The flood of applicants led many political and educational leaders to announce that higher education was facing a funding crisis: how could colleges cover the costs of educating far more students and offering a broader range of programs without charging higher tuition, which would push higher education even farther beyond the reach of many? Many colleges offered to let students borrow a portion of the money they would need; that is, student loans were administered by the individual colleges.

However, students used only a fraction of the funds that colleges made available for loans. Students—and their parents—shared a "widespread belief that to borrow money for college is to mortgage the borrower's future." During the 1950s, popular magazine articles chided "middle-income Americans, a get-now-pay-later breed when it comes to the iceboxes and TV" for "still clinging tightly to the pay-as-you-go idea on college education." Higher education, the articles insisted, was a sound investment: "A college education actually provides the increased income that more than pays for itself," while "college is a far better investment than a car, and borrowing to pay for college entails a smaller commitment than is usually involved in a mortgage." To be sure, not all students had equally bright financial prospects: "If you are headed for a comparatively low income field such as teaching or the ministry, you will probably want to borrow only as a last resort." Female students, in particular, were said to worry that "a debt would serve as a negative dowry": "They figure their chances of marriage are a lot better if they are financially chaste. [But] the more tolerant attitudes toward young working wives increase their chances of being able to pay off their debts even after marriage."[8] These articles encouraged families to accept the idea of borrowing for college.

During the mid-1950s, a few states began to devise their own guaranteed student loan programs. Although there were calls for the federal government to do more to support higher education, these proposals met with considerable resistance. Some warned that the federal funds might come at a high price, that colleges might have to surrender control over their curriculum or other activities to the government. Other critics worried that any federal program to aid colleges would be very expensive, and there were disagreements regarding the appropriateness of the federal government assisting—or refusing to assist—private or religious colleges. Race raised still other issues: southerners who favored existing systems of racially segregated higher education feared that federal authorities might interfere with those arrangements, even as liberals sought to ensure that, at a minimum, any new federal policies would treat Negro colleges fairly. There was no consensus regarding what the federal government ought to do—or even whether it ought to do anything. No wonder a 1949 National Education Association poll of leaders at nearly one thousand colleges found that fewer than half favored a program of federally guaranteed student loans.[9]

In the aftermath of World War II, it was clear that the nation faced a dilemma: the demand for higher education was growing, and there was general agreement that society needed more highly educated people; yet the costs of college blocked many people from achieving their aspirations, and there was considerable skepticism about the federal government's ability to offer a solution. So how did student loans emerge from this confusion as the principal means by which the federal government supported higher education?

THE PATH TO FEDERAL STUDENT LOANS

The story of how the United States arrived at federal student loans is one of those convoluted tales that often characterize histories of policymaking. These tend to be accounts of long series of negotiations, as different actors struggle to get their interests recognized and incorporated into whatever policy emerges. Rather than try to detail the ins and outs of every effort to shape federal support for higher education loans, we have chosen to highlight four early policies, beginning with one that supported college education without relying on loans.

The GI Bill (1944)

The Servicemen's Readjustment Act of 1944, familiarly known as the GI Bill, was designed to forestall the sorts of protests that angry veterans had mounted following the First World War. World War II had mobilized far more men and women, who had been away for a longer period of time. The nation needed to reintegrate millions of veterans into American society and its economy, and the GI Bill offered a range of benefits, including loans to help them purchase homes, farms, and businesses, and payments—not loans—for education.

Although the GI Bill is recalled fondly as a policy triumph, it was the subject of considerable debate when the law was being crafted.[10] Education was by no means the bill's central focus; rather, the principal concern was to award veterans "mustering out" pay ($500 in cash, the equivalent of about $6,450 in 2013 dollars) intended to help support them until they could find employment. The initial proposals for the new law featured limited support for higher education: only those veterans who had interrupted their college educations to serve in the military would receive aid for education. However, negotiations expanded the scope of the education benefits. By the time the GI Bill passed, it offered far more generous provisions: all veterans would be eligible for support if they chose to further their educations. The government would pay educational costs (tuition and fees, books, room and board) directly to colleges, and veterans would receive an allowance (initially $65 per month for unmarried veterans—that amount would be increased—plus additional sums for dependents).

Nonetheless, people worried. Colleges weren't sure that the veterans would be able or willing to do college work. Conservative legislators opposed a government program that would boost the life chances for some individuals but not others. The bill's proponents overcame the opposition, partly because it was easy to argue that veterans deserved generous benefits to repay them for their wartime service, and partly because even the most optimistic projections wildly underestimated the number of veterans who would choose to take advantage of the educational provisions.

By the time the program had run its course, 7.8 million veterans— nearly one in two—received some educational benefits. Not all of them became college undergraduates; some used their GI benefits to pay for vocational schooling, while others received advanced training in graduate or professional schools. Nor did everyone who started an educational program graduate. Scholars continue to debate the program's impact. After all, college attendance was rising before World War II began, and many veterans undoubtedly would have chosen to attend college even without a GI Bill. The question is how many veterans completed college who would not have done so had the GI Bill not existed. A survey of ten thousand college students in 1946 reported that only about 20 percent of veterans judged they probably would not have gone to college had there been no GI benefits; however, a group of non-black veterans surveyed in 1998 were much more likely to report the program's support as having been important: more than half agreed that the GI Bill made it possible for them to afford college. Overall, the consensus is that the GI Bill increased the nation's stock of college graduates by something like 450,000.[11]

Whatever the initial skepticism and however modest its contribution to the national stock of human capital, the GI Bill is generally recalled as a great success. The program produced plenty of scandals: "One-third of the $14.5 billion spent on the educational portion of the GI Bill went to fictional schools, real schools overcharging the government, or on-the-job training hoaxes." Yet those problems have vanished from our collective memory. The GI Bill's real legacy is to have established that the federal government might—even should—support individuals' efforts to gain higher education.[12]

The National Defense Education Act of 1958

Overall, the GI Bill was a success, in that millions of veterans were reintegrated into a booming economy. But America now faced a new challenge—the Cold War. The atomic bomb's role in ending World War II had led people to equate national security with scientific dominance. In 1957, the Soviet Union launched Sputnik, the first artificial satellite, an event that proved the United States was not ahead of its rival in all scientific endeavors (figure 4). Sputnik inspired a round of national breast-beating about the quality of American schools, with critics warning that the nation's educational system was failing to produce enough scientists and engineers. Longtime proponents of increasing federal support for higher education did not waste the opportunity provided by the crisis: "The significance of sputnik for the policymaking process was ... that it disarmed opposition to federal aid per se."[13]

These advocates warned that Americans were squandering a precious resource—the brainpower of its talented youth—at a time when it was most needed: "As a nation, the United States can ill afford the

Figure 4. Uncle Sam awakens to the realization he's been wasting brainpower (1957).

waste of man- and woman-power that occurs when children with the best brains are not educated to perform their optimum function. It is a well-documented fact that between 100,000 and 200,000 high school pupils in the top quarter of their class fail to go to college primarily because they lack the necessary funds."[14] Proponents seemed to agree on the size of the problem—200,000—although the meaning of that number seemed to shift. The Office of Education estimated that "over 200,000 students would be aided by loans" over a four-year period, while the *New York Times* spoke of "the 200,000 able students who drop out of school each year."[15] In any case, the Cold War demanded that America stop wasting its brainpower. This concern launched the first student loan mess.

In response, Congress passed and President Dwight Eisenhower signed the National Defense Education Act of 1958 (NDEA), which articulated its own rationale: "The defense of this Nation depends upon the mastery of modern techniques developed from complex scientific principles. It depends as well upon the discovery and development of new principles, new techniques, and new knowledge. We must increase our efforts to identify and educate more of the talent of our Nation."[16]

Title II of the NDEA created the first large federal student loan program for higher education. Funds for lending were made available to colleges (which had to match one dollar for every nine dollars provided by the federal government). Colleges were to give special consideration to "(A) students with a superior academic background who express a desire to teach in elementary or secondary schools, and (B) students whose academic background indicates a superior capacity or preparation in science, mathematics, engineering, or a modern foreign language."[17] Individuals could borrow up to $1,000 per year, to a maximum of $5,000; those who went on to teach full-time in public schools could have up to half the loan (and the interest on that portion) cancelled. It was a relatively straightforward program (see figure 5).

The NDEA's loan program proved controversial, but not because the government was taking a new direction by establishing a federal program that would allow individuals to borrow to cover their college costs. Rather, in the aftermath of McCarthyism, opposition centered on the law's provisions requiring loan recipients to sign a loyalty oath and an affidavit stating that they did not favor overthrowing the federal government. This led several elite colleges to announce that they would not

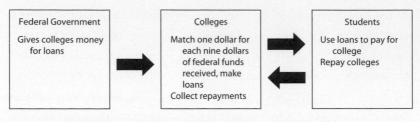

Figure 5. Student loans under the National Defense Education Act (NDEA) of 1958.

participate in the program, and various politicians called for an end to the provisions, until the affidavit was dropped in 1961. Other amendments gradually expanded the NDEA: loan recipients who taught in private schools became eligible to have half their loans forgiven, and the range of students who could qualify for loans expanded so that, by 1964, "no longer would students applying for loans have to be in the critical 'defense' fields of science, language, mathematics, or engineering to receive preference. They could, moreover, be attending commercial business schools or technical institutes or be enrolled in nursing programs."[18]

The NDEA, then, was a pivotal moment in the story of how students would pay for college. Some remained suspicious of debt; the *New York Times* covered a speech by the president of the State University of Iowa opposing "long-term-credit financing of college education": "He thought it was not good for youths to be saddled with 'enormous debts' when they come out of college. Society, he said, should pay most of the cost. The country, he went on, can afford any kind of education it wants; 'the problem is to persuade people it is important.'"[19] Similarly, in a 1962 book about higher education finances, a Harvard professor worried, "Is it not likely that whatever sense of obligation remains among young Americans for the support of their aged parents would be shaken should their obligation to their parents for their education be removed? To the extent that this would occur, the loan program would be subversive of family ties. Moreover, to increase ... people in the class of long-term debtors should be to increase thereby the popular stake in inflation."[20]

But such critics were swimming against the tide. As the lead for another *Times* article put it, "Joe College is about to receive a lesson in practical economics. He soon will be picking up the tab for his own education, experts predict, simply because nobody else can afford to pay for it."[21] As the share of young people hoping to attend college rose, colleges were becoming less exclusive and more students were from families of modest means. Demand far outstripped the money available for scholarships, and many politicians resisted having the federal government simply give money to students. Yet the Cold War and the threat posed by Sputnik seemed to require policies that would foster scientific and engineering education. Why not encourage those students studying for essential careers, but by lending—not giving—them the money needed for college?

The NDEA led to a boom in student borrowing: "In 1957, the year before the passage of the NDEA, 80,000 students borrowed money from college student-loan funds; in 1961, 115,000 students borrowed four times that amount thanks to the infusion of NDEA money."[22] And as demand proved greater than the amounts budgeted, Congress increased the funds available for loans (see figure 6). Federally supported student loans were becoming an increasingly important way for students to pay for college.

It is less clear that the NDEA transformed the face of higher education.[23] The proportion of high school graduates who became full-time college students did not change markedly (suggesting that the NDEA did not lead large numbers of low-income students to enter college). The proportion of teachers who had completed college did rise, but it is uncertain what proportion of those teachers relied on NDEA loans to pay for their training. Similarly, the number of degrees awarded in the sciences rose, but the degree to which the NDEA can be credited for this is unclear.

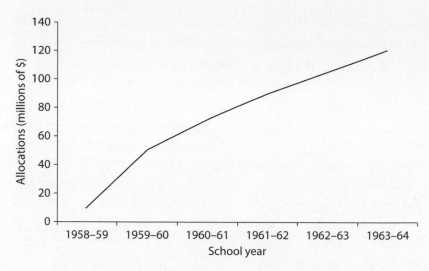

Figure 6. Allocations for NDEA student loans, 1958–1964. Includes 10 percent matching funds from educational institutions. Source: Flattau et al. (2006: table II-2).

> **MILESTONES IN STUDENT LOANS**
>
> 1962: $100,000,000 in new NDEA loans

The Cold War had provided the initial justification for a federal student loan program, and the NDEA's mandate was being expanded to benefit more students and more institutions. In the process, the federal government had now become committed to providing student loans, which set the stage for less restrictive policies.

The Higher Education Act of 1965

Improving higher education was a minor aspect of President Lyndon Johnson's broad vision for a Great Society; during the year it passed, the Higher Education Act of 1965 (HEA) received far less attention than such marquee programs as the Voting Rights Act of 1965, the War on

Poverty, and Medicare. Still, the issue was important to LBJ. He chose to sign the HEA into law at his alma mater, Southwest Texas State College in San Marcos, where he spoke at length. His remarks framed the issue in terms of individualistic benefits:

> This legislation … will swing open a new door for the young people of America. For them, and for this entire land of ours, it is the most important door that will ever open—the door to education…. To thousands of young men and women, this act means the path of knowledge is open to all that have the determination to walk it. It means a way to deeper personal fulfillment, greater personal productivity, and increased personal reward. This bill, which I will make law, is an incentive to stay in school. It means that a high school senior anywhere in this great land of ours can apply to any college or any university in any of the 50 States and not be turned away because his family is poor.[24]

He went on to acknowledge that there would also be communal benefits: "This Nation can never make a wiser or a more profitable investment anywhere. In the next school year alone, 140,000 young men and women will be enrolled in college who, but for the provisions of this bill, would have never gone past high school. We will reap the rewards of their wiser citizenship and their greater productivity for decades to come." However, LBJ's lengthy statement made no mention of the Cold War or national defense. The original rationale for federal student loans had vanished in the few years since 1958, when the NDEA passed.

Student loans appeared to be only a minor element (designated Title IV, Part B) in the Higher Education Act of 1965. The bill contained programs to support extension and continuing education programs, to improve college libraries, and to strengthen "developing" colleges (such as historically black institutions). Title IV, the section on financial aid to students, also included federally funded scholarship and work-study programs targeted for low-income students. In the original $250 million budget, money for student loans was the smallest item, with an allocation of only $15 million (about $350 million in 2012 dollars), compared to $70 and $45 million earmarked, respectively, for scholarships and work-study.[25]

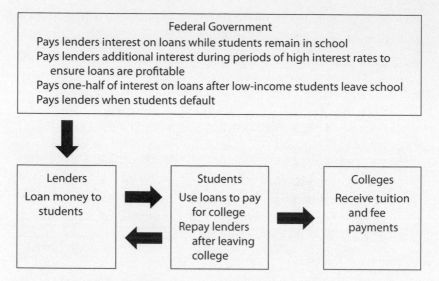

Figure 7. Guaranteed student loans under the Higher Education Act of 1965.

The HEA's apparently low student loan costs reflected a change in the way federal dollars would be used to support student loans. Under the NDEA, federal funds had been allocated to colleges, which then loaned that money to students (after matching one dollar for each nine dollars received); in other words, when a student received an NDEA loan, 90 percent of the money came from federal coffers. As the NDEA grew each year, its annual cost to the federal government rose (it reached $108 million in 1964—see figure 6). The HEA sought to provide federal support for student borrowing at a lower cost by establishing *guaranteed student loans* (GSL), in which the money for the actual loans would come from banks and other lenders, not the federal government (see figure 7). Instead of lending all the money students borrowed, the government would use its funds to make lending money to students attractive to bankers. As *Time* explained, "This program requires students to find their own private lender. The Government then pays the lender 6% interest while the student is in school and, except for high-income families, splits the 6% with the student when he repays the loan after graduation."[26]

At first glance, the HEA seemed to promise to cost the government less than the NDEA. Instead of putting up the entire loan amount, the government would be on the hook only for the interest. But there were two problems with this vision. First, the program's initial low cost was deceptive: "In a modestly growing interest-subsidy program of the [HEA] type, early years involve very small interest charges. But as the volume of outstanding loans grows, so do the interest costs."[27] And the volume of loans was sure to rise. After all, students who took out loans for their first year of college were also likely to take out additional loans during the next three years, even as new students were starting college and borrowing for their educations, so the number of students with loans, the amounts being borrowed, and the amount of interest being covered by the federal government were all sure to increase. And the number of young people entering college was increasing, both because a growing percentage aspired to go to college and because the large cohorts of baby boomers were now of college age. In addition, the loans would be larger, as college costs continued upward. There was every reason to anticipate that the program would grow each year, and that costs would balloon far beyond the $15 million budgeted for 1965.

Second, it would soon become apparent that additional federal money would be needed to support HEA student loans. The GSL program forced banks to make lots of relatively small loans, so the program was expensive for lenders to administer. And the lenders' money would be tied up: it might be several years before students graduated and started repaying the principal on their loans. Moreover, in years when interest rates were relatively high, banks did not find 6 percent student loans attractive investments. To sweeten the deal for the banks enough to ensure that students would be able to borrow money for GSL, the federal government sometimes found it necessary to pay the banks an additional 2–3 percent interest as a premium.[28]

One historian argues, "It is difficult to overstate the importance of the HEA's financial aid title."[29] Its scholarships and work-study programs (both depending on financial need) made college accessible to more low-income students than ever before; these programs democratized access to higher education and diversified the student body. As *Time* put it, "It is now true that practically no high school graduate of intelligence need forsake a college education for lack of funds."[30]

But the student loan program became particularly important because it offered federal aid to the middle class. In 1968, the *New York Times Sunday Magazine* carried a long article, "The Higher Cost of Higher Education," which argued that paying for college was becoming a "massive social problem." "Higher education is becoming less a privilege for the wealthy and more a right for everyone," the *Times* argued, so that "the broad middle class clamors at the university's gates."[31] The article's focus was middle-class families who were being squeezed between their inadequate savings and constantly rising college costs, with particular attention to the plight of parents with two or more children attending college simultaneously. Increasingly, these families needed student loans. The article quoted one lender: "Years ago, people resisted the idea of financing their children's educations with monthly payments, but when the Government got into the educational loan business it took the stigma away." The article went on to describe the HEA as "a guaranteed-loan plan aimed at middle-income and upper-income families, who have not been inarticulate in conveying to lawmakers their chagrin about mounting college costs."

This was not how the Johnson administration had envisioned the HEA's democratizing impact. In congressional hearings on the bill, Republican legislators repeatedly raised the alternative of offering tax deductions or tax credits for college expenses, only to be rebuffed. For instance, the commissioner of education responded to one Republican lawmaker, "The first order of business ... is to assure the opportunity for the children from families with low incomes to go on to higher education ... [whereas] tax credit proposals ... provide tax relief in a form which would be of benefit to families with larger incomes."[32] Yet while the HEA's scholarship and work-study programs were targeted at lower-income students, its student loans would be available to nearly everyone else. In 1966, the administration proposed making loans available to students from families earning up to $15,000 annually (nearly $108,000 in 2013 dollars), which would "make about 90 percent of the nation's college and university students eligible for this type of assistance." Commentators noted that student loans were no longer uncommon; as *Business Week* put it, "College on the cuff, like buying a car on terms, has become a way of life in the U.S."[33]

Sallie Mae (The Student Loan Marketing Association—1972)

The guaranteed student loan program's shortcomings quickly became apparent. Bankers weren't enthusiastic about making the loans, which involved relatively small amounts of money and lots of paperwork, so the profits weren't all that high. When interest rates were high, other sorts of lending were more profitable, and the federal government's efforts to make the loans more attractive by increasing the interest paid to lenders could be stalled in Congress. For several years, proposals to adjust rates got bogged down in debates over whether there should be restrictions against lending to campus activists. When the federal government was insufficiently nimble, students—and lenders and colleges—could find themselves waiting for the passage of last-minute legislation that would make it possible to process loans. Thus, in August 1969, President Richard Nixon complained that Congress had recessed without passing a bill to approve an adjustment before the academic year began: "It is inconceivable to me that the Congress would turn its back on 200,000 young Americans who need these loans for their education." Three years later, he offered praise when another crisis was averted: "I want to express my thanks to the Congress for responding so promptly to an urgent problem. If the Congress had not responded promptly—enacting this legislation 48 hours after I requested it—

thousands of deserving young people, ready to return to college or other post-secondary schools, might have been denied the loans they need for the coming school year." He continued, calling the HEA student loan program "an overwhelming success—more of a success than even the creators of the program foresaw," and noting that, since 1965, "loans totaling more than $4.6 billion have been made," and "in fiscal year 1972 alone, more than a million applicants borrowed $1.3 billion."[34]

> **MILESTONES IN STUDENT LOANS**
>
> **1971: $1,000,000,000 in new student loans**

The notion that, in a mere seven years, HEA loans had grown to seventeen times the program's initial size did not seem to give Nixon pause. As figure 8 demonstrates, the growth in federal support for student loans had been impressive. The graph includes the initial years of both the earlier NDEA program and the later HEA loan programs (NDEA continued, but it was renamed National Direct Student Loans and directed at graduate and professional students).

The rapid expansion in federal support for student loans—which, in retrospect, might seem to be the program's key feature—was noticed, but it mostly drew praise. These programs allowed significantly more students to borrow significantly more money. Most commentators saw this as the solution to the first student loan mess, which revolved around the problem of insufficient opportunity. Deserving young people needed help to fulfill their educational aspirations, and student loans provided that help.

Some alternatives were proposed. Some Republicans continued to promote a policy based on tax credits, just as some Democrats continued to lament that the HEA—like the NDEA before it—had not provided more federal scholarships (which would not have to be repaid) rather than loans. But the alternative that attracted the most

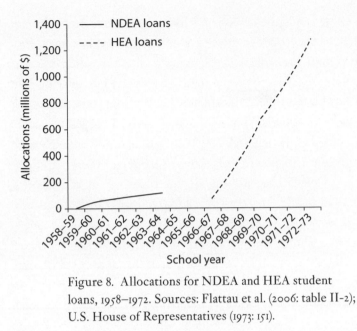

Figure 8. Allocations for NDEA and HEA student
loans, 1958–1972. Sources: Flattau et al. (2006: table II-2);
U.S. House of Representatives (1973: 151).

press attention was Pay As You Earn (PAYE). Kingman Brewster,
Jr., the celebrated president of Yale, led the campaign for PAYE; he
argued that it would "permit any student to draw down [from the federal government] an advance equal to the cost of his education, on the
understanding that he would in return have to repay a proportionately
larger income tax for the balance of his life." Under the plan, borrowers would agree to pay additional taxes equal to 0.4 percent of their
income per $1,000 borrowed—for life. PAYE was "designed not to
penalize students who elect lower-paying careers.... [I]f a student
borrows $5,000 and later earns $10,000 a year, he will repay $200 annu-
ally. If he earns $50,000, he will repay $1,000 per year." In some ver-
sions, repayments would stop after thirty years. PAYE drew praise
from both liberals and conservatives. The *New Republic* noted that "the
burden for paying a large part of [public institutions' operating] costs
would be removed from taxpayers, and placed on the beneficiaries
of higher education," while the *National Review* argued that "deferred

tuition in public and private colleges looks like a step toward fiscal sanity and greater freedom of choice and will, we hope, become one of the facts of college life."[35]

PAYE proposals attracted some media coverage, but they did not inspire federal policymakers. Presumably, it would have been difficult to gain support for the plan, both because it would have led to people with higher incomes paying back much more than they borrowed even as those with lower incomes might never fully repay their loans, and because repayments in the form of higher taxes would continue for thirty years—or longer. In theory, PAYE offered substantial long-term communal benefits; in future years, the additional tax revenues might be sufficient to cover the cost of loans to successive generations of new students. However, individuals might balk at agreeing to pay a lifetime of higher taxes, especially because college costs could be expected to rise. It was one thing to envision a $5,000 loan resulting in an additional 2 percent tax on income, but a student who borrowed $25,000—an unimaginable amount in 1970, but one that would soon seem less far-fetched—would be expected to cough up additional taxes equal to 10 percent of personal income to cover loan costs.

Instead, policymakers' attention focused on a more immediate problem: the frequent need to adjust federal payments to make student loans attractive to lenders. Whenever interest rates rose, Congress was under pressure to quickly pass legislation authorizing higher payments, and those bills could be derailed whenever opponents tied them to other issues, such as refusing loans to student radicals. Moreover, lenders disliked student loans because they lacked liquidity—it might be several years before students who borrowed money to support their first year of college began to repay their loans. Proponents began to call for the establishment of a secondary market.

These proposals called for the creation of a new agency similar to the Federal National Mortgage Association (known as Fannie Mae), to be called the Student Loan Marketing Association (or Sallie Mae). Banks would lend money to students (the primary market) but then sell

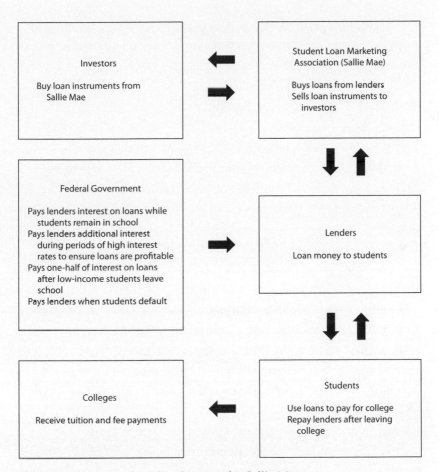

Figure 9. Guaranteed student loans under Sallie Mae.

their loans to Sallie Mae (thereby giving cash back to lenders so that they could relend the money) rather than having to wait years for their loans to be repaid (see figure 9). In turn, Sallie Mae would issue "its own government-guaranteed debt in the capital markets," creating a secondary market where investors could purchase bundles of student loans as long-term investments. As *Business Week* explained:

> Sallie Mae will have two major roles to play. Most important, it will help lenders meet the soaring demand for student loans.... Sallie Mae also will

stand ready to pump money into the student loan market when all credit is expensive and hard to get.... The interest limit [on guaranteed student loans] is 7%, but at HEW's discretion up to 3% more can be charged as a "special allowance." Lenders, it is hoped, will keep making student loans when market rates on other investments are higher simply because they will be very "liquid."[36]

There was now an arrangement whereby more students could borrow more money with less uncertainty. The first student loan mess seemed to have been resolved; prospects seemed bright.

REVERBERATIONS: EXPANDING CONSUMER CREDIT

By 1972, federal student loans, which had been relatively rare only ten years earlier, were far more common. More students, many of them from families of modest means, aspired to higher education, even as college costs were rising; the marketplace featured more people—increasingly people with less money—demanding something that was becoming more and more expensive. No wonder student loans seemed to offer a solution. It was a solution with broad support: both LBJ and Richard Nixon called for expanding student loan programs.

It is important to place these developments in their larger cultural context. The 1960s saw Americans becoming more comfortable with the idea of borrowing. To be sure, most people already accepted the notion that they would probably need to borrow to buy their homes, their cars, and often their major appliances. But those loans were against tangible assets; if someone failed to make their payments, the bank could foreclose, seize the house or car, and resell it. Loans were considered appropriate for big-ticket items; it would take too long to save enough to pay for a house. But there was a widespread sense that people shouldn't borrow to pay for most other items, which explains those 1950s magazine articles insisting that it was appropriate to borrow to pay for college and offering reassurance that education was a good investment because the increased income college graduates earned would more than pay for the cost of any student loans.

But Americans also were becoming much more comfortable with borrowing and credit. Consider the dramatic spread of bank cards. Bank Americard (which would become Visa) and Master Charge (which would become Master Card) took off in the late 1960s; they encouraged consumers to borrow for virtually any and all purchases, and they signed up a growing number of businesses—all kinds of businesses—to display little logos announcing which credit cards they accepted. There was no need for merchants to assess the borrower's qualifications to make each purchase. These loans were not guaranteed by whatever was purchased; failure to pay a credit card bill would not result in the bank reclaiming the groceries you'd bought with the card. Rather, the loans were guaranteed by the cardholder's income. Credit was increasingly a way of life, a routine aspect of managing one's money.[37]

For many people, this was—as the advertising campaigns for the cards proclaimed—a convenience. There was no need to carry cash; you could simply whip out a credit card when you wanted to buy something and pay off the balance when the bill arrived. But, of course, the lenders were quite pleased if you chose to carry a balance, paying just part of what you owed, because next month's bill would include an interest charge on the amount you still owed. This became the new normal: it was not uncommon to owe money on your house via a mortgage, on the car you'd purchased on payments, and on last month's purchases tallied in your credit card statement. So it didn't seem all that odd to take out a loan to help pay for college. After 1970, magazine articles stopped trying to convince readers that student loans made sense; they simply assumed people understood that.

And so, we have the first student loan mess, a product of individuals' aspirations to improve their prospects—and their leaders' designs to strengthen the nation's human capital—through higher education. At the individualistic level, more young people wanted more education, even as that education was becoming more expensive. Meanwhile, politicians acknowledged the communal value of increasing levels of education, and they created student loan programs to give those young people the opportunities they deserved. The first student loan mess, based on concerns that the cost of college discouraged promising students and wasted the nation's brainpower, would be resolved through the federal government's support of student loans. But attention was already shifting to another mess.

CHAPTER TWO

Disillusionment and Deadbeats

The Second Student Loan Mess

In 1964, before the creation of Sallie Mae, even before LBJ's Higher Education Act of 1965 passed, *Newsweek* noted that "an alarming percentage of students have been lax in repaying government loans under the National Defense Education Act of 1958.... [S]ome $1.3 million ... was overdue, a sum large enough to cause considerable concern in Washington."[1] Inflation makes this amount seem deceptively small— $1.3 million 1964 dollars equals $9.8 million 2013 dollars—but even that corrected sum seems like small change for the federal government.

Yet concern that student loans weren't being repaid would become the centerpiece of the second student loan mess. Whereas commentators had typified the original student loan mess in terms of wasted brainpower—bright young people who wanted to go to college but could not afford to do so—once federal student loan programs were in place, people began worrying about a new, troubling figure: the *student deadbeat*, who ignored the obligation to repay college loans. In 1977, *Newsweek* ran another story ("Study Now, Pay Never") accompanied by a graph titled "The Rise in Student Deadbeats," while a *U.S. News & World Report* story ("Time of Reckoning for Student Deadbeats") featured a similar graph labeled "How Defaults Have Zoomed." Ten years later, *U.S. News* ran yet another story that spoke of "rampant deadbeatism" and "welshers"; that story's graph was headed "Stiffing Uncle Sam."[2] Such press coverage blamed the student loan program's problems on irresponsible borrowers. Political leaders were equally likely to focus on the students' irresponsibility. President Jimmy Carter spoke out: "One of the things that has endangered the entire college aid program has been the deliberate cheating by college students off the taxpayers." Similarly, President Ronald Reagan noted: "While we do our part to help finance college education, students must do their part and act responsibly. Most do, many do not."[3]

To understand why attention turned to student defaults, we need to appreciate what was at issue. The initial NDEA loans involved direct expenditures by the federal government. Washington sent money to colleges for loans. In turn, the students who received those loans were to begin to repay them upon graduation, and the money that was repaid was to be used for future loans, thereby reducing the burden on the federal government. But NDEA was succeeded by the Higher Education Act of 1965, and its guaranteed student loan (GSL) program. Under GSL, students received loans from banks, and the federal government's immediate expenditures were limited to the interest payments while the students remained in school. But—and this was the real issue—these were *guaranteed* loans.

Guaranteeing the loans meant that the federal government—which is to say, the taxpayer—was on the hook if students failed to repay their loans. After all, it wasn't possible for lenders to repossess the education that students had received. It was necessary to reassure prospective lenders that they would get their money back, and that reassurance took the form of the federal government promising to make good on any losses.

Any lender understands that there is some risk that a loan won't be repaid. Stuff happens—borrowers die, they get seriously ill, and so on. Lenders try to take those risks into account; this involves calculating that past borrowers defaulted on about X percent of loans and then setting interest rates high enough that lenders can anticipate still making a profit on the proportion of loans that will likely be repaid. So long as lenders make accurate assumptions about the likelihood of default, they can minimize the risks of lending.

Now put yourself in the federal government's shoes. You budget for a student loan program using a set of assumptions: that there will be X students needing loans, that they will borrow Y dollars, and that only Z percent will fail to pay back their loans. If those assumptions are good, the risks associated with the program should be low. But notice that a variety of things could increase your risks, including an increasing number of borrowers, individuals taking out larger loans, or an unexpectedly large proportion of borrowers who default on their loans. In hindsight, it seems obvious that, in the case of student loans, all of these were likely to occur.

It was a certainty that there would be more borrowers and that the amounts each would borrow would increase. The number of borrowers would inevitably rise as more and more people pursued the dream of getting a higher education (recall chapter 1's data on the increasing proportion of young people completing college). The sums they were borrowing were also sure to grow for two reasons: first, tuition and other college costs were rising; and second, the additional people who wanted to go to college tended to come from lower-income families (because they were the ones who in the past had been unable to afford college), and on average, they were likely to need to borrow a larger share of their college costs. Even if every student loan was repaid on schedule, the program's costs were certain to grow year after year.

Less predictable was the proportion of borrowers who failed to pay back their loans. Let's say you anticipate that some low percentage of borrowers will default—say 2 percent. Now suppose that, in fact, 4 percent default. One way to look at that outcome is to be pleased that the vast majority of borrowers—96 percent—are making their scheduled payments. But that misses the point: a 4 percent default rate means that the lender's costs are twice as high as anticipated. (This is what happened in the Great Recession of 2007. About 90 percent of people with home loans continued to pay on their mortgages. Only a relatively small percentage defaulted, but the losses from those defaults were much larger than lenders had anticipated, and that helped throw the global economy into a tailspin.)

In other words, if an unexpectedly large proportion of students defaulted on their loans, it could be seen as a big deal. These concerns emerged almost as soon as federal student loan policies started, with the NDEA program; they were central to the discussions establishing the GSL program; and they remained a principal concern after the establishment of Sallie Mae. This chapter begins by examining how people understood and tried to address defaults in terms of those "deadbeat students." But this chapter also considers some unanticipated consequences of federal student loan programs: the reactions of for-profit educational institutions and of borrowers, state legislatures, and the colleges themselves. Arguably, policymakers' concentration on defaults obstructed their view of other, more important developments that would not only exacerbate the second student loan mess but set the stage for the messes still to come. First, however, we need to establish the context within which the deadbeat debate took place.

STUDENT LOANS CONTINUE TO GROW

Although concerns about student loan defaults emerged early and continue into the present, this chapter will focus on the period from the creation of Sallie Mae in 1972 through the passage of the Higher Education Amendments of 1998 (which made it impossible for most borrowers to discharge student loans by declaring bankruptcy). During this period, discussions of student loans tended to concentrate on the problems posed by deadbeats—what we're calling the second student loan mess.

This was a period of dramatic growth in student loan programs. As noted in chapter 1, the proportion of young people pursuing higher

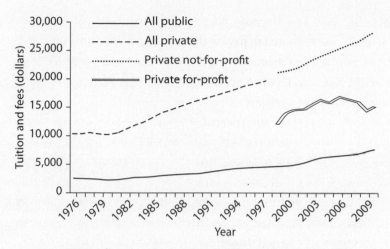

Figure 10. Average tuition and fees at four-year public and private institutions, 1976–2010, in 2013 dollars. Source: National Center for Education Statistics (2012: table 349).

education was increasing. And the costs of attending college were growing. Figure 10 shows the dramatic rise in tuition and fees at both public and private four-year colleges between the 1976–77 and 2010–11 academic years. Notice that through 1998–99, the graph shows costs for all private schools; beginning in 1999–2000, this category is subdivided into traditional private not-for-profit institutions and for-profit colleges. This is an extremely important graph; we will have occasion to return to it, both later in this chapter and in future chapters. Figure 10 tracks college costs in constant 2013 dollars—that is, it takes inflation into account.

Thus the average in-state tuition and fees at a public four-year institution rose from $617 in 1976 to $7,136 in 2010, but Figure 10 shows this increase in constant 2013 dollars—from $2,524 in 1976 to $7,618 in 2010. If tuition costs had simply kept up with inflation, the lines in Figure 10 would be horizontal. The graph shows that through the early 1980s inflation-adjusted costs at both private and public institutions remained fairly stable, but thereafter college costs rose much faster than the cost of living. But note that the lines not only rise (indicating that college costs climbed faster than inflation), but they get steeper (meaning that costs were outpacing inflation at an ever more rapid clip). In fact, between 2000 and 2013, the rise in college tuition and fees outstripped increases in the costs of health care, housing, and all the other components in the Consumer Price Index.[4] As student loans became more common, their very availability must have exacerbated these increases; colleges could raise prices without worrying that students wouldn't be able to afford to enroll.

As college costs rose, fewer students were able to muster the resources needed to graduate from college debt-free. To be sure, some parents earned enough—or had saved enough—to pay for their children's college, while other students worked summers or part-time during the school year to pay for college. Lots of students relied on some combination of personal savings and earnings, plus money their families had saved or earned, plus scholarships, grants, and other forms of financial aid that did not involve federal loans. But while students from relatively privileged upper-middle-class homes might graduate with no debt, rising tuition (and the associated costs for books, room and board, and so on) made it ever more difficult to complete college without borrowing some of the money needed.

It is hard to find data that permit year-to-year comparisons of how students financed college and that go back far in time. In 1975, a report from the Congressional Research Service estimated that one in eight college students had a federal loan.[5] The first year for which reasonably complete data are available is 1992–93, twenty years after the establishment of Sallie Mae and toward the end of the period covered by this chapter. By that time, a substantial minority of college students were using federal student loans; nearly a third—31.3 percent—of full-time undergraduate students received federally guaranteed student loans. The type of institution made a big difference in the likelihood that a student would have federal loans: in 1992–93, only 24.8 percent of students at public institutions had federally guaranteed loans, compared to

43.6 percent at higher-cost, not-for-profit private institutions, and 52.4 percent at for-profit private institutions (these for-profit colleges will receive considerable attention in chapters 3 and 4).[6]

Use of federal loans would continue to rise. In 1999–2000, only seven years later, the percentage of students with federally guaranteed loans had climbed from 31.3 percent to 44.3 percent. And, in 2007–8, fifteen years after the start of our comparison, nearly half of all undergraduates—49.6 percent—had federal student loans; this included 40.7 percent of those at public institutions, 60.9 percent of those at private, not-for-profit institutions, and 88.7 percent—virtually all—of the students at for-profit institutions. Continually rising costs made it harder and harder for students to graduate debt-free. Whereas federal student loan programs once affected only a small minority of students, the typical student now has such loans.

MILESTONES IN STUDENT LOANS

1986: $10,000,000,000 in new student loans

In sum, recent decades have been marked by three interrelated trends: an ever-larger share of young people attend college; the costs of college have been rising; and a growing share of college students have student loans. These trends made it almost certain that more people would fall behind on paying back their loans. Why? Think back to the early years of the twentieth century, a time when perhaps 5 percent of young Americans went on to college. Maybe they weren't the smartest 5 percent or the richest 5 percent, but on average, they would have tended to be pretty good students and to come from families that were reasonably well off. Democratizing higher education—opening college doors to a much larger share of the population—meant that, again on average, students would have weaker academic qualifications and come from families that were less prosperous.

But when we think about the risk of a borrower defaulting on student loans, we realize that a more diverse student body has higher risk of default. Those with weaker academic skills are more likely to have trouble doing college work; they are more likely to get lower grades, leave college before completing their degrees, and have more trouble getting high-paying jobs. (Again, we want to emphasize that we're speaking of averages. Obviously, there are exceptions—students who do much better or much worse in college than they did in high school.) Similarly, students who come from less well-off families are likely to be vulnerable to various family emergencies; for instance, when family members get sick or laid off, students may find it necessary to interrupt their educations. We hasten to add that we are not suggesting that society should not encourage people from diverse backgrounds to attend college. Still, if lenders anticipated student loan default rates based on previous students' borrowing records, no one should have been surprised when default rates exceeded predictions as the student population came to include more individuals at higher risk of defaulting.[7]

There was one concerted effort to slow the student loan program's growth. By the early 1980s, critics were drawing attention to the growth in and long-term costs of what they called *entitlement programs*. As part of this campaign, the Reagan administration sought to make the terms for loans to higher-income families less generous. As President Reagan explained:

As things stand now, our nation provides some aid to college students from the highest income families.... This defies common sense, insults simple justice, and must stop. Government has no right to force the least affluent to subsidize the sons and daughters of the wealthy. And under our proposal, this will change. Those whose family incomes are too high to qualify for guaranteed loans with heavy interest subsidies will still have access to guaranteed, but unsubsidized loans of up to $4,000. And every qualified student who wants to go to college will still be able to do so.[8]

Some Republicans worried that loans were going to students and families who didn't need them. Representative Albert Quie, for instance, pointed to the issue's equivalent of the welfare Cadillac: "A student ... who admitted to the Congressman that he had used his guaranteed loan to buy a red Corvette. Quie's view of the program was shaped by this example, which he recounted several times."[9]

Still, the growing dependence of middle-class families on student loans meant that politicians were reluctant to reduce access to the program.[10] Given the program's popularity, both Democratic and Republican presidents tended to campaign by taking credit for its growth. Even Ronald Reagan, after having made concerted efforts during his first term to limit the student loan program, declared at a 1984 campaign rally on a college campus: "Now, here at this school, for instance, there are a number of students who are receiving some sort of Federal financial aid for their tuition, and, believe me, they're students who really need that help. And their student loans haven't been cut. In fact, we recently asked the Congress to increase to $3,000 the grant aids for the truly needy." Similarly, in his 1992 re-election campaign, George H. W. Bush noted: "We have increased programs for the funding for student loans," just as Bill Clinton pointed to his record during his 1996 reelection campaign: "We have put in place an unprecedented college opportunity strategy. Student loans can now be given directly to people who need them.... This is a dramatic change which is making loans more accessible to young people who did not have them before."[11]

In sum, more students were receiving federal student loans, and this meant the federal government was committing much more money to student loan programs. Because these programs were popular with middle-class voters whose family incomes were too high for their children to qualify for grants or work-study programs, few politicians were willing to call for curtailing guaranteed student loans, and eliminating the program had become unthinkable. If student loans had problems, they needed to be solved.

THE DEADBEAT DANGER

Rather than worrying about the student loan program's swelling size, critics focused their attention on the risk of defaults—the problem of student deadbeats, whose irresponsibility in not paying back their loans was portrayed as the loan program's central problem.

As noted in the opening of this chapter, concern about defaults first emerged regarding the NDEA (the initial student loan program). The risk of defaults received a good deal of attention during congressional hearings regarding the proposed Higher Education Act of 1965, although Texas Democratic senator Ralph Yarborough suggested that defaults were an inevitable result of the decision to promote higher education through loans rather than grants:

> I was on the committee in 1958 when this was discussed. It was anticipated there would probably be some high delinquencies. The bill started out as a pure scholarship bill. We lost by about two or three votes, and this was changed to a loan program.... We pointed out these students would have no income, would be from low-income families, it would take them years to get established. They would probably be slow in paying. That doesn't mean they are deadbeats.[12]

Nine years later, Rhode Island's Claiborne Pell, another Democratic senator, held a hearing on defaults, and he, too, began by lamenting the decision to rely on loans:

> It was the original intent of the Congress that [grants and work-study] would be of primary importance and the then-new loan program would be a supplemental standby mechanism. Over the years, due to niggardly funding of the [other] programs, the Guaranteed Student Loan Program was utilized to meet more and more of the main responsibility for Federal student assistance.... It should be understood that, if we allow the Guaranteed Student Loan Program to grow, it will be one of the major Federal sources of funds for student assistance, since it is an open-ended program rather than grants. There should be a conscious choice made with regard to this program, rather than an inexorable growth which will suddenly confront us with an accomplished fact, on which no real decision will have been made.[13]

Pell added:

> I think the concept of loans for undergraduate education is fraught with
> problems and maybe we ought to get on with the idea of Basic Educational
> Opportunity Grant and the right of people to 16 years of education, a floor,
> not necessarily paying for Yale or some other high-cost place, but a floor of
> education just like they have for 12 years at high school. We could go on
> with that and get rid of a lot of employees [dealing with loan defaults] and
> save the taxpayers some money and not have a fifth of our young people
> starting out in life as cheats.[14]

Although Pell spoke only two years after the creation of Sallie Mae, it
was already too late; student loans had become the centerpiece of federal higher education policy. The issue was no longer whether the government should rely on student loans but rather what needed to be
done to strengthen the program.

By the mid-1970s, references to deadbeat students had become the
standard way of characterizing the student loan problem. This language implied that irresponsible student borrowers could be blamed for
the program's problems. Thus John Silber, the president of Boston University, warned of "a new coming of age": "It will be a rite of passage ...
separating adolescent students from true adults. This rite will be a
financial bar mitzvah in which young Americans will declare bankruptcy at about 25 years of age and thus be freed of all debts incurred in
obtaining their education. This new rite of passage will undermine the
concept of financial responsibility, which is closely related to personal
integrity."[15] Such comments—like talk about deadbeats—implied that
the real need was for tighter controls that would compel students to fulfill their responsibility to repay their loans.

And controls were unquestionably weak. The guaranteed student
loan program was organizationally complex, involving money flowing
among students, lenders, educational institutions, and the federal government (recall figure 9 in chapter 1). Students were not obliged to
begin repaying loans until 120 days after completing their schooling; at
that time, they might have moved, they might not yet have a job, and

so on. Who was responsible for keeping track of a student's loan? Everyone's answer to that question seemed to be, somebody else is responsible. In one congressional hearing after another, witnesses testified that many educational institutions were more interested in signing up students than in weeding out high-risk applicants; that neither federal, state, nor private accrediting agencies could be counted on to certify the quality or stability of the institutions students sought to attend; that because the loans were guaranteed, lenders did not always screen applicants with the care they used for other sorts of loans; that the means of keeping track of borrowers (whether they were still enrolled or had dropped out, where they were living, and so on) were inadequate; and that the dramatic growth in the numbers of students receiving loans had swamped the relatively few federal employees charged with collecting student loans.[16] Moreover, many of these problems seemed intractable. Was it better to allow students to receive loans to attend schools of dubious quality or to give government officials the power to judge which sorts of education were worthy of federal support? Was it better to process loan applications quickly so as not to impede a student's enrolling in the next term or to give each application careful and possibly time-consuming scrutiny? It was easy to denounce deadbeats but far more difficult to design a system of averting defaults.

PROBLEMS WITH PROPRIETARY SCHOOLS

Even as the attention of the media and policymakers focused on the character flaws of deadbeat students, there were critics describing the default problem in somewhat different terms. Public discussions of student loans tended to refer to loans for attending traditional colleges, that is, not-for-profit institutions of higher education offering degrees in the liberal arts or such professions as engineering and education. These were educational programs designed for the brightest, the most promising young people, multiyear programs that provided training for society's most lucrative careers, although that training came with an ever-higher price tag. Discussions of student loans naturally tended to be about helping talented young people achieve lofty goals.

Even today, only a minority of Americans complete four or more years of college education. What about the rest? Wasn't the federal government also obliged to help young people who were not college bound to achieve their dreams? In 1965, LBJ noted: "Fewer than half of our young people go to college; the quality of life in our country—and the strength of our economy—cannot depend solely upon this minority," as he signed the National Vocational Student Loan Insurance Act, which paralleled the Higher Education Act of 1965 by establishing federally guaranteed loans for vocational training.[17]

But vocational education differed from colleges in important ways. In general, those who entered college had better academic records, came from higher-income families, and were more likely to go on to higher-paying careers than those who became vocational students. All this meant that college students posed lower risks of not repaying their loans than their vocational school counterparts. But there was another important difference: although some vocational training occurred at not-for-profit community colleges, a large share of vocational education came from for-profit, proprietary institutions.

Proprietary schools lobbied to be included in federal student loan programs, and it is easy to see why. Students who previously couldn't afford to pay for vocational training could now borrow the money they needed, and with the federal government guaranteeing the loans, the schools ran no risk of not being paid. Existing schools expanded, and new ones opened their doors; their advertisements promised to help students get the loans they'd need to complete their programs and insisted that this training would be the route to a bright future.

In no time, problems with student loans to attend proprietary vocational schools became apparent. As early as 1973, the *Washington Monthly* wrote that the federal student loan program has become a parody of the way to tackle a social problem.... Because the government turned on the money without watching where it was going, roving packs of charlatans and con men moved in to fill the gaps in the educational system. Not only are these hustlers tolerated as they grow fat at their victims' expense, but they are actually abetted by government policy. The secret of their success is the knowledge that the federal government will bail them out when they need help, serving as the collection agency of last resort.[18]

Critics argued that many proprietary schools offered worthless programs that, even when completed, all too often failed to prepare students for the sorts of good jobs promised by the schools' ads. The schools took care to get the money from loans up front, so that even students who dropped out almost as soon as they started a program— or sometimes even before starting—might find themselves owing for an education they never received: "If you get a federal loan to go to a vocational school and then find that the school's promises were a hoax, this has no effect on your obligation to repay the loan."[19] In many ways, these critiques foreshadowed the claims about predatory lending in the twenty-first-century mortgage crisis; they depicted unsophisticated borrowers being flimflammed into taking out loans they had little hope of paying back.

And federal loan money made this all possible: "A new breed of proprietary school has evolved—schools at which nearly every student, and thus the school itself, is dependent upon government aid."[20] Retaining access to loan money became the schools' central goal. When the government tried to require that students receiving loans attend schools meeting some sort of accreditation standard, proprietary schools quickly established their own accrediting agencies. Moreover, students applying for loans were not particularly price sensitive; schools found that they could raise prices without frightening away prospective students. The results were predictable: although vocational education students received a relatively small proportion of federally guaranteed student loans, they accounted for a much larger share of defaults. *The*

Nation argued, "The only equitable solution is to wipe out these debts owed by students cheated by vocational schools."[21]

In 1975, the Senate Committee on Government Operations held hearings on the broad topic of guaranteed student loans, although the testimony concentrated almost exclusively on proprietary education. Senator Henry Jackson described "an approximately $8 billion ... program with perhaps $1 billion in potential defaults. I say 'approximately' and 'perhaps' because, incredibly, precise figures on this program are not available because of the apparent failure of the Office of Education to maintain adequate records." The hearings argued that inadequate government supervision opened the door for "a small group of unscrupulous individuals who prey on unsuspecting young people and parlay Federal funds into financial empires," "certain fly-by-night promoters," and "unqualified schools" that were "dependent upon the student loan program for their survival."[22] Much of the hearing testimony concerned "West Coast Schools," an interconnected set of proprietary vocational schools. One man testified that he had seen their ads for a television repair course, met with an admissions officer, and signed loan papers for $1,300 (about $5,600 in 2013 dollars): "The next day, I went back to the school and told the woman who had signed me up the day before that I wished to withdraw from the course and cancel the loan. She told me not to worry about anything and that the loan would be terminated."[23] However, the man later discovered that the loan had been processed. Although he had never received any training, when he contacted the federal government, he was told he had to repay the loan.

Such stories helped explain why proprietary vocational education— or, to use the term preferred by those in the business, *private career schools*—accounted for a minority of student loans but a disproportionate share of defaults. In 1974, 29.6 percent of the total amount loaned by the federal government went to proprietary schools, yet they accounted for 58.0 percent of the total defaults.[24] The same study reported that private colleges and universities had a default rate of 11.2 percent, only slightly lower than the 11.9 percent at their public counterparts, whereas proprietary specialized and vocational schools had a 48.1 percent default rate. Only a year later, Massachusetts Republican senator Edward Brooke claimed that proprietary schools "account for nearly 60 percent of the default claims."[25]

The last few paragraphs have shown that proprietary vocational schools attracted a good deal of critical attention for abusing the student loan program during the early 1970s. They were the subject of critical journalism and congressional hearings. Flash forward to the early 1990s. Once again, proprietary schools came in for a new wave of essentially the same criticisms. *Consumer Reports*, for instance, presented a 1992 exposé that listed the same sorts of deceptive practices used to entice students to take out loans that the *Washington Monthly* had detailed in 1973.[26] And there was a new round of congressional hearings. At one 1990 Senate hearing, an official from the General Accounting Office estimated that proprietary schools accounted for 22 percent of student loans but 44 percent of defaults—figures not that different from 1970s estimates.[27]

Policymakers made various efforts to constrain the proprietary schools' worst excesses. The 1992 amendments to the Higher Education Act contained an 85/15 rule, which required that a school receive no more than 85 percent of its revenue from student loans—that is, a school could not depend on student loans for *all* its income. This limitation was watered down in 1998 with the introduction of a 90/10 rule.[28] The federal government also instituted audits of the largest proprietary schools to determine whether some schools' students were particularly likely to default on their loans (which might indicate that those schools were not in fact preparing their students for employment). Originally, schools with default rates exceeding 20 percent might lose their eligibility for student loan funding, but this constraint was also loosened, so that only schools with 25 percent default rates for three consecutive years would be affected.[29] However, these measures hardly settled matters. Proprietary higher education was taking new forms (as discussed in chapter 3) and would become the focus for considerable attention yet again (see chapter 4).

NEW POLICIES

Concentrating on defaults and emphasizing the role of deadbeat students led to a series of policy changes that in turn shaped the future of student loans. In general, policymakers recognized the student loan program's popularity and sought to retain it. Even the Reagan administration, which sought to curtail the program by restricting student loans to only the neediest families, found that this goal received little support from either the public or Congress.[30] Student loans had become a popular middle-class entitlement program, easily defended as fostering the American Dream. As a consequence, policy recommendations during the second student loan mess betrayed two rather contradictory impulses: to discourage defaults yet make it easier for more people to borrow larger sums. This section begins with several efforts designed to bring student loans under control and hence reduce the number of student deadbeats—efforts that often came under attack for doing more harm than good. But the section continues by noting other policy changes that had the opposite effect, making it even easier for more students to borrow more money.

Strengthening Loan Collection Efforts

The complex organization of the student loan program following the creation of Sallie Mae (recall figure 9 in chapter 1), coupled with the growing number of students graduating with student loans, the difficulties of keeping track of graduates who were on the move and often changing jobs and addresses, and the limited earnings of recent graduates at the beginning of their careers, made collecting loans challenging. In response, the Department of Education continually expanded its efforts to track down students in default. They also

Figure 11. Deadbeats confronted with tougher collection measures (1982).

adopted other measures, such as publicizing the names of prominent people in default when suits for repayment were filed against them and cracking down on government employees who had not repaid their loans (figure 11).[31] Although the government's debt collection efforts might become more efficient, the constantly growing number of borrowers—to say nothing of the continuing increases in the amounts owed and the proportion of high-risk borrowers—made it almost inevitable that statistics about the number and size of defaults would show things getting worse.

In contrast to those 1950s articles encouraging borrowing to pay for college, popular magazines now began reminding their readers that they were obliged to repay their loans, warning them that the debt collectors would be coming and urging them to make arrangements to repay before it was too late. As *Glamour* put it, "You might have thought there was no rush to repay your debt.... Today, however, that's all changed."[32] Stories profiled defaulters, some insisting that they were the victims of mistaken identity or other bureaucratic mix-ups, some struggling to make ends meet, a few unrepentant. (*Rolling Stone* quoted one of these: "If you owe money to a large corporation or big government, your conscience can allow you to forget about paying it. They can afford it. You can't.")[33] Still, year after year, congressional hearings featured Department of Education officials insisting that they intended to do more to reduce defaults and force deadbeats to pay what they owed.[34] Related measures designed to increase the pressure to repay student loans included having the Internal Revenue Service divert defaulters' tax refunds toward loan repayment and reporting the identities and Social Security numbers of defaulters to credit bureaus (thereby damaging their credit ratings).[35]

While there was general disapproval of student defaults, efforts to restrict access to student loans were subject to criticism, because those borrowers who were most at risk of defaulting could also be characterized as the most socially vulnerable, those who most needed the government's help. *Ms.* magazine criticized the Reagan administration's efforts to restrict student loans and asked, "Will Americans have to watch their children abandon the pattern of upward mobility through education?" while *Time* noted that "reduction in [guaranteed student loans] may keep lower- and middle-class students from attending expensive private colleges, turning such schools into exclusive preserves for the rich."[36] Increasingly, Americans assumed that the federal government should make student loans available, even for middle-class students.

Exempting Student Loans from Bankruptcy

Many young people with student loan debt found themselves in difficult circumstances: they owed money for their loans, they were often facing the additional costs of launching families, yet they were typically earning much less than they would once their careers had had a chance to develop. There was a temptation to declare bankruptcy, discharge their existing debt, and start over. In 1974, *Business Week* reported that students declaring bankruptcy accounted for 5 percent of losses on educational loans.[37]

Obviously, bankruptcy posed a considerable risk to the student loan program. Lenders needed to be assured that they would be repaid, and the federal government sought to do this by making it increasingly harder to shed student loan debt through bankruptcy. In 1976, Congress amended the Higher Education Act of 1965 by forbidding borrowers to discharge student loans through bankruptcy during the first five years of their repayment periods; in 1990, the ban was extended to seven years. But as bankruptcies—fueled by credit card debt and other financial problems, as well as student loans—rose steadily in the late twentieth century, worries about bankruptcy as a method of avoiding student loan debt continued. Finally, the Higher Education Amendments of 1998 made student loan debt nondischargeable through bankruptcy unless the debtor could clear the relatively high bar of demonstrating undue hardship.[38]

Giving Educational Institutions and Lenders a Stake in Reducing Default Rates

Other critics blamed the organizational complexity of the student loan program for high default rates. With guaranteed loans, lenders and educational institutions were rewarded when more students took out loans—lenders had more borrowers, and schools could enroll more students, without either bearing any risks. In effect, high-risk students were not their problem; the federal government would deal with defaults. This led to various proposals to have lenders or educational institutions bear a share of the risks.

In 1987, complaints that some institutions—particularly proprietary schools—accounted for a disproportionate share of student loan defaults led the Reagan administration to propose withholding all federal student aid from schools where the default rate on student loans exceeded 20 percent.[39] This proposal proved controversial. College administrators spoke out against the measure, arguing that colleges were not responsible for either making or collecting loans and should not be punished for high default rates. Students at many historically black colleges and universities—institutions with relatively high proportions of high-risk students—had high default rates, and *Jet* magazine warned, "Bad Student Loans May Force Most of 108 Black Colleges to Shut Their Doors."[40]

The Reagan administration also proposed reducing the share of loans guaranteed by the federal government, so that instead of making good on 100 percent of a defaulted loan, the government might cover only 80 percent of the losses. This proposal was not popular with lenders or with Sallie Mae (which had been a darling of investors precisely because its securities were backed by guarantees that made them low risk). Critics of these proposals warned that making loans riskier to lenders would inevitably lead to higher interest rates or refusals to lend to high-risk students.[41] These issues were intractable: high defaults were a by-product of using student loans to give a broad range of students access to higher education, and reducing the risk of defaults by curtailing loans to high-risk students would inevitably mean limiting access to college for young people from families of relatively modest means. As with efforts to reduce defaults through more efficient collection efforts and limiting access to bankruptcy, Americans' growing dependence on access to student loans meant that proposals to tighten up the program met with resistance.

Adjusting the Terms for Borrowing

Even as political leaders sought to slow the rise of defaults, there were pressures to continue expanding the student loan program. In particular, the inexorable rise of college costs—which were not just rising but outstripping inflation—guaranteed not just that more students would seek to borrow money but that they would need to borrow ever larger sums. In response to this demand, the federal government increased the limits on the amount students could borrow (this trend is discussed in chapter 3).

Other changes sought to make repayment less onerous. Loans specified when repayment should begin; usually, the first payments were due some number of months after the students completed their educations. Whereas this period was usually 120 days in the earliest student loan agreements, later loans often permitted longer delays—often requiring the first payment nine or even twelve months after leaving school (of course, interest charges continued to pile up during this period, so that delaying the start of payment meant that the borrowers would owe even more). Later loans often featured longer repayment schedules or gave borrowers options, such as making smaller initial payments (during the years when their incomes were likely to be lower). Of course, there was no free lunch; borrowers might make lower monthly payments but wind up paying higher overall interest charges.[42]

Program Proliferation

A self-help book, *Take Control of Your Student Loan Debt,* published in 2001, noted: "There are at least 15 different kinds of federally guaranteed student loans," and that list did not include the William D. Ford Federal Direct Loan Program (started in 1993).[43] Over the years, loan types had proliferated, as Congress sought to fine-tune the loan process. Actually, things were not quite as complex as this quotation implies because programs were renamed as they were modified, so that people might have received very similar student loans in different years but under different program titles. Still, over the years, the array of programs became more varied, with particular programs introduced to reflect the needs of different types of students or somewhat different political philosophies. What follows is only a partial list of programs, intended to give a sense of the directions in which federal student loan programs evolved.[44]

SUBSIDIZED DIRECT STUDENT LOANS.   The oldest student loan program began with the NDEA: students received loans from colleges (using a combination of federal funds and school funds). Over time, such loans came to be restricted to students who could establish financial need; interest rates on these loans were lower than for other federal student loan programs, and the program was subsidized by the federal government, which paid the interest on the loan until recipients completed their schooling. In 1986, these were renamed Perkins Loans (after Democratic representative Carl Perkins).

GUARANTEED STUDENT LOANS.   These were the sorts of loans introduced in the Higher Education Act of 1965: the student borrowed from a lender, with the loan guaranteed by the federal government. After 1988, these were renamed Stafford Loans (after Republican senator Robert Stafford). Over time, arrangements for these loans became more complex: they could be subsidized for students with financial need (meaning interest payments were covered by the federal government while the borrower remained enrolled in school) or unsubsidized (meaning that the borrower was responsible for all interest payments— although repayment might be postponed until after graduation).

PARENT LOANS.   By the late 1970s, there were proposals to establish parent loan programs (sometimes called PLUS loans—an acronym for Parental Loans for Students).[45] The logic here was straightforward: parents who had jobs and accumulated assets were likely to be lower-risk borrowers than their college-age children; they posed less risk of default and might be charged somewhat lower rates of interest. (PLUS Loans were also available for graduate and professional students— also likely to be considered low risk.) PLUS loans could be made by private lenders or as direct loans from the federal government (in which case, borrowers had to be able to establish financial need); they were not subsidized, so repayment began immediately, without government assistance.

CONSOLIDATION LOANS.   Over the course of their education, students might have taken out various loans, under different programs, from different lenders, and with different terms. It became possible to consolidate some or all of these loans so as to make repayment easier. However, there was often a fee for consolidation, and consolidated loans often extended the repayment period, which meant that while borrowers could make lower payments, they would continue owing money and paying over a longer period, so that their total interest payments might be substantially higher than if they'd simply paid off their original loans on schedule.[46]

DIRECT LOANS.   For the twenty years following the creation of Sallie Mae, guaranteed student loans were the centerpiece of federal student loan policy. Under these arrangements, most loans originated with private lenders whose enthusiasm for making student loans depended upon the state of the larger economy. Encouraging lenders to make money available to students required adjusting interest rates and otherwise ensuring that conditions were sufficiently favorable to attract lenders.

By the early 1990s, critics argued that guaranteeing student loans had proven to be an unnecessarily expensive approach and that it would be cheaper for the federal government to lend its own money to students via direct loans, thereby eliminating the costs of supporting private-lender middlepeople (in 1991, estimates were that a direct loan program might save the federal government roughly $1 billion per year).[47] When Bill Clinton became president in 1993, he proposed a program to shift federal student loan programs toward direct loans. A version of the bill passed, but after Republicans gained majorities in both houses of Congress in the 1994 midterm elections, they sought to restrict the direct loan program.

The debate over direct loans made student loan programs, which had grown in part thanks to considerable bipartisan support, a more divisive issue. The business press, which had celebrated Sallie Mae as a low-risk investment precisely because it was backed by government guarantees, warned that direct loans would prove to be a boondoggle: "The notion that some bureaucrats in the bowels of the Education Dept. could run the program more efficiently than private companies borders on the ludicrous."[48] Clinton, who spoke more often and in more detail about student loan policy than had any of his predecessors, defended direct loans: "The students are better off, the [college] administrators are better off, the Federal Treasury's better off, and the country's better off because now we're going to have more people borrowing money and going to school. But the bankers aren't better off, and they've persuaded the House of Representatives to get rid of the program, go back to the old system. And now it's under assault in the Senate." He added:

> The new majority in the Congress got the people who run their budget office to pull an incredible gimmick. They said that in calculating the cost of the direct loan program, as compared with the cost of the old student loan program, the guaranteed loan program, we had to calculate the administrative costs of the direct loan program and put it in, but we couldn't count anything of the administrative costs that we paid for the guaranteed loan program to try to make the direct loan program look more expensive than the guaranteed program when everybody knows it's cheaper. It is bizarre.[49]

To be sure, there had been differences between Democrats and Republicans throughout the evolution of student loan policy. At several points, Republicans had unsuccessfully proposed tax deductions or tax credits for college expenses (measures that would have provided greater benefits for families with higher incomes), while Democrats had sought to expand grants or at least make lower-interest loans available to students with lower incomes.[50] But the broad dependence on federal student loans and the fact that loan programs, once in place, lived on until all the loans had been paid off meant that the array of loan options tended to expand.

REVERBERATIONS: WHAT HAPPENED WHILE ATTENTION FOCUSED ON STUDENT DEADBEATS?

Thus far, we have argued that, during the second student loan mess, attention focused on defaults and deadbeat students. This was not a trivial topic—billions of federal dollars were at stake. But the discussion over how to deal with defaults took the continued existence of federal student loans for granted. Millions of students had taken advantage of these programs; the college aspirations of millions more probably depended on the continued availability of federal support of some sort. When policymakers focused on those students who did not pay off their loans on schedule, they were saying in effect that this was a generally successful program that needed a little fine-tuning.

But even as politicians called for getting tough on student deadbeats, the steady growth in federal student loans had other effects. The availability of billions in student loan dollars changed the scenes within which all sorts of people operated. Not just students and their parents, but legislators and various sorts of colleges found themselves living in a world in which federal student loans were a fixture, and they reacted in ways that reflected the new situation. In many cases, their reactions served to make things worse, to increase the pressure for an even larger student loan program.

Reverberations for Borrowers

Underpinning all student loan programs is the assumption that individuals would prefer not to borrow money if they could avoid doing so. Why take out a student loan, incur a debt, and wind up paying interest if you could pay college costs outright? After all, there were lots of other ways to pay for college: help from parents, personal savings, income from part-time jobs, no-interest loans or outright gifts from rich relatives, and so on. If not the last resort, taking out a student loan at least seemed to be somewhere down the list of attractive ways to cover college costs.

Still, student loans could change the ways students and their families thought about paying for higher education. The rising costs of college posed very different challenges for those at different income levels. In 1971, tuition at a four-year public college was equal to about 12 percent of income for families in the lowest quintile of income; by 2008, tuition costs equaled about 42 percent of their income—an astonishing rise. In contrast, for families in the highest-income quintile, the same tuition increases were barely noticeable: tuition would eat up only about 2 percent of their income in 1971 and only 4 percent in 2008.[51] While this might suggest that the upper middle class would not find loans attractive or necessary, there were other troubling trends. Families were under other stresses: although "every year more than a million families take out a second mortgage on their homes just to pay for educational expenses," "the nation's higher divorce and separation rate has had an effect on parents' ability and willingness to pay for their children's educational costs."[52] Some economists worried that loans could disrupt an established *intergenerational compact:*

> In principle, a stable system of family finance of higher education could be run by having each generation either pay for its own education or pay for that of its successor generation. . . . Any one generation can get off scot-free by accepting its parents' largesse and refusing to help its own children. . . . [I]f, at any time, a society wishes to move in the direction of having its children pay for more of their own education through student loans—as there is some reason to think our society is beginning to do—there is an awkward problem of managing the transition fairly.[53]

Even if parents assumed the principal responsibility for funding their children's education, federal programs for guaranteed student loans created new incentives, particularly in periods of high inflation. Consider a 1979 article in *Money* magazine titled "College Loans at 7%—for Everybody" with the subheadline "A high family income no longer disqualifies applicants—and the repayment terms are irresistible." In 1978, Congress had ended the rule that restricted eligibility for student loans to families earning no more than $25,000 per year (more than $89,000 in 2013 dollars); all families were now eligible for federal loans. The article explained:

> Even a family that has put aside enough to pay for college can hardly turn down a loan. Assuming an average rate of inflation of 7% for some years to

come—which may be conservative, considering that the current rate is 13%—a $2,500 loan to a freshman will be whittled down to $1,772 in today's money nine months after he graduates. In the meantime, the $2,500 the family didn't spend on school fees could have remained invested, earning interest or making capital gains.[54]

The article conceded, "Guaranteed student loans may be a bargain for the borrower, but they cost the taxpayer plenty: $600 to $1,000 for each $1,000 loaned." Similarly, Jane Bryant Quinn warned that "opening the program to everyone, regardless of income ... sounds nice and democratic. But it also means that the wealthy can now keep their money ... and borrow for college at low rates subsidized by taxpayers."[55]

The consequences of making guaranteed loans available to everyone, regardless of income, were dramatic. Quinn later noted that her earlier prediction had been correct: "Loan volume quintupled as well-to-do parents invested their own money and borrowed the government's cheap money instead."[56] By 1982, the federal government had reinstated limits on eligibility: student loans would be available only to families earning less than $30,000 (about $72,000 in 2013 dollars). But there was a lesson: loan terms should not be so advantageous that the government wound up allowing individuals to profit by borrowing. The availability of student loans encouraged families to consider different ways of financing higher education.

Reverberations for State Legislatures

Public institutions of higher education were intended to democratize higher education by making it possible to go to college at low cost. In the early 1970s, many state institutions had low tuition and fees. Legislatures assumed that providing inexpensive educations would produce long-term communal benefits. That is, a state legislature would pump money into the state's colleges and universities, which could in turn charge students far less than the cost of providing the education. (This was why out-of-state students were often charged vastly higher tuition than students who were considered state residents.) In turn, those educated students would begin careers and become taxpayers, whose taxes would in turn fund the education for the state's next generation of students.

The problem with this scheme was that educational costs were continuing to rise, which put greater stress on state budgets. Take another look at figure 10—that graph showing the rising costs of tuition and fees (in 2013 dollars) at different sorts of four-year colleges, from 1976 to 2010. As we would expect, public colleges had lower costs than private schools, and you might look at figure 10 and conclude that costs rose faster at the private colleges. But that impression is wrong: after taking inflation into account, tuition and fees rose 302 percent at public colleges, compared to only 273 percent at their private counterparts. Public schools, although they cost less, were getting more expensive faster.

Why did costs rise faster at state-supported schools? A variety of factors were at work. For instance, state governments had to cover other costs—particularly, Medicaid and prison programs.[57] Moreover, the wave of campus protests that began in the 1960s made students less sympathetic figures. It was one thing to subsidize the studies of deserving young people trying to make something of themselves, but it was quite another to support draft-dodging, dope-smoking protesters. But even more important, it was now possible to ask whether the state needed to subsidize higher education in an era when student loans were available.

Should higher education be understood primarily as a communal benefit (which, after all, was the underlying justification for states covering most of the costs of public colleges and universities), or were the benefits primarily individualistic (given that those who gained more education would, on average, go on to earn far more than their less educated counterparts)? Student loans encouraged people to think about the individualistic benefits of education. But then why subsidize public education? After all, students who went to private colleges did not receive public subsidies; nor, for that matter, did those young people who didn't attend college.

Of course, state legislators did not simply stop funding public education. In fact, state funding per student remained roughly stable.[58] But if states continued funding higher education at about the same level while overall costs rose, someone else was going to have to pick up the slack. The responsibility for paying the rising costs of college fell to students and their families. The share of public colleges' budgets that came from tuition rose markedly, so that the state's share of a public college's budget declined while tuition's share rose. Gradually, the burden of funding college shifted from the taxpayers to the students through a process of gradual *privatization*.[59]

Shifting costs to students created a feedback loop and increased their dependence on loans. As the costs of college rose and the proportions of those costs covered by students increased, students found themselves faced with ever higher bills. Increasingly, they turned to student loans. As a larger share of students found it difficult to pay their college costs out of savings or earnings, they joined the ranks of borrowers, and the amounts they borrowed began to rise.

Reverberations for Colleges

The availability of student loans encouraged far more students not just to consider attending college but to choose among a broader array of colleges. Whereas many students continued to attend a reasonably affordable institution not too far from the home where they had been raised, more began to think about other educational options.[60] Similarly, once some parents began to view loans as a way to reduce the amount they needed to contribute toward their children's college costs, they were more willing to support decisions to attend costlier schools.[61] If college was a good investment, many reasoned, the better the college, the greater the potential payoff. The publication of guidebooks to help prospective students and their parents make college choices took off. *U.S. News & World Report*, which began ranking colleges and universities in 1983, was soon publishing rankings for a host of categories, such as national universities, liberal arts colleges, regional universities, and so on. And there were more services to help students and their families game the application system—SAT preparation courses, guidebooks for writing college application essays, and on and on. This information encouraged people to make comparisons among colleges, to view one school as better than—worth more than—another, which in turn encouraged borrowing so as to be able to afford the superior education.

Because students were now more likely to be considering several colleges, colleges began struggling to make their wares more competitive, in what has been called "the arms race for ephemeral national prestige."[62] Often this involved improving amenities: "The quality of life and education on campus keeps improving—with food courts, state-of-the-art classrooms, modern living-learning residence halls, and new fitness centers. These improvements are often viewed by campus leaders as essential in recruiting and retaining top students, and they come with a high cost that is generally paid through higher tuition and fees."[63]

Student loans made both colleges and prospective students less concerned about these higher prices. As it became increasingly common for students to borrow money to pay for higher education, colleges began to appreciate that students were becoming less price sensitive.[64] Once students came to the realization that they were going to need to borrow some of what they would need to pay for an education, it became easier to justify borrowing a bit more. That is, once students had accepted the idea that it would be necessary to borrow, say, $5,000, they were unlikely to balk at the prospect of borrowing $6,000. These circumstances encouraged colleges to spend—and charge—more to make their campuses attractive to prospective students.[65]

While student loans are not the sole reason college costs have risen faster than inflation, they undoubtedly contribute to the process. Loans enable many young people to attain educations that otherwise would be far beyond their—or their families'—means. If prospective students were less likely to draw the line at high costs, colleges found it easier to charge more. As we will see, these developments had the most dramatic effects on for-profit schools.

All these reverberations were predictable. As early as 1980, Stephen P. Dresch, an economist, listed some "behavioral effects of student loan programs," predicting that they would

- encourage potential students to select schooling over other activities;
- encourage students to select higher-cost schooling options and to substitute borrowed funds for their own earnings in the financing of schooling;
- encourage parents to reduce their contributions to their children's schooling;
- encourage institutions to increase student charges (tuition, fees, room, board) and to reduce institutionally awarded grant aid; and
- encourage governments to reduce grant aid and other aid to students and institutions.[66]

As a piece of social scientific soothsaying, this list holds up remarkably well.

This chapter really tells three stories. The first involves the dramatic expansion of federal student loan programs during the twenty-five years following the creation of Sallie Mae, with more students borrowing more money to pay for ever more expensive educations. The second concerns the attention paid to defaults during this period. Policymakers and the press focused on the need to control deadbeat students; this was the visible student loan mess, the one people worried about and tried to bring under control through a variety of policy reforms. But the third story is in many ways the most interesting: the barely noticed ways that people and institutions responded to the growing importance of student loans, the ways that legislatures began to shift the burden of paying for public higher education from taxpayers to students, and the ways that colleges were able to increase costs. (Chapter 3 will consider yet another reverberation—the expansion of for-profit education beyond the realm of vocational education, into institutions competing with traditional not-for-profit colleges and universities.) All these shifts ensured that student loan debt would rise rapidly—more rapidly than the cost of living, more rapidly even than the cost of education. And this would set the stage for the third student loan mess.

CHAPTER THREE

Outrage and Crushing Debt

The Third Student Loan Mess

Even as policymakers concentrated on reducing defaults by student deadbeats during the second student loan mess, a new concern—what we'll call the *third student loan mess*—was taking form. It was already visible in 1994, when President Clinton argued that the direct loan program he'd advocated "will decrease the debt burden that crushes too many."[1] By the beginning of the new century, references to student loans as "crushing debt" would become commonplace.

As the twentieth century came to a close, self-help books aimed at those dealing with student loans began to appear, with titles such as *The Guerrilla Guide to Mastering Student Loan Debt* (1997) and *Take Control of Your Student Loan Debt* (first published in 1999).[2] These manuals listed the types of loans and gave strategies for dealing with debt. Soon there would be more critical books about the situation of those paying for student loans, featuring angrier titles: *Strapped: Why America's 20- and 30-Somethings Can't Get Ahead* (2005); *Generation Debt: How Our Future Was Sold Out for Student Loans, Credit Cards, Bad Jobs, No Benefits, and Tax Cuts for Rich Geezers—and How to Fight Back* (2007); and *The Student Loan Scam: The Most Oppressive Debt in U.S. History—and How We Can Fight Back* (2009).[3] These analyses—all by young authors—began with personal accounts that described either their own or their friends' struggles with heavy debt. More recently, there have been testimonials—such as *Destroy Student Debt: A Combat Guide to Freedom* (2012), which recounted how the author repaid $90,000 in student loans in only seven months, and *Debt-Free U: How I Paid for an Outstanding College Education without Loans, Scholarships, or Mooching Off My Parents* (2010)—and even a "time-travel murder mystery" (*Death by Student Loan,* 2010) in which the heroine faces $100,000 in loans.[4]

Photos of the 2011 Occupy Wall Street demonstrations featured protesters with homemade signs, such as "Is 'Following Your Dream' supposed to be this terrifying? $60,000+ in debt from my student loans," and "I have $80,000 in student loan debt. How can I ever pay that back now?" Editorial cartoons portrayed student loans as outsized bullies, giant backpacks, or other crushing burdens. The new student loan mess focused not on bright young people blocked from achieving their dreams or on irresponsible deadbeats but on former students who had pursued the American Dream of higher education, only to find themselves in hock to their eyeballs.

WHY STUDENT LOAN DEBT BECAME "CRUSHING"

All federal student loan programs have placed limits on the amounts that can be borrowed. Recall that under the initial loan program—the National Defense Education Act of 1958—a student could borrow up to $1,000 per year; thus four years of loans would total $33,815 in 2013 dollars.[5] Over time, student loan regulations allowed students to borrow ever-larger sums. For example, in 1988–89, a dependent student (that is, one deemed financially dependent on parental support) could receive subsidized Stafford loans (that is, loans for which the federal government would cover the interest payments so long as the student continued to be enrolled in school) up to a total of $13,250 for four years of study (over $23,000 in 2013 dollars); ten years later, such students could borrow a total of $17,125 (about the same—$23,000 in 2013 dollars). In 1998–99, independent students (those deemed not reliant on parental support) could borrow an additional $18,000 in unsubsidized Stafford loans (meaning that the accrued interest would be added to the principal); that is, such students could borrow up to $35,125 for four years of study (about $48,000 in 2013 dollars), although with the interest from their unsubsidized loans added to the principal, they would graduate owing more than that.[6] And the limits continued to rise: in 2012–13, a dependent undergraduate student could receive direct loans totaling $31,000 (with $23,000 of that subsidized) over four years; an independent undergraduate could borrow $49,000 (again with $23,000 subsidized).[7] Much higher amounts were available for those going on to attend graduate or professional school.

In other words, the limits on what students could borrow increased. But why did this come to be viewed as a problem? Three factors were at work.

Limits on Student Loans Weren't Keeping Up with Rising College Costs

Raising these borrowing limits was necessary if student loan programs were to remain relevant. For starters, inflation required that students be allowed to borrow more; a $1,000 loan could go a long way toward paying for a year of college in 1958, whereas by 2012, a $1,000 loan would make only a modest dent in a year's tab, even at most public institutions. And, of course, college costs had been rising even faster than inflation (recall figure 10); even if the borrowing limits on student loans had some cost-of-living adjustment, this would not have kept pace with college costs.

Table 1 illustrates the failure of student loan programs to keep pace with the costs of being a residential student at a private college.[8] A first-year student in 1958 who borrowed the maximum over four years could cover about half the costs of tuition, fees, and living on campus. By 1988, loans for dependent students would cover only about a quarter of those costs; today, about a fifth. Although it might seem like loan limits more or less kept up with inflation (in that the maximum students could borrow in 1958 and in 2013 both amount to about $30,000 in 2013 dollars), they have fallen well behind rising college costs.

TABLE 1

Maximum Available Loans Have Not Kept Pace with
Average Costs at Private Colleges

Program	Maximum Loan (four years)[a]	Average Cost (four years)[a,b]	Maximum Loan as a Percentage of Average Cost
NDEA (1958)	$4,000	~$8,000	50%
Stafford (1988)	$13,250	$51,250	26%
Stafford (1998)	$17,125[c]	$86,600	20%
Direct Loan (2012)	$31,000[c,d]	$145,500	21%

[a]Assumes student enrolled in four consecutive years beginning with the date given.

[b]Average cost of tuition, fees, room, and board at private, four-year institutions (data after 1999 include only not-for-profit institutions). Source for data after 1988: National Center for Education Statistics (2012: table 349).

[c]For dependent students (higher loan limits available for independent students).

[d]Includes both subsidized and unsubsidized loans.

Loans Became Harder to Pay Off as Economic Growth Slowed for the Middle Class

The students who took out those early student loans left college to enter a rapidly expanding economy featuring not just relatively high inflation but also rising real incomes. In 1958, median family income was $5,100 (about $40,970 in 2013 dollars); in 1968, it was $8,630 ($57,575 in 2013 dollars). This meant that taking out a $1,000 NDEA loan in 1958 didn't pose such a savage burden, both because the dollars paid back weren't worth as much and because people were earning more dollars. That is, $1,000 borrowed in 1958 was equal to nearly 20 percent of the median household's income. Imagine still owing that money ten years later: $1,000 was less than 12 percent of the now larger median household income. This made student loans seem like less of a burden. By the 1990s inflation rates were lower and real income growth was much reduced, so that the long-term burden of student loans now seemed much greater.[9]

There Was Less Slack in the System

The second student loan mess—the concern about student deadbeats—led to a variety of tougher rules intended to ensure that students would repay the sums they had borrowed. To be sure, there were provisions for canceling some loans. People who were engaged in public service, such as some teachers or law enforcement officers, could have some or all of their loans canceled. In general, cancellation provisions were more generous for those with Perkins loans (intended to assist lower-income students) than for those with Stafford or direct loans (also available to middle-income students). For instance, one guidebook noted: "If you are a full-time elementary or secondary school teacher serving low-income students, you can cancel up to 100% of your Perkins loans." However, cancellation terms for borrowers with Stafford or federal direct loans were less favorable: "If ... you are not in default on your loans and you have been employed as a full-time teacher for five consecutive years in a school that qualifies for loan cancellation under the Perkins program ..., you can cancel up to $5,000 of the total amount still outstanding after you have completed the fifth year of teaching."[10]

There were also various arrangements that offered some flexibility by stretching repayment over longer periods, so that a borrower's monthly payments would be lower (although slowing the rate at which the principal was reduced meant additional interest charges, thereby increasing the total that would have to be repaid). But by and large, a student who borrowed money was going to have to pay it back, and many students wound up owing large sums.

> **MILESTONES IN STUDENT LOANS**
>
> 2011: $100,000,000,000 in new student loans

As a result, as the twenty-first century began, complaints about the burden of student loan debt grew louder. The first student loan mess was typified by a bright young person who could not afford to pursue an education, and policymakers rushed to establish loan programs to bring college into reach of all. The key figures in the second student loan mess were those deadbeat students who needed to be compelled to meet their responsibilities and repay what they'd borrowed. Now the focus shifted yet again, this time to young people no longer in school but crushed by the burden of student loan debt.

CONTINUAL EXPANSION OF STUDENT LOAN PROGRAMS

Trends that were already well established during the last decades of the twentieth century continued into the new millennium. The proportion of young people seeking more education continued to rise. This increase occurred in every income group; although the gap between the rates at which high school graduates from low- and high-income families entered college remained substantial, it was growing smaller.[11] And as we saw in chapter 2, democratizing the college population meant that there would be more students at greater risk of default.

Moreover, federal grant programs—designed to support the education of the lowest-income students—were shrinking. In 1980, the maximum Pell grant covered 69 percent of the cost of tuition, fees, and room and board at a public four-year college. By 2010, the largest Pell grant would cover only 34 percent of those costs.[12] The share of all federal financial aid supplied by grants had fallen from 55 percent in 1979 to only 26 percent in 2007, even as student loans' share of financial aid rose from 39 to 64 percent.[13] As grants became harder to come by, more high-risk students were encouraged to borrow.

At the same time, the cost of college continued to outstrip inflation (see figure 10), which ensured that a growing proportion of students would need to borrow money for their educations. In particular, the trend for public institutions to shift an ever-larger share of the costs of college onto students continued. Nationally, between 1990 and 2010, state support per student fell more than 25 percent.[14] Yet costs continued to rise: "From 2001 to 2011, ... tuition and fees at state schools increased 72 percent.... Ohio's flagship university, Ohio State, now receives 7 percent of its budget from the state, down from 15 percent a decade ago and 25 percent in 1990."[15] With state support declining even as college costs rose, a growing share of students at public colleges needed to borrow money.

And as noted above, borrowing limits rose to meet the increased demand for loans. With students—who were on average less able to afford the costs of college—facing ever higher costs, it is easy to understand why more students were borrowing more money. A 2010 study by the Project on Student Debt compared students with loans who graduated in 1996 with their counterparts in the class of 2008. In 2008, 10 percent had borrowed at least $40,000; in contrast, only 3 percent of the 1996 students had that much debt (calculated in 2008 dollars). Moreover, the Great Recession made things even worse when new graduates found it harder to get jobs: "Borrowers with such high levels of debt are more likely to have difficulty repaying their loans, especially in tough economic times when high-paying jobs are hard to find. The unemployment rate for young bachelor's degree recipients was a sizable 5.7% in 2008 and rose to 8.8% by 2009, the highest on record."[16]

Even as borrowing limits increased, the proportion of those who borrowed the maximum amounts available rose. In 1988–89, 18 percent of undergraduates receiving Stafford loans borrowed the maximum allowed (including both subsidized and unsubsidized loans); in 1999–2000, loan limits were higher, yet the percentage of students borrowing the maximum rose to 52 percent.[17] Inevitably, this meant that borrowing was increasing most among students from families with relatively high incomes. Student loans had always been intended to boost the prospects of those from lower-income backgrounds, while those from higher-income families were better able to pay for college without resorting to incurring debt. Thus, in 1989–90, among dependent students with Stafford loans who came from families with incomes in the lowest quartile (remember that these students might also be eligible for

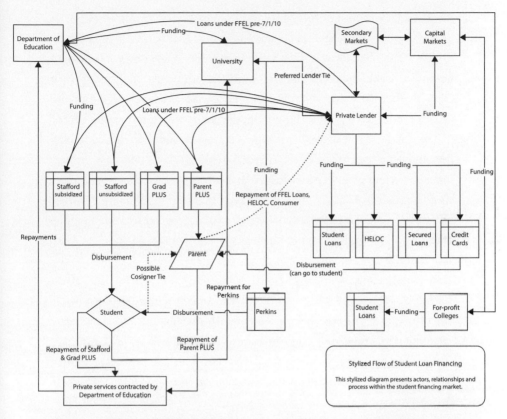

Figure 12. The market for student loans (2013). Source: Adapted from Edmiston, Brooks, and Shelpelwich (2013: figure 1).

other student aid programs, such as Pell grants and lower-interest Perkins loans), 29 percent borrowed the maximum amount possible, compared to only 6 percent of those from families with incomes in the highest quartile. By 1995–96, the percentage borrowing the Stafford loan maximum rose modestly among those whose families had the lowest incomes, from 29 to 34 percent, but more than tripled among those from the highest-income families, rising from 6 to 20 percent.[18] Student loan debt was spreading farther into the middle class.

Not only did student loan programs expand in size, but the array of programs available also grew; in 2013, the Federal Reserve Bank of

Kansas City presented a bewilderingly complex diagram that sought to give an overview of the student loan system (see figure 12). And it is important to remember that federal student loans were only one way to help pay for an education. Students and their families also used money from work and savings; colleges might award them reduced tuition; they might receive grants; they might get loans from their state or from private lenders; and so on.[19] Just how students financed their educations depended upon a host of factors, such as their academic records and financial circumstances, and where and what they studied. Still, over time, a growing share of students were relying on federal student loan programs, and they were borrowing ever-larger sums. No wonder attention began to turn to the burden of loan debt.

CLAIMS ABOUT CRUSHING DEBT

Obviously, student loan debt is not evenly distributed among all students. In fact, the distribution is so uneven that statistics about *average student loan debt* need to be treated with considerable care. Remember that some students complete their education with no debt. We might suspect that these fortunate students tend to come from better-off families, which have sufficient income or savings to cover college costs without borrowing. We might also suspect that debt-free graduates tend to have attended less expensive institutions and have studied for shorter periods of time. That is, a student who completes an associate's degree at a public community college will be less likely to take out student loans than someone who attends only private institutions for however many years it takes to complete an undergraduate program plus graduate or professional training.

One common way of calculating average student loan debt is to include students without any loans in the calculations. This can give a poor picture of the problem. Imagine that we take ten students: five have no debt, and the other five each owe $10,000. If we calculate the average student loan debt by dividing the students' total debt ($50,000) by the number of students (10), we discover that the average debt is $5,000, but this is not a terribly useful figure, since the students with debt all owe twice as much as that average. A better way to frame the question is to ask what is the average student loan debt *among those students who actually have loans;* in our example, of course, the answer would be $10,000—a figure that gives a clearer sense of the challenges facing those borrowers.

Note, too, that the students in our example who owe $10,000 may experience repaying their debts in very different ways. Students who graduate and find jobs that pay well may find their student loan debt completely manageable. Others—such as those who graduate when the economy is in difficulty and well-paid jobs are hard to find, or whose degrees don't qualify them for such jobs—may wind up with lower incomes, such that paying off their loans does become a burden. The American Council of Education advocates using "a more accurate measure of the student borrowing challenge": "Debt burden, measured as a percentage of income that must be dedicated to loan payments after graduation, provides a more balanced look at both sides of student borrowing—the debt and the payoff."[20] Having a debt burden of 7 percent or less is deemed *manageable,* whereas 8 percent or more is considered *less manageable.*[21] Of course, most workers' incomes rise over time. Assuming their loan payments remain constant, their student loan debt burden is likely to be greatest just after they complete school and then become more manageable as their incomes increase. But saying this ignores the likelihood that many of these borrowers will face other increasing costs as they seek to start families or own homes. Even a "manageable" debt burden can remain a considerable constraint.

Some critics warn that educational debt serves to reproduce patterns of social inequality.[22] Everything else being equal, those from high-income families have less need to borrow and are more likely to enter the workforce with no—or at least manageable—debt burdens. One analysis from 1997 found students' family income inversely correlated with their ability to be debt-free: while less than 40 percent of students who came from lower-income families had no educational debt burden, this was true for over 60 percent of those from upper-income families.[23] Further, African American households had higher average debt burdens than white households.

Student loan programs had been understood as a way to open a route to achieving the American Dream, so that young people who faced disadvantages, whose families couldn't afford to pay for college, would still have access to higher education. But being able to borrow to continue one's education did not mean that all inequalities would somehow be erased. It should not have surprised anyone that students who could pay for college without borrowing would start postcollege life on a more comfortable footing than those who had found themselves racking up five- or six-figure student loan debts.

One common criticism of loan debt was that it forced students to make troubling choices. These choices began before the students even entered college. One 2006 estimate was that "200,000 qualified students every year put off college for financial reasons"—the same number used in those wasted-brainpower claims that people had made nearly fifty years earlier, which inspired the establishment of student loan programs (see chapter 1).[24] The hard choices continued once students were actually on campus. The critics pointed to evidence that, while most undergraduates at four-year colleges held part-time jobs, those with student loans were more likely to work, and to work more hours, than their counterparts without loans—probably not the most surprising finding, since we might assume that students who borrowed would be those in greater need of money.[25] In addition, critics worried that the need to pay off their debts would lead many students to forgo careers they might find attractive in favor of taking less satisfying but higher-paying jobs, and hence there would be "a slight 'creeping up' of the correlation between debt and the pressure felt by undergraduates to go into certain careers."[26] Even after graduation, being in debt might lead young people to move back in with their parents or to postpone continuing their educations, buying houses or cars, getting married, or

Figure 13. Crushing debt has consequences for students and their families (2011).

having children (figure 13).[27] The stresses might spread to parents who had taken out PLUS loans with the understanding that their children would pay them off, only to find their own credit ratings suffering.[28] Debt didn't have to be unmanageable to affect borrowers' lives, but in dramatic cases, it could come to dominate their existence.

It was easy to portray those with crushing debt as sympathetic figures.[29] After all, they had pursued higher education to better themselves, in line with the urgings of authority figures ranging from their parents to a series of presidents. If they had chosen more expensive private colleges, it was because those choices had been encouraged as the most promising route to a lucrative future. If they had borrowed money, it was only because it was necessary: they had no control over tuition costs and often had no realistic way of saving enough or earning enough to cover those ever-rising bills. In short, student loan debt need not be understood as the result of people rushing headlong into irresponsible borrowing; it could be portrayed as the product of rational choices made by young people to get the educations they sought.

Still, the results could be nightmarish. Books about student loan debt described their authors' firsthand experiences coping with their loans. *Strapped* opened with the author and her husband broke: "We had not a dollar between us and payday was three long days away.... [B]ecoming adults had left us with $57,000 in student loan debt and $19,000 in credit card debt."[30] The author of *The Student Loan Scam* began his book by detailing his own student loan history:

> Over the course of earning three degrees in aerospace engineering at the University of Southern California, I managed to accumulate about thirty-eight thousand dollars in student loans. In 1998, when I graduated, these loans had grown to fifty thousand dollars.... In late 1998, I found a job at an exceptionally good college, Caltech, as an aeronautical research scientist. The salary wasn't high, ... and my monthly student loan payment ... amounted to about 20 percent of my take-home pay. [He fell behind in his loan payments and left Caltech, but found himself unable to find a higher-paying job in his field, and his loans went into default. He eventually contacted the U.S. Department of Education.] I told them I'd repay the principal and accrued interest and even offered to pay at an increased interest rate of 10 percent if only they would remove some of the penalties.... Sallie Mae had already made well over twenty-five thousand dollars on my original thirty-eight-thousand-dollar loan—why should they need more? [He was refused.] ... [B]y mid-2005, my balance had swollen to $103,000.[31]

An account such as this one—describing someone who trained for a career in a demanding and presumably well-paid profession but who wound up with a debt burden equal to a fifth of his take-home pay (remember that payments above 7 percent are judged "less manageable"), who fell behind in his payments, who left one job in hopes of landing a better-paying one only to find that the job market had dried up, who tried repeatedly to renegotiate the terms of his loan, and who wound up still owing more than twice as much as he'd borrowed—

makes harrowing reading. At least for some students, the student loan program, which had been intended to boost opportunities, instead trapped borrowers in inescapable long-term indebtedness, a twenty-first-century version of, if not slavery or indentured servitude, at least owing one's soul to the company store. Tamara Draut, the author of *Strapped,* called it the "debt-for-diploma system."[32]

Increasingly, critics argued that the program had lost sight of its purpose, that it operated to protect lenders against losses at the quite literal expense of the borrowers. Thus, an article in *Academe,* the magazine of the American Association of University Professors, drew parallels between student loans and indentured servitude, and concluded:

> College student loan debt perverts the aims of higher education, whether those aims are to grant freedom of intellectual exploration, to cultivate merit and thereby mitigate the inequitable effects of class, or, in the most utilitarian scheme, to provide students with a head start into the adult work world. In practice, debt shackles students with long-term loan payments, constraining their freedom of choice of jobs and career. It also constrains their everyday lives after graduating, as they bear the weight of the monthly tab that stays with them long after their college days.[33]

An NYU professor warned: "Foreclosing the future of young people is a callous act, and a self-destructive path for any society. But allowing Wall Street financiers to feed off their predicament is beyond any moral compass."[34]

Such critiques could lead to proposals not just to somehow end the reliance on student loans in the future, so as to keep future students from being trapped by crushing debt, but even that existing debts should be forgiven, freeing those burdened by paying off their loans. Why not declare a jubilee, write off the loans, and free up those with loan debt to boost the economy by purchasing homes and other goods? The Occupy Student Debt Campaign (part of the larger Occupy movement) articulated principles that included "free public education, through federal coverage of tuition fees," "zero-interest student loans, so that no one can profit from them," and "the elimination of current student debt, through a single act of relief."[35] The campaign invited borrowers to sign a pledge to withhold loan payments after a million other people had signed. *The Debt Resistor's Operations Manual* declared: "To the financial establishment of the world, we have only one thing to say: We owe you nothing.... [E]very dollar we withhold from the collection agency is a tiny piece of our own lives and freedom that we can give back to our communities, to those we love and we respect. These are acts of debt resistance."[36] The manual's section on student loans warns: "If we fight this system alone, the best we can hope for is to keep our heads above water. The good news is that those suffering with student debt have begun to organize. Collective action is the only true solution."[37] In comparison to these far-reaching proposals, federal efforts to address crushing student debt fell far short of resolving the third student loan mess.

ADDRESSING CRUSHING DEBT

The third student loan mess received more public attention than its predecessors, and it became a more contentious topic. To be sure, student loans enjoyed broad support. There were now many more students relying on student loans, many of them from middle-class families, so the program had a large, broad constituency. Most policymakers accepted that higher education brought important communal benefits, and they understood that their constituents depended on access to student loans, which made them reluctant to cut back the program in major ways. But there were increasing partisan tensions: during the Clinton administration, Democrats had favored offering more direct loans, while many Republicans defended guaranteeing loans from private lenders. And as the program grew and student loan debt emerged as an issue, Republicans worried about the costs of an ever-growing social program, while Democrats seemed more concerned with making the terms of student loans more favorable to borrowers. These differences led to more open, more rancorous debates than had characterized earlier student loan policymaking.

Republican ambivalence toward student loans was apparent in George W. Bush's administration. During an early 2002 discussion on education issues, President Bush seemed to acknowledge that students were accumulating more debt: "Right now our Government forgives up to $5,000 in student loans. If someone is willing to teach math, science, or special ed in a school that is having trouble recruiting teachers, then we ought to forgive up to $17,500 in student loans."[38] He was referring to the $5,000 forgiveness available to Stafford loan recipients after teaching five years in a low-income school. The limit was indeed raised to $17,500 for "highly-qualified math, sciences, and special education teachers" in those schools.[39]

However, the Bush administration also sought to slow the growth of the student loan program as part of its efforts to rein in domestic spending, and this invited criticism. The Deficit Reduction Act of 2005 promised to "shave $12.7 billion out of the federal student loan program, in large part by locking in interest rates often at a higher level than the current variable rates. 'This bill is the largest raid on student aid in history,' said Rep. George Miller (Calif.), the senior Democrat on the House education committee."[40] Even the usually conservative commentator Dick Morris criticized Bush for signing the measure:

> In the accompanying press release, the president said that the bill was about "Improving Federal Student Loan Programs and Increasing Benefits to Students." And yet these "improvements" actually *cut* student loan funding—by a net $13 billion!—while socking student borrowers with huge interest rate increases which they must pay in order to get the education that the government keeps telling them they need to compete in today's global economy.... In fact, of the $40 billion in spending cut under [the act], the largest share by far came from the cuts in student loans. This thoroughly iniquitous piece of legislation rolls back decades of federal policy bent on encouraging students to ... continue their education.[41]

Reducing federal domestic spending may have been a desirable goal, but policies that led to student borrowers paying higher interest rates could be criticized for only making the crushing debt mess worse.

However, these denunciations simplified a complex policy issue. Borrowers, of course, prefer low rates of interest, but interest rates fluctuate with the economy. When loans are taken out in years when interest rates are low, borrowers would prefer to lock in their payments at a fixed rate, but when interest rates are high, they prefer loans that offer variable rates so that their payments fall if interest rates decline. On the other hand, lenders favor variable rates for loans made when interest rates are low and fixed rates on loans made when interest rates are high. Things become more complicated when we realize that students usually take out a new loan each year, possibly with very different terms than for their previous loans if the economy has shifted.[42] So the sorts of terms borrowers and lenders favor may shift from year to year.

In 2001, Congress had agreed that, beginning in mid-2006, Stafford loans would have a fixed interest rate of 6.8 percent: "Lawmakers, higher education associations, and student advocate organizations championed the bill because ... 6.8 percent ... was lower than estimates of what borrowers would pay" under the current variable rate. However, the economy shifted and interest rates fell sharply, so that a 6.8 percent fixed rate no longer seemed especially favorable. The bill Bush signed maintained the fixed-rate formula, and "some observers interpreted Congress' decision to maintain the rates as a Republican-led Congress charging higher interest rates on student loans to reduce the deficit."[43] During the 2006 campaign, some Democrats promised to cut student loan interest rates in half, to 3.4 percent. Student loans now touched a larger share of the American population and had emerged as a campaign issue.

Democrats regained control of both houses of Congress in the 2006 elections. Faced with Congressional Budget Office estimates that fulfilling their pledge to cut interest rates on a wide range of student loans to 3.4 percent would cost $52 billion over five years, they backpedaled and passed a narrower, much less costly bill that applied a 3.4 percent rate only to subsidized Stafford loans for undergraduates issued during the 2011–12 academic year. This in turn set up a new crisis for 2012—

would Congress extend the lower rates?—with President Barack Obama pressuring Republicans ("This should be a no-brainer") during the run-up to that year's presidential election. The lower rate was extended for one more year, which set the stage for an annual congressional drama in which Democrats could call for extending lower rates and criticize Republicans for their willingness to burden students.[44] These dramas were overwrought in that they concerned only loans from one federal program taken out in a particular year, and maintaining the 3.4 percent interest rate saved the typical student with a subsidized loan of less than ten dollars per month.[45] In 2013, Congress and the president agreed on a new variable rate that would cover several loan programs and would result in students paying lower interest rates, so long as the economy remained favorable.[46]

Although slashing interest rates on all student loans proved impossible for congressional Democrats during Bush's last years in office, they were able to draw attention to a seemingly more straightforward issue—corruption and inefficiency in the guaranteed loan program. A recent series of scandals had exposed questionable links between private lenders and colleges. Many students looked to college financial aid offices for guidance in choosing a lender, and colleges often distributed lists of recommended lenders. It was revealed that lenders were paying colleges for favorable placement on those lists. In some cases, individual financial aid officers were found to have received stock options or consulting fees from particular lenders. In other cases, it was the colleges that benefited from the kickbacks: "In one egregious attempt to persuade the University of Maryland to list it as a 'preferred lender,' loan giant Nelnet gave the school a $50,000 'donation.' Several lenders created 'revenue sharing,' which kicked back a portion of the profits on student loans to schools, meaning that universities like Duquesne were directly profiting from helping to drive their students into debt."[47]

During the 1990s, the Clinton administration had tried to promote direct loans, arguing that they would prove cheaper for both borrowers and the federal government, because ensuring that there would be profits for lenders inevitably raised the cost of guaranteed loans. The scandals involving colleges that received kickbacks for recommending particular private lenders suggested that the guaranteed loan market was tainted by corrupt practices and fell far short of an efficient free market where competition among lenders kept interest rates low. For its critics, the guaranteed loan program might have been designed simply to profit lenders. *Rolling Stone* argued, "The system essentially operates as a lucrative form of corporate welfare, offering a guaranteed rate of return for banks and other middlemen who provide capital for student loans," while, according to the *New Yorker,* "the government hands out billions of dollars in subsidies to lenders every year, all but insuring them a steady profit. In effect, lenders get a guaranteed return with very little risk."[48]

Even conservative and business periodicals—predictable advocates for the superiority of private enterprise over government programs— found it hard to oppose direct loans. *Business Week* conceded, "Lenders insist that they provide valuable services, including running financial-literacy programs that help students budget payments. But the default rate for federal student loans made by private lenders is 7.3%, compared with 5.3% for direct federal loans, according to the Education Dept.," while the *Weekly Standard* called guaranteed loans "a textbook example of crony capitalism" and declared, "Direct lending saves the government money—no really, it does—by reducing fees and other handling costs, savings which can then be passed on to the poorer borrowers," before adding, "though they never are."[49]

In contrast, direct loans became the centerpiece of the Obama administration's response to the third student loan mess. More than any of his predecessors, Obama made frequent reference to student loans, even turning the new ubiquity of loans into a laugh line at a commencement address at Arizona State University in 2009: "Maybe you've got student loans—no, you definitely have student loans."[50] In 2010, the Obama administration ended federal guaranteed student loans and committed the federal government to making only direct loans. In legislative maneuvering, student loans were attached to the administration's healthcare reform, and there were provisions to shift some of the revenue from student loans toward making up anticipated shortfalls in healthcare costs.[51] The shift to direct loans was popular, and Obama made frequent reference to it during his 2012 reelection campaign:

> Education is the only reason I'm standing on this stage. It's the only reason Michelle was able to do what she did. And so we haven't forgotten that we needed some student loans to get through school. That's why over the last 4 years, we've helped millions of students pay less for college because we finally took on a system that was wasting billions of dollars on banks and lenders. We said, let's cut out the middleman; let's give the money directly to students.[52]

The Obama administration recognized that direct loans might reduce the amounts borrowers owed, but they would hardly eliminate crushing debt. It offered a range of other programs designed to make debt more manageable. Policies to forgive some loans for people who entered careers in public service had never vanished, but now there were calls to qualify more careers for forgiveness. The *Weekly Standard* complained that "only a certain kind of graduate would be denied this splendid perk of an education: the idiot who went to work in the world of buying, selling, investing, making, and producing."[53] In 2012, Obama proposed a "Pay-As-You-Earn" option that would allow participants to cap their payments as a percentage of their income; after twenty years of payments, the balance would be forgiven. The effect of this program would be to make repayment more manageable for those who wound up earning more modest incomes.[54]

However, the new program would hardly make the issue of crippling debt vanish. Imagine a student graduating in 2012 with the average student loan debt ($26,600—the median debt among those graduates with student loans), made up of subsidized loans (basically the least costly type of student loan); further imagine that she takes a job paying an average salary ($44,259—the median entry-level salary for college graduates). Her basic cost-of-living expenses (defined as 150 percent of the poverty level—$16,755 for a single person without dependents) would be exempt, and she would pay a maximum of 10 percent of her remaining income to pay down student loan debt. Taking inflation and annual increases in her salary into account, she would pay off her student loan debt in 118 months—that is, just within the normal ten-year period for paying off loans.[55] In other words, the program would work out well for her: she would be able to repay what she needed without experiencing crushing debt.

But this is an idealistic scenario—average debt load, least expensive loan type, starting an average-salary job immediately after leaving college. In fact, even switching our student's loan type from subsidized to unsubsidized loans (so that the interest on the loan accrued while she remained in school) would increase her debt enough that this hypothetical student would still owe $7,209.11 after 120 months—obliging the federal government to forgive that amount. And things can get much worse. For students who have borrowed more than average, earn less than average salary, or—a particular concern during the weak economy of the Great Recession—are unable to find and keep jobs, it is likely that they will not be able to retire their debt within ten years, so some of it will have to be forgiven.

The reality is that many students will have problematic loans. Some people advise students that they can afford to have student loan debt equal to their expected starting salary—or even more.[56] But for a student who borrowed an amount equivalent to the average starting salary in unsubsidized loans and also earned that average salary upon graduation, the total balance owed would actually rise during the first three years of repayment in this program. After ten years, the student would still owe $41,775.34 in principal based on a $44,259 original loan (that is, this student would have repaid $32,637.12 but only reduced the principal by $2,483.66). Note, too, that once there is a policy that debts still owed after ten years will be forgiven, there is almost no incentive for borrowers not to borrow as much as possible—because each additional dollar of debt will likely be forgiven.

The Obama administration also began pressuring colleges to make the costs of education more transparent.[57] The president's State of the Union messages began warning colleges that continued support from the federal government might depend upon their bringing costs under control. In other words, the Obama administration's solution to the third student loan mess—to crushing debt—was to minimize interest payments through direct loans, make payments more manageable, forgive some debts, and call for colleges to do a better job of informing students about the cost of higher education. Such piecemeal measures could reduce some pressure on some borrowers, but they could not address the underlying issues: the costs of higher education continued to rise, even as more people sought its benefits.

Following the passage of the bills setting 3.4 percent interest rates on subsidized Stafford loans, first for 2011–2012 and then for 2012–13, there were calls for more fundamental changes. In 2013, several Democratic House members proposed the Student Loan Fairness Act, which would cap all federal loans at 3.4 percent, establish a "10–10" standard repayment plan (under which borrowers would repay an amount equivalent to 10 percent of their discretionary income for ten years, after which any remaining debt would be forgiven), and further reduce repayment obligations for people who entered public service in underserved communities.[58] Under such rules, individuals who borrowed substantial sums and went on to earn modest incomes would be very unlikely to repay all the principal—let alone the interest—on their loans. Such proposals challenged what had, during the second student loan mess, seemed to be a growing consensus that education was an individualistic rather than a communal good so that individuals could expect to pay a growing share of those rising costs. Now the menace of crushing debt was calling into question whether individual borrowers should be obliged to repay all their educational costs. While attention focused on that issue, other developments, both in higher education and in the lifestyles of college students, were attracting less notice.

REVERBERATIONS: THE EMERGENCE
OF PROPRIETARY COLLEGES

Just as the availability of federally guaranteed loans for vocational institutions had led to an expansion in proprietary trade schools during the 1960s and 1970s, once student loans became a standard way of financing higher education, proprietary colleges began to emerge.

The idea of for-profit colleges was not new. In the mid-1960s, as the Vietnam War escalated and young men could receive student deferments from the draft, media attention focused on Parsons College in Fairfield, Iowa. The college's president argued that, through innovative policies (such as offering large classes, heavy teaching loads, and admission to students who had flunked out of other colleges but could retain their draft deferments by enrolling at Parsons), Parsons could make a "profit." In fact, the college retained its classification as a nonprofit institution, although journalists speculated about whether this might be the beginning of a shift toward higher education becoming for-profit.[59] Nonetheless, Parsons folded in 1973.

Only three years later, another for-profit institution, the University of Phoenix, opened its doors. In 1989, it began offering online courses, although it did not attract much national attention until the late 1990s.[60] Phoenix targeted older, working students and awarded them credits for life experiences. The *New Yorker* quoted its president: "The people who are our students don't really want the education. They want what the education provides for them—better jobs, moving up in their career, the ability to speak up in meetings, that kind of stuff. They want it to *do* something for them."[61] Or as *Fortune* put it, Phoenix had "a solid business mindset.... Their customers (students) expect to get what they pay for (a job)."[62]

Although the new for-profits presented themselves as colleges and universities, offering undergraduate and even graduate degrees, they resembled traditional proprietary vocational schools in that their emphasis was on career training. And while *Fortune*'s article cheerfully noted that for-profits cost less than "traditional private colleges," they were more expensive than public higher education (recall figure 10). What drew students were the programs designed to accommodate those with jobs—classes taken one at a time and lasting just a few weeks, and scheduled in the evenings, after working hours. These students often had not gone on to college directly after high school; on average, they had weaker academic credentials and fewer financial resources and might have had difficulty being admitted to traditional not-for-profit colleges. They were, in short, high-risk students who were likely to need help paying for college, which meant that for-profit colleges depended on students having access to loans. The press coverage tended to ignore the importance of federal loans for these schools, although *Fortune* did mention that for-profits needed to "fulfill federal requirements for granting student aid" by demonstrating "low student loan default rates."[63] Of course, this was not setting the bar all that high; colleges' resistance to federal requirements regarding defaults (discussed in chapter 2) meant that students could qualify for federal student loans to attend colleges whose students had default rates as high as 20 percent.[64]

For for-profit colleges to show the sort of growing profits that would appeal to investors, it was necessary to continually expand their enrollment. Inevitably, this meant admitting students who were—again, on average—at ever-higher risk because they had weaker academic skills or fewer financial resources. In 2001, for-profit colleges enrolled 766,000 students; by 2010, this figure had more than tripled—to over 2.4 million, with the University of Phoenix having the largest share, or about 475,000 degree-seeking students. The Department of Education ranked Phoenix at the top of its list of colleges with the highest enrollments (in comparison, Arizona State University, the largest not-for-profit institution, had 68,000 students).[65]

A 2010 Senate report noted that for-profits' dramatic growth depended on federal dollars:

> Along with this growth in enrollment, the amount of Federal student aid dollars that taxpayers provide to these companies each year has increased

dramatically. In the 2009–10 academic year, $32 billion in Education Department grants and loans were paid to for-profit colleges. Ten years ago, that figure was about $5 billion. For-profit colleges now collect almost 25 percent of total Federal student aid money (up from 12.2 percent in 2001), over a third of GI bill education benefits to veterans, and half of all active duty servicemember tuition assistance dollars.[66]

During the third student loan mess, most commentators ignored these issues; they tended to marvel at the for-profits' popularity and speculate about the future of online higher education. (However, for-profits would soon become a focus of concern, as detailed in chapter 4.)

REVERBERATIONS: THE AFFLUENT STUDENT LIFESTYLE

It is important to appreciate that, only a generation ago, being a college student was a less expensive proposition than it has become. Useful word-processing programs for personal computers have been around for only about thirty years, the Internet as a widely accessible source for e-mail and information for about twenty. Today, virtually all college students are equipped with at least one personal computer. Cell phones have become ubiquitous, and relatively expensive smart phones are nearly as common. It would be difficult—probably not impossible, but quite challenging—to be a student today without having both a cell phone and a personal computer.

In other words, twenty-first-century students are equipped with more technology than their counterparts just a couple of decades ago. It costs money to purchase and maintain computers and cell phones. These devices also cost colleges, which need to create and manage the infrastructure so that students have high-speed access to the Internet, and of course those costs are passed along to students in the form of higher tuition and fees. But, as we have noticed, students have become less price sensitive. Students expect to need to borrow to attend college; if they need to borrow a bit more to have essentials like cell phones and computers, they are likely to view those expenses as just the normal costs of college.

It is relatively easy—particularly for younger college students and their parents—to view spending and borrowing as a normal part of the college experience. In 2006, retailers projected that college students heading back to campus would spend $36.6 billion. Companies like Bed, Bath & Beyond stock all manner of supplies for dorm rooms and run sales at the beginning of each academic year.[67] A host of firms sell clothing aimed at college students; anyone who looks at the students in a college classroom will spot a remarkable proportion displaying the logos of clothing brands. Many students own cars. Conspicuous consumption—what one critic calls *premature affluence*—is routine.[68] And just to ensure that students will be able to purchase the goods they want when they want them, the student union often has tables where students can sign up for credit cards. Like other retailers, banks target young adults, who are less likely to have established brand loyalties. Obviously, some students manage their money with care and graduate without either student loans or credit card debt, but there are others who borrow not just to afford the cost of college but to maintain a particular lifestyle while attending college.[69] Like all Americans, college students live in a culture that both values consumption and fuels spending through easy access to credit. And student loans, which often include checks to the students to cover expenses related to their education, can enable a more expensive lifestyle and encourage consumption, which only increases the need for additional borrowing.[70] Even those who have graduated and found jobs may rack up additional credit card debt on the assumption that they now ought to be able to afford all of the trappings of adult life.

No wonder the various self-help books intended to help people manage their student loan debt typically devote several chapters to basic information about money management, including discussions of budgeting, cutting costs, and avoiding credit card debt. Student loans are consistent with a larger culture that celebrates consumption as central to establishing and maintaining lifestyles—and easy access to credit as the means for making this possible.

Like earlier concerns about wasted brainpower and deadbeat students, claims about crushing student loan debt focused public attention on particular aspects of the student loan problem. However, the third student loan mess attracted more public attention and seemed more serious than its predecessors. A growing proportion of the student population was facing substantial debt, and the policies designed to alleviate the problem seemed to be stopgap measures. The new arrangements might make repayment a little less onerous, but they did little to address the underlying trends: if more people continued to seek ever more expensive higher education, the burden of student loan debt was likely to get worse. Yet public attention was already shifting, with warnings about a fourth, potentially even more serious, student loan mess.

CHAPTER FOUR

Dread and the For-Profit Bubble

The Fourth Student Loan Mess

The first years of the twenty-first century were not kind to those who believe in the fundamental rationality of markets. The new millennium kicked off with the collapse of the dot-com bubble, only to be followed a few years later by the start of the Great Recession after the housing bubble burst. People had become bubble conscious, and they began to interpret student loans within that framework, in the process identifying a fourth student loan mess.

A financial bubble occurs when people begin to pay increasingly higher prices for something, such as houses or dot-com stocks, because they expect the price to continue to rise. That is, they believe that what they've bought will soon be worth far more than they paid for it. To put it in more technical language, market participants are willing to pay above market value for some good because of greater predicted future benefits.[1] Thus the housing bubble involved people paying high prices for houses because they were convinced that real estate prices would continue to rise, so that their houses would soon be worth still more, making buying a house—even at a high price—a good investment.

The housing bubble, a major cause of the global economic collapse in 2008, was fostered by a combination of developments, including reduced government regulation of the financial sector (particularly through much weaker requirements for the amounts banks had to hold in reserve and rules regarding documentation for mortgages); the growing availability of easy credit for home loans, even for people who were at high risk of defaulting; and lenders who profited not from the repayment of loans but from commissions on loans and from repackaging those loans into securities that could be sold to investors. The Great Recession was a bipartisan accomplishment: Democrats favored making home ownership available to a larger share of the population, even as Republicans favored reducing governmental regulations on lenders. When the housing bubble burst, the economic shock was so great and the resulting recession so deep and enduring that they inspired prolonged debate over the causes of the collapse, as well as calls for policies that would ward off similar crises.

It did not take long for some critics to identify student loans as the next potential bubble. Commentators began to draw attention to parallels between the causes of the Great Recession and the market for student loans.[2]

Several trends we identified in earlier chapters were continuing. The sheer number of students attending college was increasing. Remember that when student loan programs started in the late 1950s, advocates worried that too many of the nation's best brains—half of those in the top quarter of their high school graduating classes—weren't going on to college, that their talents were being wasted. But fifty years later, with more than half of young people continuing their education after high school, the 50-plus percent of students entering college obviously could not all come from the top 25 percent of high school graduates. If, in general, the best students are the ones most likely to succeed in college (at relatively low risk of failing, if you will), then admitting ever more students meant admitting higher-risk students.

And those higher-risk students—who, on average, came from families with less money—were likely to need student loans. The number of students receiving loans was increasing each year. In addition, college costs continued to mount, and the average amounts students borrowed were increasing. So, more loans, for larger sums, to higher-risk borrowers—it was not difficult to notice parallels with the housing bubble. And just as Democrats had favored promoting home ownership, they supported making student loans widely available. For instance, their party platforms emphasized increasing access to higher education: "We should make a college education as universal as high school is today" (2000); and "We will make college more affordable, so that more young people get higher education, and more of those who graduate get relief from the crushing burden of debt" (2004).[3]

And there were other parallels as well. Remember that the money for student loans doesn't wind up in the students' pockets; most of it becomes income for educational institutions. Virtually all colleges get a percentage of their income from student loans; at some institutions, loans account for close to 90 percent of income (the maximum allowed under federal regulations). Thus colleges have good reasons to facilitate students' borrowing, just as those housing bubble lenders had incentives to write more home loans. In addition, critics noted parallels with the financial industry: just as, during the housing bubble, home loans were bundled and securitized for resale to investors, investment banks began to securitize and sell bundles of student loans. And just as they had in the case of home loans, Republicans resisted efforts to apply tighter regulations to the student loan market. Thus their party platforms called for less government interference with higher education:

> We call upon campus administrators to search for ways to hold down that [college cost] price spiral; and, in fairness to them, we propose a presidentially directed study on the effect of government regulation and paperwork demands. (2000)

> The federal government should not be in the business of originating student loans; however, it should serve as an insurance guarantor for the private sector as they offer loans to students. Private sector participation in student financing should be welcomed. Any regulation that drives tuition costs higher must be reevaluated to balance its worth against its negative impact on students and their parents. (2012)[4]

MILESTONES IN STUDENT LOANS

2012: Total student loan debt exceeds $1,000,000,000,000

The parallels with the housing bubble led commentators to speak of a student loan bubble. In 2012, the total amount owed on student loans reached $1 trillion—a sum now greater than total credit card debt.[5] Critics warned that college costs were rising faster than the cost of living and that the constant expansion of student loans—with more people borrowing more money—could not continue forever; hence, there must be a higher education bubble. This could be framed as a broad critique that questioned whether students would soon stop being willing to spend so much for all sorts of higher education—and we will address these broader concerns in chapter 5. Initially, however, most claims about a student loan bubble focused on for-profit colleges. Warnings that for-profit schools threatened the long-term stability of the student loan system—the fear that there was a for-profit student loan bubble—became the focus of the fourth student loan mess.

This chapter focuses on those criticisms and details why people worried about a for-profit bubble. However, remember that these concerns were yet another student loan mess, in which critics focused narrowly on particular aspects of the larger student loan problem. The critics emphasized the ways for-profits differed from traditional colleges, but we view those as differences in degree, not in kind. If current trends continue, the rest of higher education will grow to look more and more like for-profit colleges. We view for-profits as an early warning system, canaries in higher education's coal mine. If for-profits pose narrowly defined challenges for federal student loans today, those problems may become bigger and more widespread in the future.

FOR-PROFIT COLLEGES
AND STUDENT LOAN DEFAULTS

Chapter 3 described how the Internet fostered dramatic growth among for-profit colleges. During the ten years between 2000 and 2010, the number of bachelor's degrees awarded by for-profits grew 388 percent, vastly greater than the 29 percent increase at public institutions or the 24 percent rise at private not-for-profit colleges and universities.[6] While there were far fewer students at for-profit institutions than on traditional campuses, their numbers were swelling. These developments captured the imagination of many commentators, particularly political conservatives who argued that a profit motive encouraged innovation and efficiency in higher education.[7] They portrayed traditional colleges as, well, traditional—as hidebound brick-and-mortar institutions that were slow to adapt to new technologies and the changing demand for education, whereas for-profits were nimble, comfortable with change, and accessible to the apparently limitless individuals who desired college educations yet were underserved by traditional institutions. However, these positive assessments tended to ignore the centrality of student debt at for-profits.

Presumably, college students want to graduate. Indeed, early advocates assumed this would be for-profits' strength. For instance, in a 2002 *New York Times* interview, a financial analyst for a major bank forecast that "graduation rates for most of these companies will be in excess of 50 percent, with some as high as 60 percent. That is because they enroll working and adult students."[8]

But this was not the actual outcome; instead, the vast majority of students leave for-profit schools not by graduating but by dropping out. Recognizing that some students cannot complete college within four years, people in higher education often use the percentage of students graduating within six years as a measure of an institution's success in producing bachelor's degrees. By that standard, for-profit schools perform badly: in 2009, only 22 percent of for-profit students enrolled in bachelor's degree programs graduated within six years. By comparison,

the six-year graduation rates for public and private not-for-profit institutions were 55 percent and 65 percent, respectively. Retention rates—
that is, the proportion of students who continue in school rather than
dropping out—are another standard measure of a college's success in
educating students; for-profit schools have lower retention rates for
both full- and part-time students than not-for-profit colleges.[9] Another
crude index of institutional performance compares a college's graduation rate (which ideally should be high) with the student loan default
rate of its former students (which should be low). A 2013 report found
one hundred four-year for-profit colleges with default rates that were
higher than their graduation rates.[10]

That for-profit students are more likely to drop out should not be a
great surprise; as noted in chapter 3, their academic preparation is on
average weaker than that of students who enter not-for-profit institutions. The for-profit industry acknowledges that it accepts students
who would not be admitted in traditional colleges; thus the Association
of Private Sector Colleges and Universities responded to one critique
of low for-profit graduation rates by stating, "The only 'apples and
apples' comparison is between those schools educating large percentages of high risk students. For instance, when the graduation rates of
similarly situated students are compared, the results favor career colleges."[11] However, the accuracy of this claim is unclear: comparing the
least selective colleges—those that admit all applicants—reveals six-
year graduation rates of 31 percent at public institutions and 36 percent
at private nonprofit schools but only 11 percent at for-profit institutions,
which suggests that for-profit colleges have less success, even with
high-risk students.[12]

Students at for-profit colleges and universities may not be graduating, but they certainly are borrowing. Again, recall that students at for-
profits tend to have fewer financial resources than their counterparts at
not-for-profit schools. Thus for-profit students are more likely to qualify for Pell grants than students at traditional colleges. The Congressional Budget Office notes:

The proportion of Pell Grant recipients is much higher at for-profit institutions in part because so many of those students come from low-income families.... [A]lmost all eligible students at for-profit schools (a proportion estimated at 94 percent in 2007–2008) apply for the grants, perhaps because for-profit institutions can be significantly more expensive than public institutions and perhaps because they are better at helping eligible students submit applications.[13]

But even if they qualify for federal grants, they still need student loans. In 2008, 92 percent of students at for-profit four-year institutions took out federal student loans, compared with 49 percent of students attending public colleges and 61 percent of those attending not-for-profit private schools. Often those federal loans couldn't cover their educational expenses, so that 46 percent of for-profit students also borrowed from private lenders. (Obviously, if 92 percent of for-profit students had federal loans, a large percentage of students must have had both sorts of loans.) Moreover, the average amount borrowed by for-profit students was higher than the average loans to students at either public or private not-for-profit educational institutions.[14]

Taken together, these elements—higher-risk students who borrow larger sums but rarely finish their degrees—almost guarantee that loans to for-profit students will result in higher rates of default. In chapter 3, we suggested that, under current arrangements, students who graduate with an average student loan debt should find it possible to repay their loans, assuming that they take jobs earning the average salary *for college graduates*. But let's consider the situation of the average student who has attended a for-profit college. The average for-profit student has taken out federal student loans; in fact, each year he or she attended college, the average for-profit student borrowed more money than the average student at either public or private not-for-profit colleges. And remember, the average student at a not-for-profit institution becomes a college graduate; the average student at a for-profit college does not. Having graduated, the average not-for-profit student will then qualify for those higher-paying jobs that require a college degree, while the average for-profit student, having dropped out, won't be eligible for those same jobs. The implications of having student loan debt are very different for our two average students. Because most students leave for-profit institutions with no diploma, their employment and earning prospects are little better than they were before they enrolled; on average, a student who leaves college without a degree will earn a much lower salary than a college graduate, which means that our average degreeless for-profit student will have a much harder time repaying his or her loans and will be at much greater risk of default than the average not-for-profit student (who, remember, will have graduated).[15]

Let's step back and consider what this means for taxpayers. Students at for-profit educational institutions are least likely to graduate but are borrowing higher sums than their peers at public and not-for-profit private colleges and universities. Even if graduates from for-profits were just as likely to have successful careers as their peers who graduate from traditional colleges, for-profit graduates would be at higher risk of default simply because they've borrowed more money (and because, remember, they had fewer financial resources when they began). However, for-profit students are not just as likely to succeed as their peers, because the great majority do not graduate. Having taken on college debt without having a degree to show for the experience may make these former for-profit students worse off than they would have been had they not attended college at all. Throughout the different student loan messes, discussions of debt burden have tended to focus on those who graduate, but for-profits produce large numbers of people who find themselves paying back student loans yet have little beyond debt to show for their education.

All this means that we as a society (and as taxpayers) are transferring debt straight to those least likely to be able to repay it, while simultaneously sending money directly to the coffers of for-profit institutions that are admittedly failing a majority of their students year after year. This may not have been a big issue when for-profit colleges were smaller operations, but the situation has changed: three of the five largest degree-granting institutions in the United States are for-profit.

Today, there are close to half a million people leaving for-profits—either graduating or dropping out—and entering repayment each year, and 11 percent of those who attended four-year for-profits wind up in default within two years.[16] Moreover, default rates only get worse over time: in 2012, the Department of Education released its first annual report on *three-year* default rates: "For-profit institutions had the highest average three-year default rates at 22.7 percent, with public institutions following at 11 percent and private not-for-profit institutions at 7.5 percent."[17] And even these percentages understate the size of the problem: these two- and three-year default rates do not take into account former students who applied for or received deferrals (presumably because they would find it difficult to repay their loans and would likely default without the deferral); moreover, for-profit colleges have been criticized for covering up defaults by, for example, repaying a student's federal loan (so that it was not in default) and then demanding that the student repay the college directly.[18]

Nor are things likely to get better. The business model for for-profit education requires continued growth in revenues, and this is most easily accomplished by constantly increasing the number of students at these schools. With most high school graduates already entering higher education, increasing for-profit enrollments almost inevitably means attracting students who will be at even higher risk of failing to graduate and being unable to repay whatever money they borrow.[19]

THE PROSPECT OF A FOR-PROFIT BUBBLE

All this may be troubling, but why have critics warned about a for-profit *bubble?* Remember that bubbles occur when people bid up prices, when they pay ever-increasing amounts for something until, finally, they discover that no one is willing to pay higher amounts. What does this have to do with higher education? Obviously the costs of attending college have been growing steadily higher, but so far students have been willing to pay the higher tuition prices, in part because there is a widely shared assumption that higher education is one of the best routes to achieving the American Dream, but also because the ready availability of student loans makes it easy for students to borrow what they need on the assumption that they will be able to repay later, after they land one of those high-paying jobs available to college graduates.

Student loans, then, are important for the expansion of higher education generally, but they are absolutely essential to for-profits. The federal government sends for-profit schools about $32 billion a year for student loans and grants, and the nongrant portion is backed by student borrowers' obligation to repay that money (figure 14).[20] The bulk of these funds goes to a few giant institutions. In the 2010–11 academic year, the University of Phoenix received more than $5 billion in Title IV funds (this included some Pell grants, although student loans accounted for the great majority of this money); three other for-profit schools each received more than $1 billion, another seven more than $500 million apiece, and thirty-two more proprietary schools each got more than $100 million dollars in federal funds. These forty-three schools received more than $19 billion in federal money; more than two thousand smaller schools split the remainder. While $32 billion a year is a lot of money, that amount in itself is not enough to create a bubble. For the most part, going to college still easily pays for itself (as will be discussed in chapter 5); most student borrowers are able to repay their loans. But as we've shown, students at for-profit schools are in a more precarious position: they pay higher tuition, take longer to complete college, are less likely to graduate, and carry higher debt loads than their counterparts who attended public or private not-for-profit institutions. While a college education—at least at a public college—remains a reasonably good investment in that it will likely pay for itself in higher earnings, the case for purchasing for-profit higher education is less compelling. It is not clear that the expected value of enrolling in a for-profit college is likely to be greater than the cost of attendance.

It is not that students at for-profit schools are acting irrationally, but they may be overestimating the value of the education they're likely to

Figure 14. *Doonesbury*'s Walden College considers going for-profit. © by
Garry B. Trudeau (August 7, 2012). Used by permission of Universal Uclick.
All rights reserved.

receive, particularly if they assume they will graduate. If students become more skeptical about the value of these degrees or government policies restrict for-profits' access to the billions of student loan dollars proprietary schools rely upon for their very existence, it is quite possible that students will begin to flee the for-profit sector, revealing a for-profit student loan bubble. At this point, we need to consider how the different actors—the students at for-profit schools, the institutions themselves, and the government—have helped to create what may turn out to be a bubble.

Students and the For-Profit Bubble

While some critics argue that many for-profit degrees are not worth what they cost and are certainly not worth the amount of debt they require, hundreds of thousands of students still enroll every year. These students have grown up understanding that it is impossible to get ahead in life without a college degree. Yet with weaker academic records and fewer financial resources on average than those able to gain admission to public and private not-for-profit institutions, they are at higher risk of not graduating and of defaulting on their student loans.[21]

Often these high-risk students don't get much guidance (recall the bewildering complexity of the contemporary student loan market illustrated in figure 12). Their parents are less likely to have attended college and are almost certainly unfamiliar with the range of educational opportunities and payment methods available at both colleges and vocational schools.[22] These students may have attended high schools where guidance counselors see fewer college-bound students and have less experience helping students find the most favorable funding opportunities. Filling this void are the for-profits' advertising campaigns featuring the smiling faces of people whose for-profit degrees opened pathways to personal success. What is clear is that the students who choose for-profit universities overwhelmingly choose loans (especially federal direct loans) to finance their educations. The percentage of for-profit students paying for their educations out of pocket is very low: "Only 4 percent of bachelor's degree recipients at for-profits graduate debt-free, compared with 38 percent and 28 percent at public and private nonprofit institutions."[23]

Unfortunately, the statistics on borrowing rates do not tell the whole story about the fate of for-profit students. Students *who earn degrees* at for-profit colleges may qualify for jobs that pay higher salaries than those they might have earned without a college diploma, such that their higher incomes more than cover the costs of attending college. But for the majority of for-profit university students, who leave *without earning their degrees* and who can't command the higher salaries college graduates receive, attending a for-profit college may well not have been worth the cost.

Once enrolled at a for-profit college, it is difficult to move to a less expensive institution. Students who leave for-profits prior to graduation find it hard to transfer their credits and continue their educations at traditional not-for-profit schools:

> Many for-profit colleges hold national accreditation, meaning that they are accredited by an agency that traditionally handles vocational or distance learning schools. Holding this type of accreditation, however, generally means that the credits earned are rarely accepted at regionally accredited schools, which include all major not-for-profit and public universities and some for-profit colleges. And even credits awarded at regionally accredited for-profit colleges may not transfer to other regionally accredited nonprofit and public colleges.[24]

Even the for-profit students who do complete their programs face challenges. For-profits do not necessarily prepare their students well; students who complete programs in nursing and other fields where graduates must then pass licensing exams have lower pass rates than students who completed not-for-profit programs.[25] Graduates also find that for-profits offer few services to help them find jobs; for instance, "the University of Phoenix, with a student population of nearly half a million, has no career placement staff at all."[26] Nor do these students find employment easily. A 2009 study compared students who had started studying at for-profit institutions in 2004 with those who had entered public and private not-for-profit schools: those who had attended for-profits had a much higher unemployment rate (23 percent), and those former for-profit students who were employed were earning less than their not-for-profit counterparts.[27]

In short, for many students, reality falls far short of the bright prospects described in for-profits' advertisements. Too many leave for-profits with no credentials but plenty of debt. As critics draw public attention to the problems with these programs, it becomes less likely that students will be willing to pay the high costs of for-profit education. If students flee the for-profit marketplace, the bubble could pop.

For-Profit Colleges and the Bubble

While it is easy to blame the students at for-profit universities for making poor educational choices, the reality is that for-profit schools systematically misrepresent their product. Most not-for-profit universities restrict enrollment because they have limited classrooms, faculty members, and so on. In general, they hope to attract about as many incoming students for next fall as they drew last fall and to have enough applicants so that they can choose to admit only the best-qualified students. But the situation is very different at for-profit universities. Their leaders—and their investors—are likely to think that bigger enrollment is better; after all, the easiest way to increase profits is to serve more students/customers. Attracting new students is essential because so many students drop out:

> For-profit colleges must enroll an enormous number of new students each year to meet Wall Street investor expectations of enrollment growth. This practice is known in the industry as "churn." For example, Corinthian Colleges, Inc., began 2010 with 86,066 students and ended with 110,550, a growth of 24,484 students. But, in the same period, 113,317 students left the company (some by graduating or completing programs), requiring Corinthian to enroll 137,831 new students to achieve that growth.[28]

The need to attract enough students leads for-profits to spend nearly a quarter of their budgets on marketing and recruiting. Recruiting staff are hired for their experience in sales rather than any educational credentials they might have, and they are encouraged to engage in aggressive and sometimes deceptive recruiting practices.[29]

The way the United States pays for education with loans encourages for-profits to recruit any and all potential students, even those who have little chance of succeeding in college. Each semester (or "block" at many year-round for-profit institutions), students commit to taking a particular number of courses and paying for them by a certain date (usually a few weeks into the term). Once that date passes, the educational institution gets paid, whether the student gets an A or an F, or makes a late withdrawal. This gives colleges an incentive to get students to enroll, but little incentive to make sure students do well or even complete their classes.

Academia's traditional system of trust goes out the window when the major purpose of a university is to make as much money as possible. At most not-for-profit universities, a student's academic performance is central to earning a degree. Most schools, conscious of their reputation, try to admit only students who are likely to do well, and they are more than willing to push out students who cheat, plagiarize, or generally do not do the work required to complete courses and earn their degrees.

But the for-profit model creates a different set of concerns, in which the focus is on attracting students and retaining them so they continue to pay tuition. This results in different incentives. Instead of competing on prestige or the quality of their academic programs, for-profit universities benefit from being as relaxed as possible about academic standards, not only for admission but in classes. Ultimately, for-profits are in a race to the bottom, where the least selective schools can earn even greater income by attracting larger numbers of marginal students, who may aspire to receiving a degree but have rather less interest in getting an education.[30]

Therefore, for-profits are encouraged to maintain the minimum educational standards required to retain some form of accreditation (necessary to qualify for the government loans that allow for their continued existence). If they make graduation requirements more difficult, they will lose students to competitors, but if they make them so easy that they lose even token accreditation, they will be forced to compete with even cheaper, albeit nonexistent, universities that offer diplomas for cash.[31]

The federal government has made some efforts to rein in for-profits. The 90/10 rule (described in chapter 3) states that colleges cannot receive more than 90 percent of their revenue from Title IV funds (primarily Pell grants and direct loans). However, schools that find themselves constrained by this provision have ways around it. The current GI Bill provides federal grants for veterans' education, and there are other defense-related programs to support the education of current members of the military and their families. However, grants for veterans and servicemembers are not counted toward the for-profits' 90 percent limit on federal money but rather as *nonfederal* student aid. That is, a college that received 90 percent of its income from student loans and the remaining 10 percent from veterans' benefits would be in compliance with the limit that no more than 90 percent of income come from federal funds, even though every penny came from the government. This results in for-profits actively working to attract veterans interested in attending college on the GI Bill. One recent analysis found that the top seven recipients of GI Bill dollars in 2009–11 were for-profit schools.[32]

It is difficult to exaggerate for-profit colleges' dependence on federal funds: "When all Federal educational benefits are counted, including money disbursed from the military Tuition Assistance program and the veterans post-9/11 GI bill program . . . , the 15 publicly traded for-profit education companies received 86 percent of their revenues from Federal sources. This allocation means for-profit education institutions collect a higher proportion of their revenues from Federal student aid funds than most public and non-profit colleges."[33] To remain profitable, for-profits must attract ever-increasing numbers of ever higher risk students to enroll in educational programs that are more expensive and have lower graduation rates than those offered at traditional not-for-profit institutions. This would be impossible without the students' access to student loans, GI benefits, and other federal funds.

The Federal Government and the For-Profit Bubble

As we pointed out in chapters 2 and 3, federal officials—in both Congress and the various agencies that administer education policy—have long been aware of problems with for-profit schools and student loans. For-profits have troubling default rates: for decades, students at for-profit schools have accounted for roughly an eighth of all students and a quarter of all student loans, but about half of the defaults. In addition, there have been concerns that the education offered by some proprietary schools has little value, that too few students graduate and launch successful careers.

At the same time, the federal government has generally sought to avoid student loan policies that constrain students' educational choices; for the most part, students are eligible for loans regardless of what or where they choose to study, whether they choose to attend public or private institutions, whether those institutions are affiliated with particular religious faiths or political ideologies or are intended to educate members of particular ethnic groups, whether they train students for blue-collar vocations or elite professions, or whether they are nonprofit or for-profit.[34] In other words, young people are encouraged to choose their own paths toward the American Dream, and the federal government stands willing to help regardless of which path they choose.

However, given the troubling record of for-profit education, the government has tried to set some standards for institutions that wish to receive federal student loan dollars:

- Setting a maximum for the proportion of an institution's funding that can come from Title IV. The original 1992 85/15 rule (that is, no more than 85 percent of funding could come from Title IV) was revised into the less stringent 90/10 rule, and we have already noted that some federal dollars, such as veterans' benefits, do not count toward the 90 percent. Some critics have called for making benefits for veterans and members of the military count as federal funds (that is, counting toward the 90 percent) or for returning to the tougher 85/15 standard.[35]

- Setting a maximum default rate. Since the Reagan administration, the Department of Education has proposed disqualifying institutions from receiving further student loan funds if a high percentage of students who received loans to attend those schools defaulted. In recent years, the department has issued two-year federal student loan cohort default rates; in 2012, they began issuing annual reports for three-year rates (in 2012, this measured the percentage of students in the cohort of students whose loans had become due in 2009 and who had defaulted three years later). Current policy is that schools will become ineligible to process further student loans if, for three consecutive years, 25 or 30 percent of students have defaulted after beginning repayment within two or three years, respectively. In 2012—the first time three-year rates were calculated—218 schools had default rates over 30 percent, and 37 of those had default rates over 40 percent.[36]

- Establishing gainful employment rules. In 2011, the Department of Education proposed additional standards for career training programs. To remain eligible for Title IV funds, a program would need to meet at least one of three standards: 35 percent of former students are repaying their loans; students' annual loan payments do not exceed 30 percent of their discretionary income (that is, income above 150 percent of the poverty line); or the payments do not exceed 12 percent of a typical graduate's total earnings (at current rates, this would require an outstanding balance of no more than about 1 to 2.5 times the graduate's salary depending on salary and loan terms).[37] Although no program would lose eligibility until 2015, when the government issued its first report in 2012, about 5 percent of programs were found to have not met any of the three standards.

- Encouraging standardized financial aid letters. Complaints that the letters colleges send to newly admitted students are sometimes written in ways that obscure the real costs of college led to calls for colleges to adopt a standardized financial aid letter that would allow students to compare offers from different campuses. An online, standard-format College Scorecard first became available for students admitted in 2013.[38]

Many of these regulations were introduced or strengthened during the Obama administration; it is still too early to assess their impact.

These measures encountered resistance from for-profit educators. They lobbied and made political contributions, particularly to Republicans opposed to excessive regulations on businesses.[39] They also challenged some government regulations in court; in one successful challenge, a federal judge ruled that the standard of 35 percent of former vocational students repaying their loans was arbitrary.[40] In other cases, for-profits have tried to work around regulations. For example, one way to ensure that less than 90 percent of an institution's income comes from Title IV funds has been to *raise* tuition so that even the maximum available federal loan amounts cannot cover the costs of college, thereby forcing students to come up with the additional cash through other means, such as borrowing from private lenders. In some cases, for-profit colleges have provided such loans for their students.[41]

That is not to say that the government never acts. In 2012, three schools were declined further federal aid for exceeding the 90/10 rule two years in a row.[42] The institutions were the Suburban Technical School in Hempstead, New York, the Healthy Hair Academy in Inglewood, California, and the College of Office Technology in Chicago, Illinois. Together, these facilities received about $15 million in Title IV funds in the 2011 school year. While this seems like a drop in the bucket, another $129 million in aid went to schools that had slipped above the

90/10 threshold for the first time, and $20.1 billion went to schools with more than 80 percent of income coming from Title IV funds (meaning these institutions are largely dependent on federal dollars). Twenty billion dollars is a staggering amount of aid going to schools that seem to be at some risk of exceeding the threshold, and this only refers to aid distributed in a single year.

Still, the long-term trend has been for the federal government to gradually tighten the restrictions under which for-profit colleges operate. One possible effect of these measures is to make for-profits less attractive to prospective students, so that the danger of a for-profit bubble again grows.

TOO BIG TO FAIL?

If for-profit higher education turns out to be a bubble, it will not be because officials and the media failed to raise questions about the schools' problematic relationship to student loan programs. After all, Congress had been holding hearings on student loan defaults and for-profits since the 1970s, yet the for-profit sector continued to grow. Why didn't someone rein in the growth of for-profits, which were utterly dependent on the availability of federal student loan funds? Why weren't people more concerned about the danger of a bubble collapsing?

In part, the answer lay in the bookkeeping methods the federal government used to keep track of student loans. Let's say you loan ten bucks to your buddy. If you suspect that your buddy won't be able to repay you or can't be counted on to remember to repay you, you might simply think of that money as gone—your loss. Or if you consider your buddy completely reliable, you might be confident that you will in fact get your ten bucks back at some point, so you view the money you loaned out as an asset. Government accountants adopt the latter view. Imagine that the government loans $1,000 to a student. You might think of that as an expenditure, but in bookkeeping terms, the cost of lending is counterbalanced by the $1,000 (plus interest) the student owes the government. The money owed to the government is treated as an asset, at least until the loan is written off as uncollectable. Suppose the student postpones repayment: the asset grows because the student now owes additional interest. Suppose the student stops paying and is in default: the asset's value increases still further through a combination of penalties and compound interest. In other words, from a bookkeeping standpoint, lots of defaults are not a problem because they translate into big assets. And that way of thinking is not completely fanciful, because the government is powerful enough to track down student debtors and compel many of them to repay what they owe.[43]

As a consequence, even when student loan debt crossed the trillion-dollar threshold in 2012, from a bookkeeper's perspective, this did not seem all that alarming. So long as one assumed that the federal government would be able to compel repayment, all the debt individual students had accrued simply meant that the government had big assets on its books. But was that a realistic assessment? Would all those former students in fact be able to repay what they owed? Or would the government have to write off a lot of those debts and start treating them as losses instead of assets?

If the government's accounting methods could be criticized for offering an excessively rosy vision of the long-term costs of student loans to the government, critics on the left interpreted these paper assets as proof that the terms for student loans were too harsh. Thus the lead sentence in a June 2013 report in the *Huffington Post* declared: "The Obama administration is forecast to turn a record $51 billion profit this year from student loan borrowers, a sum greater than the earnings of the nation's most profitable companies and roughly equal to the combined net income of the four largest U.S. banks by assets."[44] Such critiques equated interest charges added to the books with profits and largely ignored the costs of collecting—and even possibly writing off—loans. Other accounting methods that took such factors into account suggested that federal student loan programs more or less broke even.[45]

Talk about a for-profit bubble had implications for these arrangements. In effect, the government's methods of accounting for student loan debts turned the program—at least on paper—into an asset, a profit center. But if student loan debt totals more than $1 trillion dollars, and if at some point there is an acknowledgment that some share of that debt—perhaps even a large share—cannot be repaid and must be written off as a loss, this could presumably lead to a significant increase in the national debt.

But there is another issue that particularly relates to for-profit institutions. Federal student loan policies specifically state that if a school fails and closes its doors, the loans for the students enrolled in the school will be forgiven.[46] Given many for-profits' near-total dependence on the availability of federal student loans and the federal government's efforts to reduce this dependency, we can imagine that excessively strict federal policies could cause some schools to fail, which could represent a substantial loss to the taxpayers. While the failure of a small for-profit institution would hardly make a difference in the federal budget, the collapse of a much larger institution, such as the University of Phoenix, would make a noticeable dent.

Let's talk numbers. In the 2011 school year, the five largest for-profit institutions received $9,223,280,964 under Title IV of the Higher Education Act.[47] Five schools, in just one year, received almost two billion dollars apiece. These five schools averaged 85.74 percent in Title IV funds on the government's 90/10 scale, with the highest coming in at 88.7 percent. The next five largest for-profits took in about $2.3 billion, with an average of 83.7 percent. There were eighteen more for-profit institutions that received more than $100 million from Title IV in just the 2011 academic year (averaging 83.9 percent in federal funds). These were massive line items in the student lending budget.

It is difficult to get the exact amount owed by current students (that is, not including those that have already graduated or dropped out) at these institutions, but with a few assumptions, we can get a rough picture. The ten largest for-profit schools collect at least $11.5 billion a year from the U.S. government in the form of Pell grants and direct loans. While many students drop out, large rosters of continuing students with loans remain. We estimate that, at any given time, the schools have current students with about $18.5 billion in student loan debt.[48]

If these schools start shutting down, current policy requires that the outstanding loans of all currently enrolled students be forgiven, and those ledger assets immediately turn into liabilities. There would be no way for the government to book these forgiven loans as future assets.

So, if for-profit schools are large enough that excusing their current debt would not be in the best short-run interest of the Department of Education, these universities essentially become too big to fail. Educational quality becomes irrelevant: no matter how good or bad a school may be, if its students have enough current debt, it makes sense not to shut it down.

This creates an odd intersection of desires for for-profit universities and the federal government. From the standpoint of the university, massive growth becomes not just a way to increase profits but insurance against too-restrictive regulations. While a school is small, attracting more students can lead to more regulatory attention, but after it reaches a certain size, every additional current student becomes a sort of insurance policy against regulators cracking down. When we think about it this way, for-profits' aggressive recruiting practices start to make even more sense.

The Department of Education has a very different set of incentives. Clearly they would like to see predatory for-profit lending halted, but bringing it to an abrupt halt could be financially disastrous. From the standpoint of the government, the ideal way to end the influence of these universities would be to get all their students graduated (and into repayment) while slowly winding down the for-profits, gradually reducing them in size.

There are signs that, even without further government pressure, for-profit enrollments will level out, if not decline.[49] It is hard to believe that there is a large untapped market of prospective students in the United States. By now, virtually every warm body interested in postsecondary education has experienced overtures from the largest for-profit educators. As a test, type a generic term like *college* into a popular search engine and see which advertisements accompany your results (in mid-2013 our search returned ads from three of the top five for-profit universities). Odds are that these schools have already tested the waters with virtually everyone open to trying them. Future growth is likely to come from two sources: recruiting students from outside the United States (who, of course, cannot qualify for federal student loans) or trying to attract each year's cohort of new high school graduates (a sizable population, to be sure, but much smaller than the cumulative pool of unconventional students that was underserved in the late 1990s, when for-profit enrollments began to boom). At a minimum, the for-profits' business model—attracting ever more students who can pay high tuition with federal student loans—is going to become harder to maintain. A quick glance at stock prices of large for-profit corporate parents paints a bleak picture, showing sharp declines in share prices since the Great Recession.[50] Whether for-profits shrink gradually or rapidly enough to constitute a noticeable bubble remains to be seen. Moreover, there are other clouds on the for-profits' horizon.

REVERBERATIONS: THE LARGER IMPACT OF FOR-PROFIT HIGHER EDUCATION

Higher education has always been a business, but this has become increasingly apparent in recent decades, as the competition for prospective students increased, fueled by the visibility of college rankings and other shifts discussed in chapter 2.[51] At the same time, there have been increased calls for colleges to demonstrate their value (we will discuss these in chapter 5). Beginning in the 1990s, *assessment* became a buzzword in the accreditation process; institutions were called upon to monitor whether their students were learning anything. The criticism of *failing schools* or *failure factories* (terms usually applied to urban high schools with high dropout rates and poor educational performances by the students who stayed in school) began to spread to higher education.[52] Legislatures demanded that public schools improve their efficiency with higher graduation and retention rates.

Much of this criticism seemed new. It had always been the case that some students who entered college fell by the wayside for all sorts of reasons, from flunking out to choosing to start software firms that would make them billionaires. Moreover, as the proportion of young people deciding to pursue higher education grew—a process that, as we have noted, brought increasingly higher-risk students to campus—there was every reason to expect that some of these students would not succeed. Basically, American colleges gave lots of people the opportunity to pursue higher education, but they didn't guarantee that all those students would complete their degrees. Increasingly, however, critics argued that anything short of graduation constituted a social problem.

The calls for colleges to behave more like businesses often were accompanied by suggestions that for-profits offered examples of the effective application of business principles to higher education. At first, traditional colleges dismissed for-profits as having weaker students, less-qualified faculty, and poorer academic programs. But the explosive growth of for-profits, in particular their ability to attract thousands of online students, led administrators at traditional institutions to look for ways to expand their online offerings. If large numbers of students were willing to enroll in online courses, why let for-profits have them all? Online education promised potentially large profits at low cost. On campus, class size is limited by the number of seats in a classroom, but the only limit on the size of a distance learning class involves finding some way to grade students' work, a problem easily solved by graduate student labor or conversion to some sort of machine grading. Not-for-profit institutions began increasing their online offerings, including establishing entire programs that could be completed without setting foot on campus.

This was not good news for for-profits. While for-profit schools had been ahead of the curve in figuring out that distance learning could lead to massive growth, traditional schools were catching up. Now, instead of having no competition, for-profit schools are finding themselves competing for students with prestigious not-for-profit universities experimenting with distance learning. Major universities began offering Massive Open Online Courses (MOOCs), creating new competitors in online education.[53] While the completion percentages of MOOCs make the worst for-profit records look admirable, there is one huge difference: MOOCs are for the most part free, so users can try courses, often only paying if they want credit for their work. While MOOCs in their current form are unlikely to replace conventional colleges, they are a significant threat to the for-profit distance learning model. Now students can enroll in courses with professors from top schools teaching in their exact areas of expertise. At this point MOOCs are much cheaper, and the credits are transferable to an increasing number of brick-and-mortar colleges.

This leaves for-profit schools in a bad position. With their dubious practices making headlines, government regulators seek to devise tighter restrictions on for-profits' access to student loan dollars for high-risk loans, without making the constraints so severe as to cause the for-profits to fail quickly (so that their loans would have to be forgiven). At the same time, there are no more easy growth opportunities. There are just not enough prospective students out there to continue the growth rates for-profits have been enjoying, and new competition from MOOCs (which, at least for now, seem not to be that interested in money) represents a barrier to increasing tuition. This all means that the for-profit education system as we know it is likely on a long-term downswing, with the cost to taxpayers still to be determined. What we do know is that there are legions of former students from these institutions who are having trouble paying back their loans, and this is an issue that the discussion of the for-profit bubble does not address.

The fourth student loan mess was largely the result of the increased popularity of college. With college having been sold as a path to a middle-class existence, private companies arose to cater to the massive increase in demand for college that was unmet by traditional higher education institutions. This caused many small problems and one big one.

The small problems have to do with what people learn from one another. Increasingly relaxed requirements for many online for-profit colleges contributed to a flood of graduates and increased suspicion regarding the value of a college diploma. The banner profits from for-profit colleges encouraged many not-for-profit colleges to mimic the profit-making behavior. Finally, the combination of many new college choices and many new college students who were less concerned about price because of the availability of loans created a sort of academic race to the bottom for many schools, which undermines the traditional mission of higher education.[54]

However, the big problem was financial. Thanks to the policy reforms discussed in the previous three chapters, for-profit colleges became some of the largest annual recipients of federal Title IV student aid dollars. These institutions encouraged high-risk students to take on large amounts of debt without—in most cases—earning the sorts of educational credentials that would translate into higher incomes. Large numbers of these students have big debts but limited prospects; many are likely to default on their loans, disrupting their lives and increasing the federal deficit. At the same time, the government's efforts to constrain for-profits—to say nothing of the diminishing pool of prospective students and the growing competition from not-for-profit colleges—could cause even some of the largest for-profits to collapse, necessitating forgiveness of their students' loans and further boosting the deficit. The resulting financial blow won't be as great as the collapse of the housing bubble, but it is likely to be noticeable, and it could destabilize student lending policies for generations.

The for-profit mess is not over, but it is already being obscured by concerns that there is an even larger bubble, one that affects higher education generally. The quick growth experienced by for-profit schools—which their not-for-profit peers are trying to replicate—did not come without significant costs. These concerns will be the subject of the next chapter.

CHAPTER FIVE

What's Next?

Prospective Student Loan Messes

We have described the history of federal student loan policy as a series of messes, each involving policymakers focusing narrowly on particular aspects of student loans while, in the process, managing to ignore other aspects that would contribute to the next mess. Through the different messes, government student loan programs have continued to grow, with more people involved and more money at stake. While the government plays a vital part in student lending, there are signs that the student loan problem has grown too large to address one smaller mess at a time. There is no reason to imagine that past reforms have finally solved the student loan problem; in fact, there are signs that the next mess will be the worst yet. This chapter tries to envision what form the next mess might take.

The future is difficult to forecast because there are several prospective messes on the horizon. One possibility is that higher education—not just the for-profit colleges discussed in chapter 4 but a large share of traditional colleges—will itself prove to be a bubble and collapse as growing doubts about the value of higher education lead large numbers of young people to forgo college. But even if people continue to pursue education, there are other risks. Colleges have become dependent on student loan dollars, and although higher education generally may endure, this hardly means that every campus will survive. Moreover, there are risks to students who, so long as college costs continue to rise, will need to borrow ever larger sums to chase the American Dream. And then there are the risks for the federal government and the taxpayers should calls for lower interest rates and more generous forgiveness terms for student debt lead to increased costs for the government, or should a lack of reform lead to extensive defaults. However, as much as we may sympathize with the plight of student borrowers, we need to understand that somebody is going to have to cover the costs of student loans, to realize that the money to pay off loans cannot simply fall from the sky without consequences.

IS COLLEGE WORTH IT?

What is the value of higher education? Most universities—and most professors—give fairly idealistic answers to this question. They talk about fostering a love of learning, making their students truly educated, turning them into critical thinkers.[1] In this view, higher education trains people to think better—to read more thoughtfully, to locate and critically evaluate information, to organize their ideas, and to communicate those ideas more effectively. These higher-order thinking skills are understood to have real value, in that college graduates should be able to apply those skills in their careers. Employers, the argument goes, will pay a premium for workers who can think better. The point is not that the material covered in college classes necessarily has direct, practical value, but rather that requiring students to think hard— whether they are thinking about Shakespeare's plays, patterns of social inequality, or experiments in a chemistry lab—lets them practice and improve their thinking skills, so that they will become generally better thinkers, and therefore better, more productive citizens.

Although professors may prefer to talk in principled terms, higher education is also understood to have a direct, practical, individualistic payoff. For decades, most Americans have shared the assumption that college is a sound financial investment, that college graduates' earnings more than pay for the costs of their education. And the data generally support that claim: there is a fairly standard social scientific finding that education correlates with income.[2] High school graduates make more money than high school dropouts; people who complete some college earn more than high school grads; college graduates make considerably more than those who leave college before graduation; and those who complete advanced degrees earn more than college graduates. These are big differences; in 2012, the average weekly earnings of those with PhDs or professional degrees were more than three times greater than for high school dropouts, while those with just a bachelor's degree averaged about 65 percent more than high school graduates. In fact, the relative advantage of having more education is even greater than those comparisons suggest, because average income figures include only those who are employed, and unemployment rates decline as education increases; for instance, high school graduates have an unemployment rate nearly twice as high as that of college graduates. Moreover, the higher education *wage premium*—the additional income college graduates can expect to receive—has generally increased in recent years.

To be sure, income also varies by college major: on average, those with degrees in engineering wind up making more than those with business degrees, who in turn earn more than those who majored in the humanities. But the data also show that every major produces a wage premium; on average, those who complete a bachelor's degree in the humanities earn about 55 percent more than high school graduates.[3]

However, in the last twenty years, more critics have challenged the assumption that college is a good investment. In 2013, William J. Bennett, a former secretary of the Department of Education, published a book, *Is College Worth It?*, and articles with similar titles have appeared in numerous magazines.[4] Even if most of those articles wind up answering the question affirmatively, the subject's popularity suggests that what was once taken for granted has become something people consider worthy of discussion.

In part, these skeptics point to the rising costs of a college education that we've documented in earlier chapters. If the price of attending college exceeds the additional income that college graduates can expect to earn, going to college might not make financial sense. Moreover, if students have to borrow a large share of their college costs—and particularly if the interest on their loans increases what they owe, so that the total amount far exceeds what they borrowed or even the entire costs of their educations, it is not difficult to imagine that some students might wind up in worse financial shape than had they chosen to skip college. Of course, we already know that private schools—whether not-for-profit or for-profit—charge much more than public institutions, and their students wind up borrowing even more to pay for their educations.

And as we have already noted, what one studies makes a difference. Students who major in programs that lead directly into careers where there are lots of opportunities for jobs—say, accounting, engineering, or nursing—are likely to earn far more than they spent on their educations. But we can imagine that students who attend expensive private colleges, borrow a large share of the cost of their education, and choose majors that don't lead into a particular career might find themselves in more precarious financial circumstances. Perhaps college might not be worth it for some, although one website examines 1,511 colleges (some counted twice to account for differences in in-state and out-of-state tuition) and finds that virtually all (1,481) provide a positive return on investment for the median student who completes a bachelor's degree.[5]

Graduates' prospects also depend upon what jobs the larger economy has available. The Great Recession has been both long and deep: long in the sense that the recovery process has been much slower than in other recent recessions, and deep in the sense that unemployment rates have been unusually high.[6] This has had several consequences for young people leaving college with student loan debt. With fewer jobs available, some graduates can't find work; others wind up taking less desirable jobs than those they assumed they'd be able to command. We have already noted that student loan debt need not be a terrible burden for those who land well-paid jobs as soon as they graduate. But those who can't find a job—or who must settle for a job that pays less—may be unable to keep up with their scheduled loan payments. They may have to arrange to make lower payments or to postpone starting to repay their loans, leading the amounts they owe to spiral upward, so that those already in the most precarious financial circumstances find their situations getting rapidly worse.

The press has made much of difficulties the Great Recession has posed for college grads. Even though most graduates end up with jobs, there are plenty of stories about unpaid internships, delays of start dates, and jobs that disappear before their start dates.[7] Other reports describe people who wish they had not gone to college, usually those saddled with massive debt who say they didn't understand how much they would wind up owing.[8]

However, even during the Great Recession, college graduates remained in a relatively advantaged situation. Their unemployment rate—although relatively high in historical terms—is lower than the rates of their counterparts of the same age who chose not to continue their educations.[9] Still, the Great Recession has been a tough time to launch one's career. Starting salaries are somewhat lower, jobs are harder to find, and there is more underemployment—highly trained college graduates unable to find work in jobs that match their skills.[10] Put simply, the Great Recession has been much tougher than other recent business cycles for young college graduates, and the higher unemployment rates help explain the recent popular backlash against college.

However, it is unwise to generalize from a few of the worst years in U.S. economic history to conclude that the value of college will continue to decline. Graduating during a recession makes things tougher at first, but in the long run most people catch up.[11] One survey of recent college graduates found considerable optimism: 48 percent expected to have more financial success than their parents (compared to 20 percent who anticipated less success); only 3 percent reported thinking that they would have been better off if they hadn't gone to college.[12] Despite this general optimism, the past few years have been the worst time in the history of democratized education to be a new college graduate. While there are clearly negative effects to graduating during a recession, the current economic climate is not sufficient reason to fundamentally change higher education. Even if the current crop of college graduates has been hurt by their reduced early-career prospects, history suggests that, once the economy improves, college will prove to have been a good investment for most of today's graduates.

IS COLLEGE TEACHING THE RIGHT LESSONS?

Recent skepticism about the value of higher education tends to come from political conservatives. Liberals responded to the Great Recession by worrying that it would make it harder for young people of limited means to attend college.[13] In contrast, conservatives worry that college is no longer a good value: "Although the cost of college has increased at three times the rate of inflation, little evidence exists that higher prices reflect higher quality."[14] They point to attempts to measure improved thinking skills that find many college students don't seem to have benefited from higher education.[15] In addition, they argue that student loans and other federal policies allow colleges to raise prices without worrying about quality.[16]

When the economy is good, people don't worry that much about what happens in college. With the exception of those majors that train people for particular careers in nursing, accounting, and the like, most of the skills required for jobs are learned at work after college. However, when the economy is bad and employers can be much more selective about whom they hire, complaints about students being poorly prepared for work environments are taken much more seriously.

We need to remember that people have been complaining for generations about what college graduates don't know, even as those graduates boosted economic productivity. While businesses would be thrilled to have prospective employees who do not require training, the reality is that this desired level of specialization is not possible in the American university, and this is a good thing. The purpose of American higher education actually is education—that is, improving thinking—a process that creates workers who are able to apply general skills to a multitude of potential jobs, even if all these future positions require additional training. Although there have been recent complaints about new college graduates lacking skills, the complaints center around their need for better critical thinking skills.[17] Employers don't want colleges to teach something completely different as much as they want them to teach what they already claim to be teaching—only better.

SIGNS OF TROUBLE

The federal direct student loan programs discussed in chapters 3 and 4 removed many barriers to student borrowing. Using direct loans, it is currently possible to take out federally backed loans with no discussion of the borrower's qualifications (beyond evidence of being enrolled in a school) and little oversight. Because equality and access are cornerstones of the direct student loan program, creditworthiness, the nature of the school, and the student's program of study do not affect access to loans, except in the most extreme cases. This naturally creates a market with borrowers who are on average less creditworthy than those in markets where lenders are more selective. High-risk borrowers who would be turned away at banks or credit unions can borrow shockingly large amounts of money directly from the federal government, often without ever talking to a human being.

Not surprisingly, some of these borrowers get into trouble. Some of them are unsophisticated borrowers who do not clearly understand the terms of their loans; others may have understood exactly what they were doing, only to find their postgraduation lives—their jobs and salaries—less prosperous than they'd envisioned.

As a whole, the borrowers who take out student loans would be considered an extremely risky group by any lender, and as a society we should not be surprised to find that they default at a higher rate than borrowers who are more thoroughly vetted before receiving mortgage or auto loans.

In chapters 2–4, we tracked people's worries about student loan defaults over fifty years. At various times, critics have cited widely varying figures for default rates; sometimes they have worried that the rates seemed to be rising, but on other occasions they've taken comfort in evidence that the rates were falling. While we might imagine that it would be a simple matter to calculate default rates, it turns out to be maddeningly difficult. In part, this is because there are so many different student loan programs, which tend to keep their own records. But this is not the largest problem.

It also turns out to be hard to define default. Let's imagine a bunch of twenty-five-year-old college graduates who have student loan debt:

- Alec found a job and is making the scheduled payments and paying down his student loan. Obviously, Alec is not in default.
- Betina also found a job but has been failing to make her payments. Clearly, she's in default.
- Claire decided to enroll in grad school (for which she's taken out even more loans). The interest on her undergraduate loans continues to mount, but payment is deferred. She's not considered to be in default.
- Don hasn't landed a job. He's applied for a deferral while he looks for work. He continues to be charged interest, so that the amount he owes is growing, but he's also not in default.

We could continue to sketch such scenarios. But notice that among our first four students, only Alec is actually repaying his loans, yet only Betina is considered to have defaulted on her loans, although if we were the ones making the loans, we might worry about whether we could count on Claire and Don to repay what they owe.

But what is the default rate in our example? We could calculate it a couple of ways. A glass-half-full calculation might say that only one of our four students with loans is in default, therefore the default rate is 25 percent. But that's an awfully cheerful interpretation; it assumes that Claire and Don will eventually repay what they owe, even though both are piling up debt. A less sanguine, glass-half-empty interpretation might say that only two students—Alec and Betina—are in repayment (that is, they are supposed to be making payments right now), and that one of them is in default, so the default rate is 50 percent. An even more pessimistic calculation could simply note that of the four college graduates, only Alec is making payments, suggesting that 75 percent are in trouble. In other words, in calculating the default rate, it all depends on what you count, and published default rates tend to adopt the most optimistic definition of default.

In 2013, a team at the Federal Reserve Bank of New York tried to deconstruct default rates.[18] Their data suggested that in 2012 the percentage of people with student loan debt who were ninety or more days behind with their payments (that is, they could be considered to be in default) was 17 percent, up from 9 percent in 2004. Seventeen percent—even 9 percent—is a high default rate. In comparison, when the housing bubble burst, the peak in mortgage delinquency resulted in less than 10 percent of mortgages that were ninety days behind or worse (the latest data show that about 7 percent of mortgages are over ninety days behind, including those in foreclosure).[19] However, that 17 percent default rate turns out to be the glass-half-full calculation, because 44 percent of the people with student loans were not in repayment (that is, they were in situations like those of Claire and Don). When the Fed team examined only those in repayment (that is, folks like Alec and Betina), they found that in 2012 more than 30 percent of all people with student loans were at least ninety days delinquent, and the percentage of defaults among younger borrowers was nearly 35 percent.

It is important to understand what a 35 percent default rate means for any loan program. For the program to break even, borrowers would have to be charged at least a 50 percent risk premium. Suppose we loan three students $1,000, and one defaults. If the one who defaults repays nothing, the two in good standing must each repay $1,500—the $1,000 principal plus $500 in additional payments—just to recover the lender's original $3,000 principal, before any interest income. Any lower rate will cause the program to lose money. We associate 50 percent interest rates with loan sharks, not the terms of federal loans. In recent years, most direct student loans have carried far lower interest rates—3.4 percent (for subsidized loans) or 6.8 percent (for unsubsidized loans). This is not nearly enough to cover the cost of the high default rate, let alone the cost of lending the money and administering the loans.

No doubt the Great Recession made the default rate worse, but remember that even without the recession, the trend has been for more, ever higher risk people to borrow ever-higher sums. This almost guarantees that there will be more people unable to pay their loans. So why aren't people more alarmed about the default rate? Here we need to return to a topic introduced in chapter 4—the federal government's accounting practices for keeping track of student loans.

Compare government loans to the way a bank handles lending. When someone defaults on a bank loan, the bank attempts to collect the debt for a while, but if they are not successful, they sell the debt to a collection agency for pennies on the dollar and write off the remaining balance (they remove the principal owed from their list of assets and take a loss on the loan). This is a relatively quick process (with the exception of mortgages, which are beyond the scope of this book). Generally, a bank is done with delinquent borrowers less than a year from the date they stop repaying their loans.

The government is much more patient about collecting on the loans it makes. The reforms described in chapter 2 have made it almost impossible to discharge student loans in bankruptcy. Although the Department of Education says that someone who stops paying an almost-impossible-to-discharge student loan is in default, it is really better described as an endless state of delinquency. Instead of getting rid of the debt and writing it off, the government records the delinquent principal as still owed by the borrower and compounds the interest that is not being paid, meaning that the total loan balance is now growing. To make matters even worse for the borrower, if borrowers attempt to get out of default by consolidating their loans, a fee of up to 18.5 percent of the total amount owed (the principal plus the accumulated interest) can be tacked onto a defaulted balance, so that the government can credit itself with even greater assets (and the former student owes even more money).[20] These terms can make it very difficult for students in trouble to ever get current on their loans (meaning that penalties continue to accrue), yet the government can record these loans as profitable although they are not currently being repaid, and even if the principal balance is never likely to be repaid. Although some of the most hopeless student loans do end up in collection, most of the time debtors can arrange hardship decisions and deferrals (where the balance continues to grow), and many of the rest of those who are seriously behind experience wage garnishment of up to 15 percent of their disposable pay, which for many low-earning people means that their loans' balances continue to go up.[21] These attributes make the federal government the most patient consumer lender in the history of the United States. This is not necessarily a good thing for the government or for student borrowers. Some of the most hopeless cases, which would be easy bankruptcy discharges for other types of debt, languish for years with incomplete payments, rising balances, and eventual forgiveness.

Not surprisingly, the Department of Education is not forthcoming about the details of student loans, and there are long deferral periods and long payback periods that can mask what is really happening in the loan markets. Reporting about lending amounts, defaults, and other indicators of what is occurring is sometimes delayed by years, and it is difficult to get a clear picture of what is happening. However, we do have some information about the state of the direct loan portfolio, and it is not good.

In recent years, the Federal Student Aid program has been audited by Ernst & Young, a prominent accounting firm. While government programs are not necessarily held to the same standards as other businesses, Ernst & Young has been pointing out problems with the FSA for years. To summarize the long and complicated audit opinions, recent Independent Auditor's Reports in the U.S. Department of Education Federal Student Aid Annual Reports list continued, significant deficiencies.[22] The Department of Education has trouble estimating the cost of the student loan portfolio year after year; there are accounting issues both with how the costs of the program are predicted and with its ability to correctly collect debt.

So, what do we know? The proportion of defaults on student loans is extremely large and has been increasing, yet the government's accounting practices view this as essentially irrelevant since, at least on paper, the growing debt is an asset, not a problem. Moreover, independent auditors have serious reservations about the accuracy of those accounts. These are signs that the next student loan mess is likely to be much worse than its predecessors. What is less clear is what form the mess will take. To really understand the state of student lending and higher education costs in 2013, we need to understand the positions of everyone at the table.

THE PARTICIPANTS

At bottom, student loans are about students paying for higher education. When World War II ended, this was relatively straightforward: students came up with the money and paid tuition and fees to colleges. However, over the past sixty-five years, the federal government has become an increasingly important intermediary in this process; today, more than half of students have some sort of federal student loan. There are lots of reasons to believe that this proportion will only grow: more young people want to go to college and college costs are rising, so we can expect more people to borrow more money, with the government receiving ever-larger IOUs from student borrowers. But, as our account of the successive student loan messes reveals, the demand for student loans has been addressed piecemeal, and this has had a number of troubling consequences: students have become less price sensitive, states less willing to support higher education, and universities increasingly comfortable charging more for their services. The result is a system that is arguably both unsustainable and difficult to stop.

In July 2007, just a couple of months before the global economy collapsed, the head of a major investment bank told an interviewer, "As long as the music is playing, you've got to get up and dance. We're still dancing."[23] This comment would attract a lot of criticism, but it can help us understand something about the dynamics of markets. When an entire industry not only is behaving badly but has come to rely on bad behavior, it can be extraordinarily difficult to buck the trend; it is easier, in effect, to keep dancing with everyone else. In a sense, all the parties in today's student loan system—the students, the educational institutions, and the government—find it hard to stop dancing so long as the music continues.

Students

CURRENT AND FUTURE STUDENTS. When we discuss what to do about student loans, our focus is almost always on current and future college students. This is natural: if we somehow change the terms for loans—if we, say, change the interest rate—it will only affect those students who take out loans under the new rules.

The current student loan system would have been impossible to imagine in the 1950s, at the onset of federal student lending. It is the product of nearly sixty years of policymaking in response to the shifting concerns that we have characterized as messes. Today, without talking to anyone, students can take out loans directly from the government that cover tuition, fees, housing expenses, and even spending money, for as long as they remain enrolled in college.

Anyone who spends time on college campuses has seen the promotions encouraging college students to sign up for low-limit credit cards. Critics worry that college students, many of them still teenagers, are unsophisticated borrowers who don't grasp the risks of using a credit card with a 29.9 annual percentage rate. Yet these are the same young people that we trust to make decisions about taking out student loans in amounts that can dwarf any tab they might run up on a starter credit card.[24]

Popular culture portrays college life as a high-consumption lifestyle, centered around leisure. This is a theme echoed by college recruiters, who invite prospective students to admire beautiful and active campuses. Off-campus housing seeks to offer even more luxury. Thus the *New York Times* describes a student contemplating spending his sophomore year in an off-campus apartment complex: "[He] had breathed the vanilla lavender-scented clubhouse air. He had seen the beach volleyball court, toured the game room equipped with billiards, Ping-Pong and air hockey tables, and learned with delight of the Friday pool parties with a D.J., free food and snow cones, spiked with rum for those of age.... 'It's like a vacation, almost,' he said. 'I'm not going to go to class—that's how I look at it.'"[25] Of course these amenities come at a price, but student loans permit having them now and paying down the road.

Many students now expect colleges and the surrounding community to offer comforts that were unthinkable a generation or two ago. While it is still possible to find students living frugally on college campuses, it is ever easier to find ones who seem to be living well. The lifestyle of today's students is very different from what their parents or grandparents remember about their college days. However, this need not be blamed on the students. *Rolling Stone* argues that "our university-tuition system really is exploitative," operating for the benefit of "the colleges and universities, and the contractors who build their extravagant athletic complexes, hotel-like dormitories, and God knows what other campus embellishments. For these little regional economic empires, the federal student-loan system is essentially a massive and ongoing government subsidy."[26]

Many students have become desensitized to the price of education because they are unaware of many of the costs. The typical undergraduate probably has no experience dealing with sums as large as his or her tab for tuition and fees, and the means by which that bill is paid—through some elaborate combination of parental help, grants and scholarships, private loans, and federal student loans—may not be well understood. In the meantime, prospective students get a lot of advice that they ought to choose a college based on how well it fits them rather than cost.

In other words, prospective students are encouraged to make choices that will make their educations more costly. They may face a reckoning—but not today.

FORMER STUDENTS. For most students, the need to begin repaying their loans begins only once they finish their educations. Whereas policymakers tend to focus on reforms that will help future borrowers, the millions of former students who now have to deal with loans get surprisingly little attention. Those who are already in repayment (and most likely in need of help) are often forgotten when new policy debates occur; few student lending reforms apply to loans that are already in repayment. In many ways, former students are the forgotten casualties of the student loan messes (figure 15).[27] Even as the focus moves on to the next student loan mess, former students are stuck repaying their loans under old terms that may now be deemed unacceptable for future students. It is no surprise that press reports of debt rage and people wishing they'd never gone to college involve former students.

For instance, the recent debates over retaining a 3.4 percent interest rate for subsidized direct student loans concerned only loans that were dispersed after the fall of 2011.[28] The interest rates for the same direct loans taken out between fall 2006 and spring 2011 range from 4.5 to 6.8 percent. Former students hear politicians talk about the importance of keeping interest rates low for today's and tomorrow's students, even as they face repaying their own loans at higher rates.

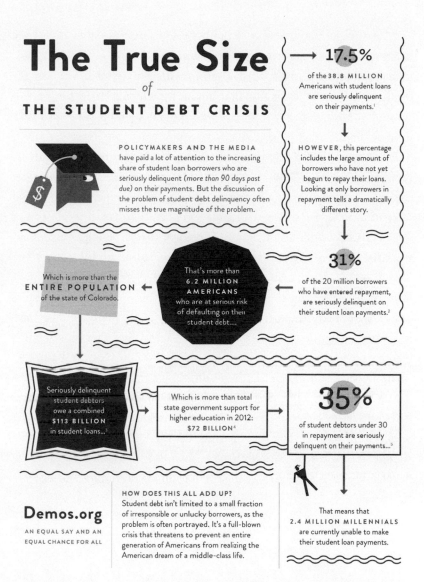

The True Size

of

THE STUDENT DEBT CRISIS

17.5%
of the 38.8 MILLION Americans with student loans are seriously delinquent on their payments.[1]

POLICYMAKERS AND THE MEDIA have paid a lot of attention to the increasing share of student loan borrowers who are seriously delinquent (*more than 90 days past due*) on their payments. But the discussion of the problem of student debt delinquency often misses the true magnitude of the problem.

HOWEVER, this percentage includes the large amount of borrowers who have not yet begun to repay their loans. Looking at only borrowers in repayment tells a dramatically different story.

That's more than 6.2 MILLION AMERICANS who are at serious risk of defaulting on their student debt....

Which is more than the ENTIRE POPULATION of the state of Colorado.

31%
of the 20 million borrowers who have entered repayment, are seriously delinquent on their student loan payments.[2]

Seriously delinquent student debtors owe a combined **$113 BILLION** in student loans...[3]

Which is more than total state government support for higher education in 2012: **$72 BILLION**[4]

35%
of student debtors under 30 in repayment are seriously delinquent on their payments...[5]

Demos.org

AN EQUAL SAY AND AN EQUAL CHANCE FOR ALL

HOW DOES THIS ALL ADD UP?
Student debt isn't limited to a small fraction of irresponsible or unlucky borrowers, as the problem is often portrayed. It's a full-blown crisis that threatens to prevent an entire generation of Americans from realizing the American dream of a middle-class life.

That means that 2.4 MILLION MILLENNIALS are currently unable to make their student loan payments.

Figure 15. Former students' view of student loan debt (2013).

Although former students are rarely the subject of debt relief, they are the ones having all the repayment problems, those whose default rates rise year after year. Ultimately, everyone with student loans eventually becomes a former student, and it would make a great deal of sense to devote more attention to the cohort of debtors that is actually in repayment.

Of course, there are reasons why former students tend to get overlooked. The terms of their loans are clearly defined under law. Maybe they are burdened by crushing debt, but the government has no legal obligation to alter the loans' terms. Moreover, there are a lot of former students who owe a lot of money: a reform that dramatically reduces what they owe is likely to have serious financial repercussions for the federal budget when billions of dollars in assets vanish from the government's books. And there is the matter of moral hazard. While it is certainly true that there are a lot of people who are delinquent on paying their student loans, it is important to remember that most people who have had student loans have repaid—or are currently repaying—them. Even if a third of today's young people in repayment are delinquent, that also means that two-thirds are managing to repay their loans on schedule. People who have met or are meeting their loan terms might well believe that they played by the rules and other people should, too. Any reform that changes loan terms for other former students risks making the folks who repaid their loans on schedule feel like suckers.

Institutions of Higher Education

FOR-PROFIT COLLEGES AND UNIVERSITIES. The fourth student loan mess focused on the problems with for-profit higher education; these were described in detail in chapter 4. Here we simply want to note that there are reasons to worry that the for-profits' problems may spread to traditional not-for-profit higher education. Again, for-profits are modeling practices that other colleges may decide to copy.

Remaining profitable gave for-profits a ferocious desire for institutional growth; they were hungry for student-customers who could supply the increased income demanded by financial markets. Not-for-profit colleges' growth is constrained by limits, such as the number of faculty and classrooms, but for-profits attempted to recruit anyone and everyone. Conventional universities watched—at first in horror and then in awe—as for-profit institutions fundamentally changed the college student market: they recruited many, many high-risk students through advertising and branding, offering products that looked very attractive to new consumers.

PUBLIC COLLEGES AND UNIVERSITIES.   In most cases, public institutions are partially funded by states, so that some portion of their operating budget comes from state appropriations. However, chapter 3 noted that state support has been shrinking as a percentage of the institutions' overall operating budgets. In response, tuition and fees have been rising faster at public schools than at their private counterparts (recall figure 10).[29]

Easy access to student loans made students less price sensitive. Public colleges and universities traditionally served the people of the states that funded them; most students came from in-state, attracted by public schools' proximity and lower tuition. But access to student loans, less expensive travel, and greater awareness of the relative prestige of different colleges led a growing number of students to consider more options before choosing a college. Private schools that once seemed out of the reach of many became accessible with combinations of public and private loans. But students having more choices meant that colleges increasingly found themselves competing for students.

In this competition, it helps to consider the perspective of the consumers, most of them teenagers who are deciding where to spend their formative years. While professors might like to imagine that students are attracted primarily by the quality of the education a campus offers, most students and their parents cannot hope to judge quality (which is why, of course, so many rely on college rankings). It is much easier to assess a college's amenities, and this creates a race between universities to have the most comfortable, trendy facilities.

The state schools of a generation ago would be considered hopelessly quaint now. Dorm rooms without air-conditioning, dining halls with limited options, and gyms only located in one area of campus are unacceptable these days. Students now expect amenities in school and around school, and many public universities have accepted this challenge.[30] This is simply the cost of competing for college students in 2013. Public universities are reinventing themselves to become more attractive choices for college-bound students by renovating aspects of the campus that have little to do with education. But how are they managing to pay for these changes?

We have already noted that public colleges and universities have been raising tuitions. But note, too, that at most of these institutions, there are tiers of students who are charged very different sums. In-state tuition is lower than out-of-state tuition. Most public colleges would prefer to admit higher-paying out-of-state students (which is why state legislatures sometimes cap the proportion of out-of-state students a school can admit). Additionally, international students are prized because they usually pay full freight, even more than out-of-state American students (who may receive discounts designed to attract desirable students). Out-of-state and international students have been a boon to public university bottom lines. Unsurprisingly, most public universities are very willing to entertain applications from these higher-paying cohorts of students; critics warn that this works to disadvantage minority and low-income local students (who probably will need financial aid from the institution).[31]

This process is not nearly as stable as it appears. While most public universities are doing very well today, their continued health depends on continued interest from out-of-state and international students, which in turn depends upon the health of the domestic student lending program and the international economy, respectively. In short, these universities have put themselves in a position where they are "betting on the come." While this may work so long as college students continue to be more feature sensitive than price sensitive, this system has the potential to collapse if student loan availability is reformed significantly or if students become more price sensitive as they worry about the difficulty of repaying student loans.

If students fall away from choosing schools based on features and return to comparing institutions on price, the long-term financial model of many public universities could fall apart, and a large number of these institutions could face a crisis. Many of the recent changes to public universities required huge capital expenditures and long-term debt structuring, justified by models that showed revenues continuing to grow year after year.[32] Much like the overleveraged housing and financial markets of the previous decade, many public universities are putting themselves in riskier positions than ever before, even though they may be experiencing record revenues.

While this picture is already bleak, it gets worse. Taking a page straight from the for-profit playbook, many public universities turn to the financial markets when they fall short of money for major renovations intended to make their campuses more attractive. From 2000 to 2006, the market for higher education debt (bonds issued by universities to investors) tripled.[33] The debt issuances, long used as tax-free ways to pay for big infrastructure projects, are growing in number, size, and frequency. In addition to needing tuition to pay for larger operating expenses, many universities now must also pay for the cost of servicing debt.

But having a large debt load decreases options for many universities, as a portion of operating income must go to interest payments and principal reduction instead of spending on new projects, personnel, and scholarships. While the academic bond market was not very exciting before 2000, we are already at a breaking point a little more than one decade later. In 2013, Moody's, one of the popular credit-rating companies, took the surprising step of downgrading the entire higher education sector.[34] According to Moody's, there are a number of issues at play. These include "diminished demand and increased price sensitivity" for "all but the most elite universities," "prolonged muted revenue growth," "revenues from state appropriations to continue to stagnate or even decline," and research funding "vulnerable to cuts in federal budget negotiations." While this already sounds like a recipe for disaster, Moody's does not stop there. They also mention rising student loan defaults, the challenges of serving low-income students, and negative accreditation actions against an increasing number of universities. Although Moody's and its peers learned a stern lesson about debt rating after the financial crisis, keep in mind that this frightening outlook about the standing of universities comes from a firm that the schools pay to rate their debt—meaning that, if anything, Moody's has an incentive to be overly optimistic.

This situation is not dire. American higher education is not going to crash tomorrow, but we cannot help but note that all the ingredients for an industry-wide downturn are present: higher costs, increasing debt loads, and questionable future demand have the potential to lead to a massive change in public higher education.

NOT-FOR-PROFIT PRIVATE COLLEGES AND UNIVERSITIES. It might seem that private schools, with their income-producing endowments and comparatively high tuition, ought to be in good financial shape. This is true for the most elite private schools, but those that are less well fixed are not doing very well.[35] These schools are dependent on the continued interest of students: most do not do a lot of funded research (an important source of income for larger universities), and of course these schools do not receive appropriations from state governments.

As a result, private schools must balance their budgets by charging higher tuition. While news reports about increased tuition suggest that this can generate a lot of money, we need to understand that paying for a private school is much like buying a car. There is a sticker price, and then there is a range of lower prices that most students and their families actually pay. One cannot simply multiply the announced tuition by the size of the student body; colleges' actual incomes are considerably lower.

Tuition discount rates are substantial, and they grew rapidly after 2000. In 2012, the last year recorded, discounts were about 45 percent for freshmen and 40 percent for all undergraduates at private colleges and universities.[36] Discounts are uneven: they are higher for first-year students (who must be wooed to choose a campus) than for more senior undergraduates (who are generally already committed to the institution and will accept slightly smaller discounts). Moreover, families that have saved for college are offered lower discounts than those with no savings.[37] In recent years, such discounts—characterized as grants or scholarships—accounted for over 35 percent of the cost of attending private schools, more than either cash or loans.[38] Tuition discounting is a private negotiation, but many students and families will eventually discover that others are paying very different prices to attend the same school. This has the potential to make students more price sensitive, which will only put additional pressure on private colleges.

Another indicator of growing price sensitivity is the decline (since 2010) in the average amount families pay for college.[39] Tuition, of course, has continued to rise, yet families are actually spending less—possibly because they are receiving loans or discounts, another troubling sign for vulnerable private institutions. Some institutions are acknowledging this by sharply reducing both tuition and discounts, experimenting with a the-sticker-price-is-what-you-pay model. However, a majority of polled families prefer the high-tuition-high-discount method.[40]

While the most elite private institutions have almost nothing to worry about, not-for-profit private colleges make up a large share of the institutions in serious financial trouble.[41] According to the National Association of College Admission Counseling, 446 private colleges and universities did not fill their entire freshman classes in 2012, meaning that their incomes fell short of what they'd budgeted. For small, nonelite private colleges, the bad days are not coming—they are here—and the problems are beginning to spread to some selective schools. Worse, college enrollment began falling in 2012–13, as the economy improved and those who had decided to

stay in school—rather than brave the Great Recession's weak job market—entered the workforce, even as the population experienced one of
those demographic blips when the number of eighteen-year-olds fell from
one year to the next.[42] The weakest private institutions are those most
threatened by the prospects of having fewer students. Because they are
charging the highest prices to customers, private colleges have become
even more dependent on their students having access to student loans (and
therefore being less price sensitive) than their public counterparts. Their
future is tightly linked to the future of student loan policy.

OTHER INSTITUTIONAL CONCERNS.   Higher education—not-for-profit
institutions as well as for-profits—is hooked on student loans. Colleges
spend money to make themselves more attractive to students, which
causes tuition to rise faster than the cost of living. So long as students were
not price sensitive, this worked, but there are signs that a reckoning is
coming. Complaints about crushing debt and the prospect of a higher
education bubble suggest that something is going to have to change.

There are a variety of apocalyptic forecasts. One business professor/
guru says, "Fifteen years from now more than half of the universities
will be in bankruptcy, including the state schools. In the end, I am
excited to see that happen."[43] Other seers argue that free online course
content coupled with certifications of completion will make traditional
college instruction obsolete.

Of course, the history of American higher education is one of growth
and expansion, even in the face of a long string of critics who have
warned that the system needs fundamental reforms, so we might suspect that most campuses aren't about to vanish. In fact, two-year community college enrollment is growing quickly, suggesting that an even
larger percentage of the secondary-education population is interested
in continuing education (slightly less than half of community college
students already have federal loans).[44] Still, discussions of student loans
tend to worry more about students and the government, while paying
relatively little attention to the situation of colleges and universities.

But students can't be expected to take out ever-larger loans to pay for ever-larger tuitions—something is going to have to change.

Creditors

DIRECT LOANS AND THE DEPARTMENT OF EDUCATION. The final category of players is creditors or lenders, and these days the biggest student lender by far is the Department of Education's direct student loan program.

We noted in chapter 4 that the government excuses loans for students enrolled in many schools that fail, but this has not posed a problem because—until now—the schools that have failed have been small. However, imagine for a moment that the professor/guru is right and that half of the educational institutions in the United States fail in the next fifteen years. In that version of the future, what has historically been a manageable problem becomes a monster.

More than ever, the federal government is now at the center of conversations about the financial future of higher education. Regardless of the exact percentage of student defaults or the exact number of schools that close in the future, it is clear that the direct lending program is in trouble. The Department of Education is no longer just an agency that makes college more accessible by lending a helping hand.[45] The government now holds the obligations for a majority of student lending dollars in the United States, which means that it is on the hook either if large numbers of students default on their loans or if lots of colleges start to close. And as we have already shown, there are signs that both defaults and college closures are rising. This dependence on the performance of students and institutions puts the department in the vulnerable position of both a regulator supposed to foster educational quality and a creditor that can't afford to see schools close.

SECURITIZATION AND PRIVATE LOANS THROUGH SALLIE MAE AND THE FINANCIAL SYSTEM. Although guaranteed third-party loans were eliminated in 2010, Sallie Mae—which became a publicly traded company in 2004—remains a major part of the student lending industry, and it does not appear to be doing all that well.[46] In April 2013, Sallie Mae was forced to cancel a $225 million bond offering because of lack of demand.[47] Although securitization of student loans remains a multibillion-dollar business, the recalled bond issuance was a sign that investors are no longer willing to tolerate the risks related to student loan repayment.[48] While bonds of this type pay an interest premium compared to more secure debt, investors apparently no longer believe that these bonds are safe.

In a move related to these market changes, Sallie Mae announced its intention to split into two companies, separating the legacy federally backed loans from the post-2010 unsecured private lending.[49] What might be surprising is the reason for the split. Sallie Mae is worried about its older federally backed loans, not the newer private portfolio. Sallie Mae wants to distance the troubled (but backed) legacy portfolio from its newer, better-performing private loans. In spite of being largely guaranteed, the federally backed loans' performance is so bad and the future so troubling that they are scaring off investors.

It appears that investors want little to do with debt that pays relatively high interest rates and is guaranteed by the federal government. If you have managed to read this chapter and remain dubious that there's a problem with student loans, this market action should be the thing that finally scares you. If you are prone to believe Sallie Mae, then the split will result in a new private portfolio with lower defaults, unburdened by legacy debt. However, we cannot forget that these private loans are right now a relatively small industry and are only made available to students and families in the best financial condition. Essentially, everyone is invited to participate in direct loans, but if you need more money than direct loans are willing to provide, you have to be one of the lucky few with a credit report favorable enough to get private loans from Sallie Mae to cover the difference.

Essentially, Sallie Mae hopes to turn into a new entity that will reverse decades of student lending policy. Instead of lending to the neediest or brightest students, Sallie Mae now focuses on lending to the wealthiest families so as to make the safest investments. While this makes more sense as a business practice than lending to all comers, it has the potential to increase the very inequities that federal student loans were designed to combat.

Nor is Sallie Mae alone. Major banks have begun announcing that they will stop making private student loans, primarily due to the rising risk of default.[50] Private loans have increased because federal loan limits have not kept pace with rising college costs, so that students wind up supplementing their federal loans with private loans.[51] To the degree that students depend on access to these loans, private lenders leaving the arena will only increase the rates charged by those willing to remain.

Unfortunately, what is good for Sallie Mae is not good for student loans. By making extra loans available to some but not all consumers, Sallie Mae will allow wealthy families to pay even more for elite schooling. The access to extra loans on top of federal borrowing limits will allow more advantaged students to pay more for college, while leaving behind the rest of borrowers, who are unable to get private loans at good terms. This process has the potential to cause even greater tuition hikes if a certain class of students has access to even more college funding (allowing colleges to raise prices), leading to more pressure for higher limits on federal loans, making the entire cost problem even worse.[52]

This chapter has identified a set of concerns, including rising student loan defaults among former students (even as the overall economy has been improving), public colleges and universities raising tuition as they compete for students, smaller private colleges unable to attract enough students, the federal government on the hook for hundreds of billions of dollars, and private lenders reluctant to hold government-backed loans. These are all serious issues. Each one has the potential to become the focus for public concern and policymakers' attention—to become the fifth, or sixth, or seventh student loan mess. And these prospective messes are not just about students. They implicate colleges and creditors, and have the potential to affect the economy as a whole.

In this book, we argue that student loans have been treated as a series of narrowly defined messes, in which people identified problematic aspects of the larger problem and devised policies to address those aspects, without thinking through how those policies—and other changes in society—might reshape the problem. The consequence of this piecemeal approach has been that, even as particular messes may have been solved, the overall student loan problem has only grown.

Today a majority of college students take out student loans, and many of them depend on loans—they could not pursue higher education without them. In turn, colleges and universities count on students having access to loans; their plans are based on the assumption that students will continue to be able to afford the tuition and fees they charge. And the federal government is counting both on those students to repay their debts and on those educational institutions to remain afloat, even as private investors seem increasingly dubious. There is, if you will, a sort of institutional codependency—students depend on access to government loans; colleges depend on students getting those loans; and the government depends on good behavior from student borrowers and colleges.

There is, then, a student loan system, and at pretty much every point in that system, there are signs of strain. Perhaps it is time to stop focusing on one mess after another; perhaps it is time to adopt a broader frame of reference.

CHAPTER SIX

Beyond Making Messes?

This book argues that the history of federal student loan policies is best understood as a series of messes in which attention became focused on some particular aspect of a larger problem and well-intentioned policies were devised to address each narrowly defined concern. These policies might even achieve their goals: after all, the creation of large federal student loan programs did solve the wasted brainpower mess, by giving every aspiring college student access to the funds needed to pay for higher education, just as making it nearly impossible to discharge student loan debt through bankruptcy addressed the deadbeat student mess. Yet even as attention focused on particular messes, the larger student loan problem—shaped both by those aspects of the larger problem that were being ignored and by other changes in society—continued to evolve until people identified a new mess, and those new messes were arguably more serious than the old ones, so that things somehow seemed to have gotten worse, not better. This cycle could easily continue. Total student loan debt reached $1 trillion in 2012 and is on course to hit $2 trillion around 2020, even as the default rate among young borrowers in repayment is about 35 percent. Thus there are several other messes—potentially really big ones—looming on the horizon. Breaking the cycle demands that we try to understand the many aspects of the student loan problem, to see the big picture. This requires taking a step back and examining taken-for-granted assumptions that provide the foundation for the student loan debate.

GOOD INTENTIONS AND DUBIOUS OUTCOMES

The people who shaped federal student loan policies were motivated by good intentions. They shared some basic, largely unarticulated assumptions. We listed these in the introduction, but it is time to revisit them. The key assumptions were:

- *Higher education is a good thing and should be encouraged—the more educated the nation's population, the better.*

It is generally acknowledged that higher education has both communal and individualistic benefits. More education produces better, more productive citizens, so that the entire society gains; this is why the first student loan mess focused on the communal costs of wasted brainpower, and why, more recently, people have worried that other nations are overtaking or even surpassing the United States' rate of college graduation. For individuals, education serves as the principal route to achieving the American Dream; this is why adults urge young people who hope to gain—or maintain—a high standard of living to do well in school.

- *Because individuals who choose to receive more education benefit directly, they should bear most of the costs of that education.*

Not everyone is willing or able to complete college, but those who do usually make more money than those who don't. Why should those who haven't had the advantage of higher education (and who probably earn less money) be expected to subsidize the future success of the college bound? This explains the appeal of student loans: they were a way to help young people get ahead, while requiring them to pay back those who had helped them.

- *Federal loan policies should not discriminate among educational institutions—young people should be free to choose what and where they want to study, and they should be eligible for student loans to attend any school that will admit them.*

American institutions of higher education take many forms. Some are funded by states or localities; others are privately owned. Some are nonprofit; others are for-profit. Some have special missions to educate people of particular religious faiths, ethnicities, or political leanings. (Don't forget that, when student loans were introduced, many southern states operated and sought to preserve racially segregated colleges.) Allocating federal funds directly to colleges would invite critics to object that this or that kind of institution does not deserve government support. But allowing students to choose which institutions they want to attend (and allowing colleges to take responsibility for determining whether a particular student meets their standards for admission) circumvents such criticism. Over time, the federal government tried to set some standards—for its students to qualify for federal loans, a college had to be accredited; no more than 90 percent of its income could come from Title IV funds; and so on—but the basic assumption has been that the government should not interfere with students' ability to choose which schools they want to attend.

- *Federal loan policies should not discriminate among borrowers—the same rules should apply to all.*

Lenders ordinarily offer terms that try to take into account the risks posed by different borrowers. Thus people with good credit ratings—those who are judged most likely to repay what they owe—can borrow more, at lower interest, and so on. No doubt there are several factors that predict the likelihood that students will be able to complete college, start appropriate careers, and repay their loans. For example, we might assume that young people who earned high grades in high school would be better risks than those who did less well. The problem is that virtually any standard we use to assess risk will work to the advantage of those who come from more comfortable circumstances: the upper-middle-class children of college graduates, for instance, probably pose lower risks than poorer children whose parents may never have set foot on a college campus. Left to their own devices, lenders would make it more expensive for those who need help the most to borrow money for their educations. But this contradicts one of the central goals of student loan programs—to give disadvantaged young people a ladder to social mobility. The solution, of course, was to pretend that all borrowers posed essentially the same risks.

These assumptions were so basic and so widely shared that people rarely talked about them. They were all well intentioned: encourage people to get more education by providing money for loans; expect the people who benefited to repay the loans they received for their educations; keep the federal government from using student loan programs to interfere with how colleges operated; and make sure that students of modest means didn't have to pay more for their loans than those from more advantaged backgrounds. By and large, these were not controversial ideas. But people avoided exploring the implications of these assumptions or considering how student loans might have very different effects on the lives of different sorts of borrowers.

Student loans have largely stood outside the realm of partisan politics. To be sure, Democrats usually call for expanding access to loans, while Republicans tend to praise for-profit colleges and private lenders, but both parties recognize that federal student loans are a popular program upon which many middle-class families depend, and increasingly both acknowledge that college costs need to be controlled. People rely on student loans, and there would be little support for abolishing the program. At the same time, the numbers—the constantly growing amount of money owed, the rising default rate, and the increasing cost of higher education—reveal that the problem is getting ever bigger and less manageable. How *did* we get into this mess? And how might we get out?

WHAT OUR ASSUMPTIONS LARGELY IGNORE

It will help to begin by returning to those agreed-upon assumptions and thinking about them a bit more critically. Doing so makes it apparent that those assumptions gloss over two fundamental, multifaceted issues: inequality and interests.

Inequality

It is all very well to pay lip service to the value of equality. Who, after all, is willing to come out in favor of inequality? Yet the reality is that we do not live in a state of perfect equality; there are real inequalities that federal student loan programs have largely ignored. It is, we think, time to confront these.

INEQUALITY AMONG INDIVIDUALS.   One way to think about inequality is to recognize that people have different abilities. This is a theme that conservatives like to invoke: they argue that some people have more discipline, more ability, and so on. Most people cannot hit a major-league curveball, but a talented few can. Or, to take an example closer to our topic of student loans, a professor who reads a stack of term papers will almost certainly find that they vary in quality—there will be some that are much better than others, as well as some that are much worse. Our professor may attribute these differences in the papers' quality to some students being smarter, or more studious, or whatever.

In general, the best predictor of how students will do in our professor's class is how well they've done in their previous classes. Oh sure, there are exceptions: maybe Susan will be a late bloomer, and maybe Tom—a stellar student up to now—will start to fade. But in general, those who have been good students tend to continue to be good students. This is why we tell children that they need to get good grades to get into a good college: colleges prefer to admit those students whose academic records indicate that they are likely to do well.

This may seem obvious, but critics of higher education often prefer to ignore inequalities in ability. Colleges vary in how selective they are; the most selective institutions take only the most promising students, whereas the least selective institutions take pretty much anyone. Higher education has democratized: more than half of today's high school graduates continue in school. This has inevitably meant that lots of people are entering colleges today who would not have done so in earlier decades. We can think of them as being higher-risk students, academically high risk in the sense that they are less prepared and more likely to fail. Of course, some of them will do fine—they'll turn out to be late bloomers. But it would be naive not to expect that a fair portion of them won't succeed, and it seems disingenuous when critics report that they are shocked—shocked!—by the low rates of degree completion at the least selective institutions, such as for-profits and two-year colleges.

These students are also higher-risk prospects for student loans. Less likely to do well in college, they are less likely to graduate, less likely to land jobs that pay well, and less likely to avoid delinquency in paying back their loans. We may agree that everyone deserves equal access to student loans, and we may want to give everyone the chance to succeed, but we shouldn't be surprised when some people fall short.

There is a second sort of inequality among individuals—inequality of resources. Just as conservatives like to talk about differences in individuals' talents, liberals like to talk about differences in individuals' backgrounds. Some children are born in advantaged circumstances: their parents are college graduates and have higher incomes; throughout childhood they were encouraged to imagine growing up to pursue higher education. They are surrounded by countless advantages. There are more books in their homes, and their families treat reading as a central and important activity; family conversations use bigger vocabularies; parents closely monitor school performance; and on and on. In contrast, other children—whose parents may love them just as much and also dream of their kids going to college—may have less money and lack a clear vision of how to prepare their children for academic success.[1]

Differences in resources translate directly into higher risks. Not only are kids from less affluent families less likely to do well in school, but their families' circumstances are more precarious. Disruptions—such as an adult who contracts a debilitating illness or loses a job, problems that a family with lots of resources might weather with relative ease—can make it extremely hard for a college student from less advantaged circumstances to concentrate on, or even stay in, school. And after leaving school, these students are at higher risk when it comes to paying off their loans, if only because they can't expect as much financial assistance from their families.

To be sure, federal student aid policies make some effort to give those with fewer resources more help than more advantaged students receive. Those from lower-income families may be eligible for Pell grants—that is, the federal government gives them money for their education. They may be eligible to earn more money through work-study programs, and they may be eligible for subsidized student loans—the loan program that offers the most generous terms (lower interest rates and no accumulating interest charges while they remain in school). For example, at the time we were writing this, a first-year student with minimal resources might be eligible for a Pell grant of up to $5,500, $4,000 in federal work-study, and a $3,500 subsidized student loan—that's $13,000 for one academic year, not a trivial amount of support. Under the right circumstances, the student could receive an additional $5,500 unsubsidized loan. Still, there are institutions where a student would have no trouble burning through that amount of money—and much more—in a year.

And there is a third sort of inequality among individuals: unequal prospects. What students choose to study—and where they go to study—affects whether they can get a job and the desirability of the job they get. Students who major in engineering, accounting, nursing, or education are being trained to do particular kinds of work; assuming there is a demand for people with those sorts of training when they graduate, they are likely to find work and be at lower risk of defaulting on their loans. On the other hand, the prospects for students with liberal arts majors are less clear; most will do fine, but some may have more trouble finding work that pays well, so that they are at somewhat higher risk.

Prospects get particularly uncertain when students choose to continue their education in graduate or professional schools. The limits on the amounts graduate and professional students can borrow are much higher; reports of student loan debts approaching or even exceeding $100,000 almost always involve students who have spent several years receiving advanced training. Some of these students may be at very high risk of default, because they may have difficulty finding positions that pay enough to allow them to repay their loans. Critics warn, for instance, that the supply of law school graduates exceeds the number of available positions.[2]

Note that students' prospects also depend on where they studied. Graduates of elite programs tend to wind up in the best-paying positions, while those who earned their degrees at less prestigious institutions are likely to have more trouble finding desirable positions—and repaying what they owe.

In other words, assuming that all students should be treated equally does not eliminate the inequalities among individuals that make some higher risks than others. Policies that pretend there are no differences in risk, coupled with rising college costs and ever more higher-risk students entering higher education virtually ensure that defaults will continue to rise.

INEQUALITIES AMONG EDUCATIONAL INSTITUTIONS. Just as not all students are equal, neither are all colleges. Elite schools have considerable advantages. They can be selective, regarding both the faculty they hire and the students they admit. They also have bigger budgets: larger endowments generate income; larger research programs bring substantial external funds to campus in the form of grants and contracts; and they can charge higher tuitions. Most states have a hierarchy of public institutions, in which the flagship university receives more generous allocations than the four- and two-year colleges. More money means more financial flexibility, so that wealthier schools find it easier to offer financial aid packages to attract the students they most want to admit.

These varying resources affect the importance of student loans at different institutions. We have already observed that for-profit colleges are almost completely dependent on federal funds, especially if we count both Title IV money and programs for veterans and members of the military. But a small, private, nonprofit liberal arts college with a limited endowment may depend on tuition for almost all its income, and its students probably rely heavily on student loans for their tuition payments; such schools are nearly as dependent on federal dollars as many for-profits. On the other hand, those lucky elite institutions with huge endowments, substantial research funding, and highly selective admissions standards are less concerned about student loan policies.

Of course, colleges differ in more than resources: they have different missions. For-profits want to make money; others, such as historically black institutions and schools affiliated with religious denominations, have been dedicated to teaching students from particular groups; still others offer specialized programs of study. Most colleges' promotional materials insist that they offer a distinctive, if not unique, educational experience. To the degree that the availability of student loans encourages more students to choose among an array of educational options, loans foster diversity across the higher education landscape.

Interests

Inequalities among individuals and institutions mean that we should be careful of overgeneralizing about the effects of student loans. It also helps to recall the central insight from economics: that individuals, institutions, and even the government make choices based on their perceived interests. In many ways, federal student loan policies have encouraged all these entities to focus on short-run advantages.

INDIVIDUALS AND PRICE INSENSITIVITY. For the reasons we have discussed in earlier chapters, it has become increasingly hard for most people to pay for higher education without taking out loans. Whereas magazine articles in the 1950s tried to convince their readers that it wasn't unthinkable to borrow to help pay for college, most of today's students expect to take on debt. And buying on credit encourages people to explore their options: "If I'll have to borrow X dollars to pay for College A, why not borrow a little bit more and go to College B." And maybe that's a good choice; maybe College B offers a better education and is worth the higher cost. But price insensitivity can be a slippery slope, so that students can decide to borrow more to attend the school with the fanciest recreation center or to afford a more comfortable on-campus lifestyle. Just as easy credit allows people to rack up purchases on their credit cards or buy more house than they need, it leads to some people running up a tab for higher education without thinking through just what might go wrong.

INSTITUTIONS AND COST INSENSITIVITY. As prospective students have become price insensitive, institutions have been able to worry less about what they charge. In fact, administrators may conclude that remaining competitive requires that their campuses upgrade (that new rec center and so on), even if those improvements mean they must raise prices. In particular, capital improvements, such as adding a new building, may be so expensive that the institution has to borrow the money—taking out its own loans and counting on its continued ability to attract students willing to pay ever-higher prices (because those students will be able to borrow whatever amounts will be needed to pay for their educations).

GOVERNMENT AND THE DIFFICULTY OF FINDING THE REGULATORY SWEET SPOT. The federal government has not been oblivious to the mounting problems with student loans: borrowers owing ever-greater sums, default rates rising, colleges giving poor value for the dollars they consume, and so on. At various times, federal policymakers have tried to do something about one student loan mess or another, but they have faced several obstacles.

First, those widely shared assumptions about treating colleges and students equally have posed an obstacle. There have been some efforts at reform, such as devising grant and work-study programs to provide extra help for low-income students, or attempting to reduce borrowing to attend institutions whose students have high default rates, but these measures have met with resistance. Congress has been responsive to middle-class voters' demands that they continue to have access to student loans, and colleges whose graduates have high default rates have protested efforts to reduce their access to student loans.

A second obstacle is the federal government's accounting rules (discussed in chapters 4 and 5), which treat student loan debt as an asset. From this perspective, mounting student loan debt does not seem to be a problem—at least not for the government. Democrats, in particular, find it easy to argue that the expanding program does not pose budgetary issues; in fact, they are not above using the anticipated profits from student loans to cover the expected costs of other programs, such as health care reform. Third, voices arguing that the federal government should not overregulate higher education have constituted an additional obstacle. This has been a theme in Republican rhetoric, but higher education has also insisted that it ought to be allowed to manage its own affairs.

These competing pressures have led to federal policies that generally kept money flowing for student loans without a lot of constraints. By increasing borrowing limits, federal policy does little to encourage greater price sensitivity among students or greater cost sensitivity among colleges. To be sure, particular worries—manifested in what we've called the various student loan messes—might lead to some action. But people have had trouble coming to grips with the vastly larger overall problem: how to provide higher education for an ever-larger proportion of the population, which, faced with ever-higher costs, needs to borrow ever more money.

OBSTACLES TO REFORM

We finished writing this book in the fall of 2013, a time when some policymakers were trying to move beyond tinkering with specific messes to
address the larger problem. Two proposals—one heavily promoted by
President Obama—attracted a lot of attention. Here, we explore these
plans and the objections to them, in order to show how difficult it will
be to solve the larger student loan problem.

Obama's Plan

On August 22 and 23, 2013, the president spoke on several campuses
about his three-point plan—what he called "major reforms that will
shake up the current system" and address higher education costs.[3] His
second and third points promoted familiar goals: "We want to encourage more colleges to embrace new ways to prepare our students for a
21st-century economy and maintain a high level of quality without
breaking the bank"; and "We've got to offer students who already have
debt the chance to actually repay it." But the first point was more novel:
Obama proposed that the federal government begin ranking colleges
on their educational performance—tuition, graduation rates, default
rates, and the like—so that families and students would have more
information to make college choices. Further, after a few years, during
which colleges would have the opportunity to improve their performance, the federal government would begin to differentially reward
campuses based on their performance: "Colleges that keep their tuition
down and are providing high-quality education are the ones that are
going to see their taxpayer funding go up."

Obama's proposals attracted a good deal of commentary. A *New York
Times* editorial characterized the plan as "a bold and important way to
leverage the government's power and get Washington off the sidelines."[4]
But the proposals—particularly the plan to rate colleges—also came
under attack from a broad range of advocates.

To no one's surprise, Obama's political opponents were critical of his proposal. Congressional Republicans criticized Obama's plan. According to the *Times:*

> Representative John Kline, Republican of Minnesota and the chairman of the House Committee on Education and the Workforce, said in a statement that he was skeptical of Mr. Obama's proposed rating system.
>
> "I remain concerned that imposing an arbitrary college ranking system could curtail the very innovation we hope to encourage—and even lead to federal price controls," Mr. Kline said. "As always, the devil is in the details."
>
> Senator Marco Rubio, Republican of Florida, said: "I'm strongly opposed to his plan to impose new federal standards on higher education institutions. This is a slippery slope, and one that ends with the private sector inevitably giving up more of its freedom to innovate and take risks. The U.S. did not create the best higher education system in the world by using standards set by Washington bureaucrats."[5]

Leaders representing for-profit colleges argued that while the president's plan was being considered, government efforts to rework gainful employment regulations for for-profit colleges should be suspended (which would halt an ongoing effort to rein in for-profits), and noted that any system for rating colleges should evaluate "their performance relative to schools with similar student populations" (so that for-profits, with their high-risk student bodies, might operate under more lenient standards).[6] Meanwhile, conservative intellectuals raised a variety of questions: Would the plan merely reward schools that performed well, or would it actually also penalize those that performed badly? Would a rating system be vulnerable to being gamed by colleges? Might insisting on higher graduation rates encourage colleges to "lower already abysmally low standards"? Wouldn't more lenient forgiveness policies simply encourage students to borrow more at the taxpayers' expense?[7]

But Obama's proposals also came under attack from those he might have hoped would be political allies. Dēmos, an organization for progressive youth, implied that Obama had missed the point and called for restoring "the levels of public support that were the formula for success for previous generations: *stable funding for instruction, and grants, not loans, for students.*" They asked, "Why don't we rate state legislatures on their per-student investment in higher education?"[8] Commentators worried that the plan would disadvantage historically black colleges: "How will metrics that reward Pell Grant recipients and punish low graduation rates benefit schools that serve the largest portion of this at-risk population? ... Rating schools without concern for historic inequities and contemporary challenges won't make college more affordable or more accessible."[9] And representatives of faculty organizations offered a range of criticisms: Obama's plan would encourage colleges to hire fewer full-time faculty, pay attention to outcomes rather than learning, reduce the quality of education offered at all but elite institutions, and discourage educational innovation.[10] These liberal critics pointed to the decline in state support for public institutions as the true cause of higher education's cost crisis, and they argued that Obama's plans would do nothing to address this shortfall.

In short, the initial reactions to Obama's proposals featured far more skepticism than enthusiasm.

Paying It Forward in Oregon

Earlier in the summer of 2013, Oregon began discussing a proposal that would allow residents to attend state institutions tuition-free, in return for paying back 3 percent of their income for twenty-five years once they started working.[11] Critics immediately began noting problems: until large numbers of students began making repayments, the program would cost the state's taxpayers a good deal; former students who earned higher incomes would pay back far more than those who earned lower incomes; those who anticipated earning higher incomes (and who thereby might generate the most future revenue for the program) might choose not to enroll in the program; the program would not help those who wanted to attend private schools; and so on. Although the idea might seem simple, designing such a program was likely to prove complicated and—at least initially—expensive. Like Obama's proposals, the Oregon effort inspired a good deal of skepticism.

Resistance to Thinking Outside the Box

Neither Obama's proposals nor the Oregon plan offered more than a partial solution to the problem of funding higher education. However, both at least tried to move beyond the sorts of narrow issues—such as arguing about the ways to calculate interest rates for some loans—that had characterized recent debates over student loan policy.

If even modest reform efforts encounter stiff opposition, more significant changes are likely out of the question. Imagine that we were to treat higher education much as we treat high school—that is, we essentially make it free for all. Suppose every student (who qualified for admission) could enter a public institution at no—or at least very little—cost. Various incentives might be built into such a program. Perhaps those who qualified for admission to a state's selective flagship campus might receive higher allocations than those who could only qualify for less selective institutions. Perhaps those with stronger academic records could receive more support (thereby encouraging students to take high school more seriously). Or it might be possible to calculate the value of the support an individual student receives toward public higher education and to give students who want to attend more expensive private institutions a voucher for that amount. (Presumably students determined to attend private schools would need to cover the remainder of their costs through savings or private loans.) But the basic idea would be to guarantee everyone access to low-cost higher education.

One advantage of such a plan is that it would give governments some leverage on college costs. The disadvantages of this option are also obvious: it would be an expensive program and would require substantial tax increases.[12] Note, however, that this need not involve increasing the total amount spent on higher education, although it certainly would shift some of the burden of paying for higher education to taxpayers who wouldn't benefit directly from the program (if neither they nor their children were college-bound). And while elite private institutions might continue to thrive, this plan would likely kill off hundreds of more vulnerable private schools. But in today's political environment, there would be no appetite for such a dramatic and disruptive change. The alternative would seem to be to acknowledge that a lot of different things need to be reformed.

WHAT NEEDS TO BE DONE

Once we decide to confront the entire student loan problem—to move beyond focusing on one particular mess at a time—and we concede that there is no appetite for discarding the current arrangements and developing an entirely new system for paying for higher education, it becomes apparent that several sorts of changes are needed. This section offers our list of suggestions. It should be clear that every one of these proposals will encounter resistance, that our recommendations can expect to face the customary there-are-some-good-ideas-here-but-the-recommenda-tions-that-will-threaten-my-interests-are-unacceptable objections. But all the items on our list contribute to the larger student loan problem.

Controlling College Costs

We begin with higher education institutions because we believe that bringing college costs under control is the single most important—and most difficult—aspect of the larger student loan problem. Tinkering with interest rates and repayment plans can't solve the problem so long as costs continue to outstrip inflation. What needs to be done?

1. *Controlling the growth in administrative costs.* Just as tuition has been rising faster than the cost of living, higher education's administrative costs have been rising faster than the costs of instruc-

tion.[13] In part, this growth reflects increased demand—often from federal agencies, accrediting agencies, and the like—for more record keeping.

2. *Reducing other noninstructional costs.* Cutting nonacademic features means not just having a less fancy rec center but examining other, almost unthinkable possibilities, such as shedding athletic programs, which lose money on all but a few campuses. Right away, we can envision challenges. Any proposed cuts will lead to opposition. The rec center, we will be told, fosters student health and teaches them to pursue a healthy lifestyle. No doubt the opposition to cutting athletics will be deafening. Still, this is an obvious place to hold down college costs.

3. *Lowering instructional costs.* Trimming administrative fat and cutting noninstructional costs can help, but instruction consumes the largest chunk of college budgets. How to cut these costs? Visionaries argue that technology (such as online instruction) offers the most promising solution.[14] When presenting his plan, President Obama made frequent reference to reducing time on campus by eliminating the third year of law school instruction or allowing high school students to accumulate college credits so that they wind up spending less time at college.[15] Many colleges have been managing costs by having more instruction handled by part-time faculty, who are much less costly than full-time professors, and there are occasional reports of colleges dropping low-enrollment programs.[16] All these plans threaten to change the face of college education, and they, too, will encounter opposition, particularly from faculty, who can argue that these changes threaten to degrade their colleges' educational missions.

4. *Encouraging family savings.* The financial aid packages that many colleges offer families actually work to the disadvantage of those who have set money aside for college expenses. Discouraging savings means that more students are likely to borrow. Colleges should stop penalizing thrift.

Shifting Government Policies

While controlling college costs is vital, it is also the case that a large share of students depend upon government support, and this is not about to change. Still, there are several steps the state and federal governments could take to help control the growth of student loans. Realistically, many of them will be opposed by various constituencies, and most of them will cost money. When we confront the larger student loan problem, we face a set of unattractive options: increase taxes, run up the deficit, cut students' access to higher education, or retain the existing program in which student loan debt and the default rate continue to swell. No one wants to choose among these options, and it is certain that all these recommendations will prove controversial.

5. *Providing more state support for public institutions.* The proportion of public colleges' budgets that comes from state allocations has declined, which has forced tuition to account for a larger share of the colleges' income. This explains why tuition costs have risen faster at public—rather than private—schools. In presenting his plan, President Obama made frequent references to the need for the states to increase their levels of support.[17] Of course, state governments are hard-pressed by growing costs for other programs, such as Medicaid and corrections; higher levels of support for higher education will require higher taxes.

6. *Adopting realistic accounting methods to address defaults.* The federal government's method of treating student loan debts as assets even after extended periods of delinquency is one of the principal reasons that dependence on federal student loans has been allowed to rise, even as default rates soared. Adopting more realistic accounting methods, especially for accounts in deep trouble, would encourage the federal government to seek to control the ever more rapid growth of ever higher risk loans, to acknowledge the true costs of student loans, and perhaps

even to confront the need to raise revenue to invest in higher
education.

7. *Restricting support for badly performing colleges* (Obama's not wrong).
The federal government ought to stop pouring money into
loans for students to attend institutions that specialize in
recruiting high-risk students into programs where they are
likely to fail. Obama's proposal tried to engineer a soft landing
by first, in 2015, instituting ratings that would make schools'
performance public (which would presumably discourage
students from choosing to attend the weakest institutions).
Then, in 2018, once the ratings were established, the federal
government would offer less advantageous terms for loans to
colleges with poor performance records.[18] Acting too quickly
would simply cause the weakest institutions to fail and leave the
taxpayers to pick up all outstanding loans from those institutions. However, allowing dubious institutions to continue at
taxpayer expense is unreasonable—something needs to be
done.

8. *Improving grant support for the most vulnerable students.* The federal
government's programs of Pell grants and work-study funds to
support the education of low-income students have not kept
up with the increase in college costs. Similarly, need-based
scholarship programs in most states have been allowed to
decline. Meanwhile, while rising college costs have meant that
high-risk students find it increasingly necessary to take on
student loan debt to supplement whatever grants they might
receive. Forcing the most vulnerable, high-risk students to
borrow money only makes defaults more likely.

9. *Making repayment terms more workable.* This has been the focus for
many recent proposals: (1) offering additional forgiveness for debts
of individuals who pursue particular careers (e.g., in teaching or
public service); (2) limiting repayments for those who earn lower
incomes or forgiving all remaining debt after some period of

time; and (3) charging low interest rates for student loans. One problem with these proposals is that they don't do much to address any of the factors that are making things steadily worse—students' price insensitivity, the rising costs of college, and the ever-increasing amounts students are borrowing. Another is that these reforms shift the burden—possibly a very large burden—to the government and the taxpayers. The money loaned to students does not fall out of the sky; to the degree that we don't get that money back (through default or forgiveness) or that we charge interest rates lower than what is needed to pay the actual costs of the student loan program, we must generate that money, either through higher taxes or by adding to the federal deficit. Note that these are not small-ticket items; we're talking about hundreds of billions of dollars. Some proposals to forgive borrowers' remaining balances after some period of time could have a troubling moral hazard effect: once borrowers realize that they will not be expected to repay all that they owe, there may be no reason for them not to borrow as much as possible.

10. *Restricting lending to high-risk borrowers.* This can involve both carrots and sticks. On the one hand, there are complaints that too many students arrive at college ill prepared and that they don't take their studies seriously. It ought to be possible to devise a system of rewards to encourage serious students and penalize those who aren't taking their studies seriously. Obama's proposals mentioned requiring students to make academic progress to qualify for continued loans.[19] But why not go farther? Why not make it possible for students with stronger academic records to borrow at more favorable terms? At the same time, there should be borrowing limits based on gradu- ates' projected earnings. While we agree that students should be free to choose what they study, that doesn't mean taxpayers have an obligation to continue making loans that may be impossible to repay.

11. *Minimizing policies that increase colleges' administrative costs* (Republicans aren't wrong, either). It is all very well for us to encourage colleges to cut administrative spending, but one reason for increasing administrative costs is monitoring institutional compliance with various federal regulations (and Obama's proposals would only increase these demands). This is part of the problem with rising costs, and it ought to be addressed.

12. *Encouraging families to save toward and cover college costs.* Borrowing should be viewed as a worst option, not a first choice. Like colleges, governments should be encouraging families to plan for college costs.

13. *Shifting costs to those most able to pay.* Higher education has substantial communal benefits, but the system used to fund higher education places most of the burden on those who attend college. We see nothing wrong with shifting that burden, investing in students who need help, and covering the costs of those investments through taxation. Instead of trying to insist that individuals be held individually responsible for covering the costs of their educations, why not accept that the tax burden will fall most heavily on the college educated? In communal terms, society at large benefits from a more educated population, and those who experience the benefits of college should be expected to provide the most support for higher education through paying taxes. Is it really a problem if taxes paid by high-income doctors and lawyers wind up covering a share of the costs of educating schoolteachers and nurses?

Encouraging Students and Their Families

Student loan policy has distorted the market for higher education, because it may take years for students and their families to understand how much college costs and how difficult it may be to cover those costs. More ought to be done to encourage these people to make wiser choices.

14. *Encouraging savings and discouraging debt.* One consequence of rising college costs is that many people come to view borrowing as inevitable, and one consequence of readily available loans is that some students begin to take on debt to maintain a comfortable college lifestyle. There is nothing wrong with preferring designer coffee, but taking out student loans to pay for lattes buys short-term pleasure at long-term cost.

15. *Understanding risks and costs.* Students and families need to think through the consequences of borrowing. More, better, clearer information could improve decision making. The efforts of some private not-for-profit organizations to offer student loan counseling for students and their families during the college search process deserve to be encouraged.[20]

Taken Together

Our point is that the larger student loan problem has many aspects. Addressing it requires confronting all aspects rather than concentrating on one aspect—one mess—at a time. Claims that *the* cause of the student loan crisis is X (X being reduced state support for public education, or rising college costs, or high default rates, or high interest rates, or whatever) are partly right (undoubtedly whatever the claim names is part of the problem) but largely false (dealing with that particular aspect of the problem, while ignoring everything else, is not going to make the student loan problem go away and will probably make it worse).

We have listed fifteen recommendations to suggest the complexity of the problem. Adopting our proposals will not be painless—for anyone. As financiers might say, what we propose will force everyone to take a haircut. But there isn't a good alternative. We continue to experience the aftermath of the global Great Recession, which was caused, in large part, by easy-credit policies that produced a housing bubble. We can't afford to repeat those mistakes by ignoring the consequences of our easy-credit student loan policy. It is time to stop getting distracted by messes and instead confront the larger problem. After all, doing nothing and just sticking with the status quo will also produce some really bad haircuts: college costs spiraling out of reach, colleges failing and taxpayers picking up the tab, ever-higher default rates, and eventually—inevitably—a collapse that will add massive sums to the national debt. It is time for Americans to have a grown-up conversation about paying for college. If we want to promote higher education, we need to find a better way to pay for it.

TREATING PROBLEMS AS MESSES

At least in the case of student loans, concentrating on particular messes allowed the overall problem to grow and grow. We would argue that this tendency to treat a bigger problem as a smaller mess is in fact fairly common, that policymaking about all sorts of problems tends to get narrowly focused on specific messes, and this is one reason social policies can wind up being viewed as failures.

We don't mean to suggest that everyone who thought about student loans was oblivious to all aspects of the problem beyond the confines of the current mess. In fact, we have noted that throughout the history of student loan policy, there have always been voices raising inconvenient issues, often worries about the long-term costs of whatever program was being proposed. However, just as in the run-up to the Great Recession, these prophets in the wilderness were unable to get people to attend to the larger problem.[21]

Still, it is easy to understand why all sorts of people—advocates and the press, but also legislators and other officials—prefer to focus on messes. Messes are relatively easy to understand; they can be presented in melodramatic terms, with central figures who are either vulnerable victims who deserve protection from some proposed social policy or menacing villains who can be brought under control. Thus the first and third student loan messes emphasized sympathetic figures—bright kids who couldn't afford to pursue an education or hardworking former students who now found themselves crushed by the debts they'd acquired while going to school. Similarly, the central figures in the second and fourth student loan messes were villains—deadbeat students and disreputable for-profit colleges, respectively. These are stories that invite consensus; lots of people want to help promising students and crack down on deadbeats. It is relatively easy to promote social policies to address such narrowly defined messes.

But what concerns about the various messes missed were the unanticipated consequences, the ways student loan policies were making things worse. Many commentators noted that higher education was becoming more expensive; in fact, the rising cost of college justified calls for expanded student loan programs. But most of these commentators ignored the extent to which student loans fostered rising costs by encouraging students to be less price sensitive, legislators to reduce the share of public education costs assumed by the states, and colleges to increase their budgets to make their campuses more competitive.

We are by no means the first observers to note that social problems tend to evolve rather than simply be solved.[22] Troubling social conditions—poverty, say, or race relations—tend to have long, complicated histories, in which a series of particular aspects of the larger problem become messes—the focus of intense concern. Often, as in the case of student loans, these campaigns lead to new, narrowly focused policies that may address the concerns regarding a particular mess, even as the larger problem remains. Perhaps ignoring the larger problem may make things better via what was once called benign neglect, but sometimes, as the case of student loans demonstrates, those good intentions allow things to grow much worse.

There is an almost constant flow of new information about student loans. We have established a website—studentloanmess.com—as a place where we can provide links to key materials, as well as occasional commentary on the issues. Please visit us.

NOTES

A NOTE ON OUR SOURCES

There is no shortage of material on student loans. Our challenge was to write something that was reasonably short, reasonably readable, and accurate. We wound up relying on several different sorts of material.

Government Documents

When we began this project, we rather imagined that there would be a table somewhere, perhaps published in the *Statistical Abstract of the United States,* that would offer annual statistics—spanning many years—on the size of the federal student loan program—maybe the amount borrowed each year, or the total amount at risk, or even the number of borrowers. You know—a table that would give us the basics. We figured that those data would allow us to present a dramatic graph showing the program's growth. We never found that table.

Federal student loans is a broad category, one that encompasses several different programs, most of which have evolved and morphed over time, changing their names, their terms, even their purposes. There are lots of ways one might measure the growth of these programs: the total federal outlays in a given year, the total amount being borrowed, the number of borrowers, and so on. But government officials tend to be more worried about the current program—its recent past and immediate future—than about tracing long-term trends. We trace the history of federal student loan programs back to 1958—over fifty-five years. But we could not find data that presented comparable, apples-to-apples figures covering that entire period. As a result, we have had to present piecemeal statistics that depict portions of the federal student loan landscape in particular periods.

In contrast, it is much easier to trace officials' public statements about student loans over the years. Transcripts of congressional hearings are valuable because these hearings often give the participants a forum where they can explain their thinking, while the online files of the American Presidency Project allowed us to search for public statements the various presidents made about student loan policies. In addition, reports from the Congressional Research Service give a sense of the information available to officials at different times.

Popular Media

We also searched for popular discussions of student loans. For the pre-Internet period, we drew on articles from a range of magazines, including news magazines, business magazines, and other more specialized periodicals. Most of our early newspaper articles come from the *New York Times,* which offers a searchable database for the entire period covered by this book. We also examined a variety of trade and self-help books about student loans. Of course, the Internet era offers a wider range of material.

Scholarly Literature

Student loans have attracted surprisingly little attention from social scientists. Sociologists and even economists haven't written much on the topic. The literature that does exist comes mostly from these who study higher education or public policy, and their works tend to be narrowly focused, often on what might be done to address the current mess. Our goal is different. We wanted to understand student loans in their broader context. In our view, it is important to understand that people have tended to focus narrowly on particular aspects of the problem, on specific student loan messes, so that their solutions to each mess often served to make the broader problem worse. Stepping back—thinking about the entire student loan problem over its entire history—offers a better way to approach the issue.

INTRODUCTION

1. E. Best (2012a, 2012b).
2. S. Best (1962).
3. Altschuler and Blumin (2009); M. Bennett (1996).
4. Gillon (2004); Steinhorn (2006).
5. Mills (1959).
6. This approach is summarized in J. Best (2013).
7. Organisation for Economic Co-operation and Development (2012: tables A3.1, B1.2).

1. GOOD INTENTIONS AND WASTED BRAINPOWER

1. Geske and Cohn (1998).
2. For instance, in 1900, the number of high school graduates was equivalent to 6.4 percent of seventeen-year-olds; that is, roughly 6.4 percent of young Americans were earning high school diplomas. That same year, the number of bachelor's degrees awarded was equivalent to 36 percent of the number of high school graduates four years earlier; so roughly 36 percent of those who completed high school also received college degrees. Multiplying the two percentages (6.4 percent completing high school × 36 percent of high school grads completing college) gives us 2.3 percent—a rough estimate for the proportion of turn-of-the-century Americans completing college (U.S. Census Bureau 2003: table HS-21).

Measuring educational attainment within a population is tricky, especially when people's schooling is increasing over time. If we ask what percentage of all adults have completed college, we will get a relatively low number because the category *all adults* includes a large proportion of older people (who were of college age in an era when fewer people attended college). But if we ask what percentage of twenty-two-year-olds have completed college, we will get a higher number because their cohort is more likely to have gone to college than any preceding cohort. Yet the percentage of college graduates in that cohort is not as high as it will be in the future, because for one reason or another, some people do not earn their degrees until they're older than twenty-two. The typical educational path—high school graduation at seventeen, followed by a college degree awarded four years later—is not all that typical. A few people zip through high school and college in less time, and many wind up taking longer. Any year's college graduates will include some people who are under twenty-two and quite a few people who are older than that. So, even if we know both the number of twenty-two-year-olds in the population in a given year and the number of bachelor's degrees awarded during that same year, we cannot simply divide the number of degrees by the number of twenty-two-year-olds to calculate the precise percentage of young adults with a college degree. Still, if we divide the number of degrees granted each year by the number of people in some segment of the population (such as twenty-two-year-olds), and we find that the resulting figures rise over time, that is clear evidence that the population is becoming more educated, even though we may not know the exact ages at which people received their degrees.

3. National Center for Education Statistics (2012: table 283).

4. Office for Civil Rights (1991). As late as 1910, less than 10 percent of the students at what were then called Negro colleges were enrolled in college courses (Du Bois and Dill 1910: 14–15). Early sociologists made two efforts to tally graduates from all-black colleges: Du Bois and Dill (1910: 45) counted 92 graduates in 1900; C. S. Johnson (1938: 8) later calculated that a total of 770 blacks received bachelor's degrees during the five years 1896–1900. Thus the number of blacks graduating from college in 1900 was undoubtedly under 200, or well under 1 percent of the 27,410 bachelor's degrees awarded nationwide (National Center for Education Statistics 2012: table 283).

5. On expectations that older children would contribute to the family income, see Zelizer (1985).

6. The data in figures 2 and 3 come from the annual Current Population Survey: U.S. Census Bureau (2012a).

7. Cost figures from *Newsweek* (1958). A 1947 survey of nearly 9,500 college graduates found that most had worked to help pay for their college expenses: "Nearly half our women graduates got their degrees as a gift from mother and dad, and only about one in six earned half her own expenses or better. But the boys, in remarkable numbers, send themselves, in whole or in part. Only a sixth were completely supported by their parents during their college days, and better than one in three earned at least half his own way" (Havemann and West 1952: 18). Although most students worked to help pay for college, many educators worried that students' jobs interfered with their learning (Axt 1952: 216–17).

8. "Widespread belief" and "middle-income Americans": *Newsweek* (1958: 87); "a college education": *Saturday Review* (1957: 24–25); "college is a far better investment": *Changing Times* (1958: 30); "if you are headed": *Changing Times* (1956: 40); "a debt would serve": Harris (1960: 9); "they figure": *Changing Times* (1954: 33).

9. On states' guaranteed loan programs, see *Changing Times* (1958); *U.S. News & World Report* (1957). On midcentury debates over federal policies, see Axt (1952); Perkins and Wood (1960); Urban (2010). The survey is reported in Thomas (1950).

10. Altschuler and Blumin (2009); M. Bennett (1996).

11. For results from the 1946 survey, see Frederiksen and Schrader (1951: 310); for the 1998 survey, see Mettler (2005:45). The sociologist Charles Nam concluded: "The GI programs were not so much prime movers in the continued educational progress of the country as they were responses to the growing demand for formal education in a society where social organization and value complexes were undergoing change" (1964: 32). Two economists, Bound and Turner (2002), calculated that the GI Bill increased the number of college graduates in the years following World War II between 4 and 10 percent. However, Olson (1974) argued that the GI Bill failed to produce as many college graduates as had been lost when the war effort forced many students to halt their educations.

12. On scandals, see Frydl (2009: 186). For an argument that the GI Bill demonstrated that federal support for higher education could improve the nation's human capital, see Yoder (1963).

13. Clowse (1981: 49); see also Urban (2010). On post-Sputnik anxiety about American education, see Bracey (2007).

14. Perkins and Wood (1960: 149–50).

15. Urban (2010: 64); Pope (1958a: 74).

16. National Defense Education Act of 1958.

17. National Defense Education Act of 1958. There had been earlier, smaller federal student loan programs. For instance, in 1942–44, the Student War Loan program aided more than 11,000 students receiving scientific and medical training (Axt 1952: 217).

18. Clowse (1981: 155); see also Loss (2012: 159); Wilson (1983: 46–47).

19. Pope (1958b: 64).

20. Harris (1962: 260).

21. Tolchin (1958: 39). See also Clowse (1981: 90–95); Flemming (1960). Directing money to students who could choose where they wanted to study, rather than to particular colleges, also allowed the government to circumvent the various debates about which sorts of institutions should or should not benefit from the policy (Wilson 1983: 45–46).

22. Loss (2012: 159). There were 4,145,00 students enrolled in institutions of higher education in 1961, so less than 3 percent received NDEA loans (Snyder 1993:76).

23. Flattau et al. (2006: II-7–10).

24. L. Johnson (1965b).

25. U.S. House of Representatives (1965). Congress envisioned the loans as a "modest benefit to middle-class college students and their families" and assumed that most federal aid would take the form of grants to poorer students (Fossey 1998: 8). It further expected that the guaranteed student loan program would be a short-lived, stopgap measure, which would be replaced once all fifty states established their own student loan insurance programs. However, once the federal government established its program, the states saw little need to assume responsibility for student loans (Stedman 1975: 63).

26. *Time* (1966: 112).

27. Hartman (1971: 30). This was no secret: Francis Keppel, the commissioner of education, presented data to the House Special Subcommittee on Education projecting that the annual costs of insured, reduced-interest student loans would rise from $15 million in 1966 to $80 million in 1970 (U.S. House of Representatives 1965: 446). On expectations that guaranteeing loans would prove cheaper than lending federal dollars, see St. John (2003).

28. *Business Week* (1969).

29. Loss (2012: 175).

30. *Time* (1966: 112).

31. Brenton (1968: quotes from 86, 32, 82–83, 85). On loans' ability to aid both the disadvantaged and the middle class, see Hearn and Holdsworth (2004).

32. U.S. House of Representatives (1965: 48).

33. Quotes from Phillips (1966: 21); and *Business Week* (1965: 47).

34. Nixon (1969, 1972). See also *Business Week* (1969). In 1971, about one in eight college students had a guaranteed student loan (Stedman 1975: 66).

35. For an example of Democrats advocating scholarships, see U.S. Senate (1965: 116); for Brewster's quote, see *School and Society* (1967: 373); PAYE quotations from *Newsweek* (1971: 69); *New Republic* (1971: 13); *National Review* (1971: 356); see also *Time* (1971). Proposals similar to PAYE would resurface periodically: Carlsson (1970); S. Dynarski and Kreisman (2013); Gladieux (1989); Kiley (2013c).

36. *Business Week* (1972: 26, 28). See also *Business Week* (1969); Simmons (1973).

37. On the rise of credit, see Hyman (2012). Evans and Schmalensee (1999) offer a history of credit cards, while Ritzer (1995) presents a sociological critique.

2. DISILLUSIONMENT AND DEADBEATS

1. *Newsweek* (1964: 67).

2. *Newsweek* (1977: 95); *U.S. News & World Report* (1977: 21); Witkin (1987: 32).

3. Jimmy Carter (1978); Reagan (1988).

4. Short (2013); Callan (2011).

5. Stedman (1975: 66).

6. National Center for Education Statistics (2012: table 358).

7. Studies routinely found that higher-risk students (such as those with weaker academic records or from lower-income families) were more likely to default on student loans (M. Dynarski 1994; Knapp and Seaks 1992; Wilms, Moore, and Bolus 1987).

8. Reagan (1985). On the Reagan administration's efforts to curtail the program's growth while insisting that loans would remain available to those who needed them, see also Fiske (1982); *National Review* (1982); Stockman (1986).

9. Gladieux and Wolanin (1976: 198).

10. One advantage of lending to middle-class students was their reduced rate of default: "As loans have been extended to more students who are likely to repay, the default rates have dropped.... Upper- and middle-income students have a high probability of paying back their loans" (St. John and Wooden 2006: 49).

11. Reagan (1984); G. H. W. Bush (1992b); Clinton (1996).

12. U.S. Senate (1965: 116).

13. U.S. Senate (1974: 1–2).

14. U.S. Senate (1974: 8).

15. U.S. Senate (1975b: 6).

16. U.S. Senate (1975a, 1975b). For an early critique of government fiscal record keeping regarding student loans, see Controller General of the United States (1976).

17. L. Johnson (1965a).

18. Kronstadt (1973: 5–6).

19. Kronstadt (1973: 10). See also Carper (1975).

20. Kronstadt (1973: 9).

21. Carper (1975: 41).

22. Quotations from U.S. Senate (1975a: 2–4).

23. U.S. Senate (1975a: 197).

24. U.S. Senate (1974: 5–6).

25. U.S. Senate (1975b: 2).

26. *Consumer Reports* (1992).

27. U.S. Senate (1990: 7).

28. Skinner (2007).

29. Schenet (1990, 1999).

30. In his account of his service as President Reagan's first budget director, David Stockman (1986: 407) notes that even congressional Republicans resisted the administration's efforts to cut student loan programs: "The Republicans insist on shoveling out big middle-class college student subsidies, and they get Democratic help."

31. Jimmy Carter (1978); Lubasch (1985); Rinzler (1985). For a list of congressional efforts to bring defaults under control in the 1980s, see Fraas (1991a).

32. Quint (1979: 224); see also Rinzler (1985).

33. Bozzo (1981: 65); see also *People Weekly* (1985).

34. For example, see U.S. House of Representatives (1973; 1988; 1995); U.S. Senate (1974; 1987; 1990).

35. Hannon (1992).

36. Jacobs and Hess (1981: 82); *Time* (1981: 89).

37. *Business Week* (1974). See also *Newsweek* (1974).

38. Chen (2007). In 1972, the year Sallie Mae was established, there were about 165,000 consumer bankruptcies in the United States. In 1998, the year the law finally forbade discharging student loans through bankruptcy, there were 1.4 million (Ellmann 2009).

39. *U.S. News & World Report* (1987); see also Fraas (1989).

40. *Jet* (1988: 22).

41. On the lukewarm response to these proposals, see Novack (1988). For examples of the business press touting Sallie Mae's success as a low-risk investment, see *Fortune* (1984); Egan (1987).

42. For a summary of the pros and cons of deferring loan repayment, see Fraas (1987).

43. Leonard and Loonin (2001: 2/6).

44. We ignore, for instance, various federal loan programs for students training to enter healthcare professions.

45. Burks (1979). On the risks parents incur by taking out PLUS loans, see Carey (2013).

46. *Changing Times* (1991).

47. Fraas (1991b); Clinton (1993); Doyle and Hartle (1986); Eglin (1993).

48. Foust (1993: 74); see also Becker (1993); Foust (1998).

49. Clinton (1995). For the case for direct loans, see Cohn (1995); Konigsberg (1993).

50. For instance, Republican president George H. W. Bush (1992a) called for making student loan interest tax deductible.

51. Heller (2011: 22, figure 1.4). McPherson and Schapiro (1991b) found that, despite student aid programs, rising college costs discouraged lower-income students from attending college but actually boosted enrollment among upper-income students.

52. Warren and Tyagi (2003: 45); Fossey (1998: 9).

53. McPherson and Schapiro (1991b: 174–75).

54. Main (1979: 83). The Middle Income Student Assistance Act made guaranteed loans available to all students: "Inflation went through the roof, and because Guaranteed Student Loans were fixed at a super-low interest rate, they were suddenly the sexiest deal around. Naturally, there was a run on GSLs" (Stockwell, 1997: 55).

55. Quinn (1979: 76).

56. Quinn (1982: 68).

57. Mumper and Freeman (2011); Zumeta (2004).

58. Heller presents data for state funding per full-time-equivalent student, in constant dollars (2006: 17, table 1.4).

59. Mumper and Freeman (2011); Heller (2006). On privatization, see Priest and St. John (2006).

60. Tierney (1980); St. John (2003).

61. Hearn and Holdsworth (2004).

62. Warren and Tyagi (2003: 46).

63. Mumper and Freeman (2011: 48). See also Taylor (2012). In turn, private off-campus apartment complexes offered increasingly elaborate amenities to encourage students to stop living in dorms (Eligon 2013).

64. Fossey (1998).

65. Many conservative analysts argue that the availability of federal student loans frees colleges to hike their prices—a natural extension of economic theory about scarcity. One sophisticated economic model—as yet unpublished at the time we were completing this book—suggests that "private colleges game the federal financial aid system, strategically increasing tuition to increase federal aid, and using the proceeds to spend more on educational resources and to compete for high-ability students" (Epple et al. 2013: abstract).

66. Dresch (1980: 81).

3. OUTRAGE AND CRUSHING DEBT

1. Clinton (1994). For an earlier expression of concern about rising debt burdens for student borrowers, see Fraas (1988). Institute for Higher Education Policy (1995) presents the results of an early survey focused on student loan debt.

2. Stockwell (1997); Leonard and Loonin (2001). For more recent examples of such guidebooks, see Gobel (2010) and Maeda (2009).

3. Draut (2005); Kamenetz (2007); Collinge (2009).

4. Mihalic (2012); Bissonnette (2010); Russell (2010).

5. Here and below, these totals take inflation during the loan period into account by totaling the 2013 equivalents of borrowing $1,000 in 1958, 1959, etc.

6. Berkner and Bobbitt (2005: 74).

7. New York State Higher Education Services Corporation (2013).

8. Obviously, students in different circumstances are affected differently. Student loan limits have always covered a larger share of costs at public institutions (which charge lower tuition and fees than private colleges), while independent students are able to borrow more than those deemed dependents, and so on.

9. Economists and sociologists have produced a large literature on postwar economic trends. Very simply, economic growth for the three decades after World War II benefited all income groups relatively equally. However, the benefits of economic growth after about 1979 were concentrated among those with higher incomes, and those with the very highest incomes benefited the most (Frank 2007; Leicht and Fitzgerald 2007). This meant that middle-income borrowers would have experienced more income growth and therefore less difficulty repaying student loans during the 1960s and 1970s compared to their counterparts in later decades.

10. Leonard and Loonin (2001: 6/8–9). On the obstacles to discharging student loans through bankruptcy, see Lieber (2012).

11. Dēmos/Young Invincibles (2011: 24).

12. Dēmos/Young Invincibles (2011: 27). Although Pell grants covered a diminishing share of college costs, the program's costs rose dramatically during the Great Recession—a reflection of people choosing to delay entering the workforce during a weak economy and the growth in for-profit colleges (where a majority of students received the grants) (Congressional Budget Office 2013). For concerns that policymakers were losing sight of the original purpose of federal student aid—increasing educational opportunities of minorities and low-income youth—see Mumper (2003).

13. Orozco (2010). For an early analysis noting that student loans had become the principal form of federal student aid, see Stoll (2001).

14. Quinterno (2012: 16). These inflation-adjusted calculations track funding per FTE (higher-educationspeak for full-time-equivalent student); thus, two part-time students each taking half a normal course load equal one FTE.

15. Martin and Lehren (2012: 20, 21).

16. Project on Student Debt (2010).

17. Titus (2005: 134).

18. Berkner and Bobbitt (2005: 83). In 1995–96, students could borrow both subsidized and unsubsidized loans, and the totals count both.

19. For an overview of trends in the various ways students pay for higher education, see the annual reports from the College Board (e.g., 2012b).

20. American Council of Education (2004: 1). For a thorough discussion of student loan debt burden, see Baum and Schwartz (2006).

21. As the amounts owed rose, more elaborate formulas for calculating manageable debt emerged. For instance, beginning in 2007, the federal government offered Income-Based Repayment options. IBR allows borrowers to exclude a cost-of-living exemption (150 percent of the poverty threshold), then limits student loan repayment to 10 percent of the remainder. Thus, in 2012, an unmarried person with no children and a salary of $30,000 might exclude $16,755 (150 percent of that year's $11,170 poverty threshold for a single-person family) and limit loan repayment to $1,325 (10 percent of the remainder), no matter how much the individual might owe in student loans (Delisle and Holt 2012). At least initially, relatively few students took advantage of IBR (Nelson 2012c).

22. Price (2004).

23. Price (2004: 86n4, 96).

24. Gertner (2006: 64).

25. Boushey (2005: 8) found that in 2003–4, 84 percent of undergraduates at four-year colleges who had student loans held jobs, compared to 68 percent of those without loans at not-for-profit colleges and 78 percent of those without loans at public colleges.

26. Gertner (2006: 64). There is some evidence to support these claims: a study of students at a highly selective university that adopted a no-loans policy of providing grants found that "debt causes graduates to choose substantially higher-salary jobs and reduces the probability that students choose low-paid 'public interest' jobs" (Rothstein and Rouse 2011: 149).

27. Martin and Lehren (2012).

28. M. Wang, Supiano, and Fuller (2012).

29. Zaitchik (2012).

30. Draut (2005: 1).

31. Collinge (2009: ix–xii).

32. Draut (2005: 34).

33. Williams (2012: 15). For an analysis drawing an analogy between student loans and serfdom, see Blacker (2012).

34. Ross (2012). He was careful to insist that "faculty salaries have been stagnant as a whole for some time now. [Professors] are hardly to blame for skyrocketing costs."

35. Occupy Student Debt Campaign (2012); see also Ross (2012).

36. *The Debt Resistor's Operations Manual* (2012: 2).

37. *The Debt Resistor's Operations Manual* (2012: 35).

38. G. W. Bush (2002).

39. Maeda (2009: 144).

40. Weisman and Murray (2005: A9).

41. Morris and McGann (2007: 251—emphasis in original).

42. Hassett and Shapiro (2004).

43. Delisle (2012: 3, 4).

44. On the 2012 debate, see Delisle (2012: 4); Baker (2012). On the 2013 replay, see A. Kelly (2013b); Nelson (2013a).

45. Alexander, Coburn, and Burr (2013); Nelson (2013a).

46. Peters and Parker (2013).

47. Dickinson (2009: 42); see also Beaver (2008); Rawe (2007); Wingert (2007).

48. Dickinson (2009: 41); Surowiecki (2007: 28).

49. Silver-Greenberg (2009: 21); Ferguson (2009: 8). Some conservatives continued to view direct loans as a boondoggle: Hannaford (2010).

50. Obama (2009).

51. Cruz (2010); Dickinson (2009). On the accounting practices that generated profits from student loan programs, see chapter 4.

52. Obama (2012).

53. Ferguson (2009: 9).

54. A. Kelly (2012b). Critics noted that these Income-Based Repayment policies could have unintended consequences. In particular, the 2011 version of IBR "significantly reduces or eliminates the financial consequences a borrower would bear in incurring additional federal student loan debt once he reaches a debt level around $30,000—even if he expects to eventually earn a

middle income or even a high income. Moreover, institutions of higher education have a disincentive to keep tuition, fees, and other costs low because ...
their students will not incur all of those costs if they finance their educations
with federal student loans" (Delisle and Holt 2012: 12). In particular, these policies favored graduate students (who can borrow more): "Once a borrower takes
on $65,000 in debt, he bears none of the incremental cost of borrowing an
additional dollar under the new IBR, even if he goes on to earn over $100,000
for most of his repayment term. The extra debt will be forgiven" (Delisle and
Holt 2013). We will have more to say about these issues in chapter 5.

55. Our assumptions for these calculations are as follows: the 2012 average
salary for a college graduate is $44,259, and we expect annual raises of 3 per-
cent each year. This would result in a first monthly repayment of $229.20 on a
loan balance of $26,600 (or higher), calculated as the monthly prorate of 10 per-
cent of the disposable income of $27,504 ($44,259 less $16,755 [the 2012 repre-
sentation of 150 percent of the poverty line for a single person]). While this is
a perfectly reasonable expected repayment amount for our hypothetical student, things start to get out of hand with periods of unemployment, higher
loan balances, or even unsubsidized loans. While the government would be
made whole by the average student in this program, the reality is that most
borrowers who use this program would be in worse situations, with high balances and unsubsidized loans, so that this program could end up being a bad
deal for everyone—the student, but also the government and the taxpayers.

56. See, for example, FinAid (2013).

57. Martin and Lehren (2012).

58. Bass (2013).

59. Koerner (1970).

60. Sperling (2000).

61. Traub (1997: 114—emphasis in original).

62. Hodges (1999: 240).

63. Hodges (1999: 244, 240).

64. The 20 percent standard was in effect in 1990, at a time when an overview of proprietary schools equated them with trade schools, not colleges
(Schenet 1990).

65. U.S. Senate (2012: 32); Fain (2012); National Center for Education Statistics (2012: table 246).

66. U.S. Senate (2012: 15). In 2009, *Washington Monthly* ran another exposé of
for-profits—this time including colleges as well as vocational schools—which
paralleled its coverage from the 1970s (Burd 2009).

67. *Crain's New York Business* (2006).

68. Shaffer (2012).

69. There are numerous studies showing that college students often do not understand the ins and outs of credit cards, "that peer pressure may cause college students to engage in compulsive buying with credit cards," although "sufficient social support decreases the likelihood of indebtedness" (J. Wang and Xiao 2009: 8).

70. Shaffer (2012). An analysis of one survey of students at selective colleges found that students with loans tended to adopt one of two college lifestyles: most were "Serious Students," who concentrated on work and school, but another substantial share were "Disengaged," who devoted relatively large amounts of time to media consumption and sleep (Rudel and Yurk 2013).

4. DREAD AND THE FOR-PROFIT BUBBLE

1. Galbraith (1990) offers a readable introduction to bubbles.

2. For example, see Gillen and Vedder (2008); Barone (2010); and Wood (2011). On parallels between policy debates about home loans and student loans, see E. Best (2012a).

3. Democratic Party (2000, 2004).

4. Republican Party (2000, 2012).

5. Mitchell and Jackson-Randall (2012).

6. Aud et al. (2012: table 46-1).

7. See, for example A. Kelly (2011); and Wildavsky (2012).

8. Gilpin (2002: B7).

9. Aud et al. (2011: 14, figure CL-7). These data come from the U.S. Department of Education's annual report, *The Condition of Education.* It is worth noting that in 2008 the University of Phoenix—the largest for-profit college—had a six-year graduation rate of 9 percent; at its largest branch, the "online campus," the figure was only 5 percent (Lynch, Engle, and Cruz 2010: 4–5). The statistics for graduation and retention at two-year for-profit institutions (most offering traditional for-profit vocational training) are considerably better: for-profits actually outperform public and private not-for-profit two-year institutions.

10. Gillen (2013). To be fair, 314 public two-year colleges—which also enroll many high-risk students—had default rates greater than graduation rates.

11. Association of Private Sector Colleges and Universities (2010). A position paper from the University of Phoenix defending for-profits argues:

"These institutions provide access to students who previously have been left behind by or excluded from the traditional higher education system" (Apollo Group, 2010: 1).

12. Lynch, Engle, and Cruz (2010: 3, table 1).

13. Congressional Budget Office (2013: 67). See also Lynch, Engle, and Cruz (2010: 2, figure 2). However, for-profit students receive less in state grants and institutional grants than students at traditional colleges (Baum and Payea 2011: 3, table 3).

14. Aud et al. (2011: 295, table A-46-1); Lynch, Engle, and Cruz (2010: 6, table 5). On the nature of private loans, see Schemo (2007).

15. Carnevale, Rose, and Cheah (2011); Department of the Treasury (2012).

16. On the largest colleges, see National Center for Education Statistics (2012: table 249). On default rates, see Aud et al. (2011: 305, table A-49-2). This figure is for fiscal 2008; in comparison, the default rate after two years at both public and private four-year colleges was about 4 percent. The default rates for two-year schools were even higher.

17. Department of Education (2012a). The following year's report showed three-year default rates increasing (Department of Education 2013).

18. Blumenstyk and Richards (2011).

19. A professional who works in an agency that provides social services for people with disabilities describes having seen dozens of clients with cognitive disabilities (IQs of eighty or less) who have been aggressively recruited to enroll in for-profit colleges and were helped to apply for student loans. These students quickly drop out when they discover they can't do the work, but of course their student loan debt remains.

20. Federal Student Aid (2012a).

21. In 2007–8, more than half of the for-profit students classified as dependents for student loan purposes came from families with incomes below $40,000—a much higher proportion than at traditional not-for-profit institutions (Baum and Payea 2011: 2, figure 2).

22. Chung (2012).

23. Lynch, Engle, and Cruz (2010: 6).

24. U.S. Senate (2012: 56). This document, which will be cited a good deal in this chapter, is a staff report for the Senate's Health, Education, Labor and Pensions (HELP) Committee, sometimes referred to as the Harkin Report. This report attracted a good deal of public attention, and it is possible to download a variety of resources, including PowerPoint slides summarizing some of the committee's findings and video clips from the hearings.

25. U.S. Senate (2012: 110–11).

26. U.S. Senate (2012: 98).

27. Deming, Goldin, and Katz (2012: 157); see also U.S. Senate (2012: 120–21). Stainburn (2009) criticizes for-profits' advertising for exaggerating their students' employment prospects.

28. U.S. Senate (2012: 77).

29. For a detailed critique of for-profit sales practices, see U.S. Senate (2012: 46–68, 81–82).

30. This critique need not be limited to for-profits. For an argument that higher education generally has grown by maximizing enrollment of large numbers of ill-prepared and poorly motivated students, see Toby (2012).

31. For example, the website Instantdegrees.com offers a "legally registered" bachelor's degree, including a stamped diploma, verification service, a cover letter from the "university you graduated from," a copy of the college or university's accreditation certificate, and a current copy of the institution's postal prospectus. This service costs $130 for a bachelor's degree. Other degrees cost from $120 for an associate's degree to $180 for a PhD. Documentation of professorships, fellowships, postdocs, and research positions are $210 each, all with the same reference guarantee. To prevent these degrees from being easily identified as bogus, you can pick your institution (or institutions) from an increasingly lengthy list, and many of these universities have websites. Instant Degrees is one of many websites offering this service. The instructions for purchasing your degree at college-degree-fast.com advise users to make sure they were of an appropriate age at their (chosen) graduation date and not to "underestimate themselves" when choosing a GPA. These admittedly more expensive services (in the $400–$500 range) offer sealed and unsealed transcripts, letters of recommendation from your dean, and school IDs.

32. U.S. Senate (2012: 27–31, 68–71). According to the U.S. Government Accountability Office (2013: 11, figure 4), VA payments per veteran are more than twice as high at for-profits as at public institutions.

33. U.S. Senate (2012: 24).

34. To be sure, the government does insist that institutions receive some sort of accreditation, but it allows proprietary schools to establish their own accrediting agencies.

35. Project on Student Debt (2012).

36. Department of Education (2012a).

37. Department of Education (2012b); Nelson (2012b). Recall from chapter 3 that many advisors recommend borrowing no more than one's expected starting salary.

38. Nelson (2012a, 2013b).

39. Burd (2004); Halperin (2012); Lichtblau (2012). A. Kelly (2012a) notes that not-for-profit colleges and universities actually spend more on lobbying than for-profits, although they are usually trying to land research funding rather than maintain generous loan policies.

40. Fain (2013). The Association of Private Colleges and Universities, which sued the Department of Education over the gainful employment rules, does not have a website but is listed on one "Diploma Mill Police" website as a fake accreditation agency. There are over forty fake accreditors listed for online schools, and the same service lists more than eight hundred fake schools in the United States (Get Educated.com 2013). In the fall of 2013, a federally appointed panel began struggling to reach agreement on a new gainful employment policy (Stratford and Fain 2013).

41. Blumenstyk (2011); Blumenstyk and Richards (2011).

42. Mogilyanskaya (2012); Nelson (2012b).

43. A study from the Federal Reserve Bank of Kansas City notes that, although the government projects getting back more than the amounts loaned, there are costs associated with collecting on defaulted loans. Still, after all the collection costs are taken into account, the government gets back about 82 cents on the dollar, so that the costs of the student loan program account for less than half of 1 percent of the federal budget. The study notes, however: "A large number of borrowers current [i.e., considered current on their loans—not in default] are still in school, in forbearance, or have deferred making payments" and warns that "continued increases in default rates could pose a more substantial burden" (Edmiston, Brooks, and Shelpelwich 2013: 26).

44. Nasiripour (2013).

45. For rival estimates, see Edmiston, Brooks, and Shelpelwich (2013); A. Kelly (2013a).

46. Federal Student Aid (2013b).

47. Federal Student Aid (2012b).

48. Assume dropout rates of 50 percent within the first year, 40 percent during the second year, and 33 percent during the third year. Say that each year, fifty students begin the first-year program. So in any given year, the student body consists of one hundred students—fifty in their first year, twenty-five in their second, fifteen in their third, and ten in their fourth year. Now

imagine a set of schools that receive $10 billion in loans (not grants) per year. We get:

first-year students have $5 billion in loans;
second-year students have accumulated $5 billion;
third-year students have accumulated $4.5 billion; and
fourth-year students have accumulated $4 billion.

That totals $18.5 billion—the amount that would have to be forgiven if the schools closed.

49. Fain (2012).

50. Examples of five-year stock price declines from July 2008 to July 2013 (covering the Great Recession and the recovery, during which the Dow Jones Industrial Average rose 33.01 percent and the NASDAQ rose 54.23 percent): APOL: Apollo Group (University of Phoenix) −69.69%; BPI: Bridgeport Education (Ashford University) +5%; DV: DeVry −38.22%; STRA: Strayer Education −75.86%. Kaplan University, in the top five, is part of Kaplan, Inc., which is a subsidiary of the Washington Post (WPO); its stock declined 16.18%, although the other business elements make this a less direct comparison.

51. Sampson (2012); Tuchman (2011).

52. Schneider (2008).

53. For a graphic representation, see *Chronicle of Higher Education* (2013).

54. Toby (2012).

5. WHAT'S NEXT?

1. For instance, see Roche (2010). This is, of course, an idealized vision. There is also a vast nostalgic literature filled with complaints that universities have lost their way and that undergraduates engage in a good deal of knuckleheaded behavior.

2. For recent overviews on the value of higher education, see Department of the Treasury (2012); James (2012); Zaback, Carlson, and Crellin (2012). For an attempt to compare the prospective value of different students' borrowing, see Avery and Turner (2012).

3. Zaback, Carlson, and Crellin (2012).

4. W. Bennett and Wilezol (2013). See also B. Kelly (2010); Melville (2012); *Time* (2011); P. Wang (2008).

5. Payscale.com (2013a). It is important to consult the methods section for this list. While there are some significant problems with the way return on

investment is calculated, the errors are not nearly large enough to make highly positive amounts or percentages negative. It may be more informative for readers to sort this list by ROI percentage instead of absolute returns.

6. Bureau of Labor Statistics (2010, 2013).

7. For example, Bernard (2009); Gerdes (2009); Greenhouse (2012).

8. An online survey of respondents with substantial student loan debt found that about two-thirds reported not understanding how much they would owe (Whitsett 2012).

9. Greenstone and Looney (2011). Among people in their early twenties, recent college graduates did better on several measures of economic well-being than their less-educated counterparts (Economic Mobility Project 2013).

10. Stone, Van Horn, and Zukin (2012); Payscale.com (2013b).

11. Oreopoulos, von Wachter, and Heisz (2006) examined the effects of graduating from college during a recession on long-term earning prospects and found that, while people entering the labor market during a recession initially earned less, they caught up later in their careers.

12. Stone, Van Horn, and Zukin (2012: 14, 20).

13. See, for example, Elliott (2013).

14. A. Kelly and Lautzenheiser (2013).

15. Again, there is a large literature. In one recent study that received considerable attention, Arum and Roska studied more than two thousand undergraduates and found that "three semesters of college education ... have a barely noticeable impact on students' skills in critical thinking, complex reasoning, and writing" (2011: 35). Following passage of the No Child Left Behind legislation, Republicans promoted reforms that would have allowed the federal government to monitor learning outcomes in higher education. Lowry (2009) explains that the complex organization of higher education led this campaign to fail.

16. Reynolds (2013).

17. FTI Consulting (2013); Sternberg (2013).

18. Lee (2013).

19. On mortgage default rates, see McBride (2013).

20. Federal Student Aid (2013c). See the bottom of this webpage, complete with sample calculations. While there is a case to be made that there are administrative costs of consolidation, an 18.5 percent servicing rate for what is essentially an unsecured loan (no calculation of backing asset value or repossession costs) seems almost predatory.

21. Federal Student Aid (2013d).

22. See, for example, "Independent Auditor's Report" in Federal Student Aid (2012a: 127–49).

23. *Dealbook* (2007).

24. Many people with student loan debt report they did not understand their loans (Whitsett 2012).

25. Eligon (2013: A11).

26. Taibbi (2013). This reporter goes on to criticize the government for making "enormous" profits from student loans.

27. As might be expected, the situations of former students vary in ways we might expect. Delinquency and default are far more common among those who failed to graduate or attended for-profit colleges (Cunningham and Kienz 2011).

28. For rates former students are paying on different sorts of federal loans, see Federal Student Aid (2013a).

29. College Board (2012a: 14).

30. Eric graduated in 2005. His alma mater is hardly recognizable less than a decade later. Many of the featureless (and non-air-conditioned) dormitories are gone, replaced with palatial new buildings complete with AC, gym facilities, private bathrooms, and extensive kitchens. The main campus gymnasium and athletic facilities have been significantly renovated. Top brands have largely replaced the private-label dining facilities, and the classrooms continue to be modernized to incorporate new teaching technologies.

31. Kiley (2013a); Marklein (2012). For a critique of increasing foreign-student enrollment, see Federation for American Immigration Reform (2012).

32. Kiley (2012); Martin (2012).

33. *Economist* (2006).

34. Moody's Investors Service (2013).

35. Even elite private institutions have taken on considerable debt and have had their credit ratings downgraded (Rivard 2013a, 2013b).

36. Kiley (2013b)

37. Vedder (2013a). Recently, there are increasing reports of colleges exploiting the financial information of prospective students. This includes factoring financial information into admissions decisions, reshuffling the rankings of wait-listed students based on their ability to pay (or get loans), and modifying aid offers based on the likelihood of the student accepting admission (Rivard 2013d, 2013e).

38. Sallie Mae (2013: 39, table 15c).

39. Sallie Mae (2013: 7, figure 2). For a 2009 presentation for college enrollment planners on the degree to which students are price sensitive showing

that prospective students are relatively price insensitive until costs reach $25,000 per year, see Maguire Associates (2009).

40. Rivard (2013c).

41. Selingo (2013); Marcus (2013); Kiley (2013d).

42. Pérez-Peña (2013). In general, there are about 4 million Americans in each annual birth cohort, but this fluctuates a bit from year to year. Thus, in 2009 there were 4.3 million seventeen-year-olds; there were slightly fewer sixteen-year-olds, and so on for each younger year, until age eleven (there were 3.9 million eleven-year-olds), then the numbers started to climb again. Those eleven-year-olds will complete high school and start college in 2015, so the competition for students should be most intense that year (U.S. Census Bureau 2012b: 14, table 11).

43. Clayton Christensen quoted in Schubarth (2013). For examples of other forecasts, see Butler (2012); Sams (2012).

44. American Association of Community Colleges (2012).

45. Miles and Zimmerman (1997) warned that a direct loan program that ignored the relative risk of borrowers could not grow forever.

46. Office of Sallie Mae Oversight (2006).

47. Yoon (2013).

48. For evidence that default rates on private loans have been increasing, see Consumer Financial Protection Bureau (2012).

49. Silver-Greenberg and Rampell (2013).

50. Carney (2013). In a 2010 meeting with federal officials, Morgan Stanley presented data that showed very high default rates for securitized student loans.

51. Most analyses of student loans say little about private lending. For an exception, see A. Johnson, Van Ostern, and White (2012). In 2013, a government ombudsman issued a report critical of practices among private loan lenders (Consumer Financial Protection Bureau 2013).

52. For an argument that the ability of the wealthiest students (the "top 1 percent") to pay drives up tuition prices, see Hill (2013). For a rebuttal, see Eden (2013).

6. BEYOND MAKING MESSES?

1. On class differences in children's upbringing that shape their prospects for higher education, see Lareau (2011).

2. Smith (2013).

3. Quotes from Obama (2013a); see also Obama (2013b, 2013c).

4. *New York Times* (2013: 26).

5. Shear and Lewin (2013: 18).

6. Fain and Jaschik (2013).

7. Quote from Vedder (2013b); see also A. Kelly (2013c); A. Kelly and Hess (2013).

8. Dēmos (2013—emphasis in original).

9. Jarrett Carter (2013). Similarly, community colleges, which also have lots of high-risk students, worried about the effects of the proposed rankings (Stratford 2013).

10. Fichtenbaum and Reichman (2013); Flaherty (2013).

11. Kiley (2013c). For a similar proposal for a nationwide policy, see S. Dynarski and Kreisman (2013). Income-based repayment plans are used in other countries, including Australia, New Zealand, and the United Kingdom (Hillman 2013).

12. Some crude, back-of-the-envelope calculations: in 2010, there were about 18 million undergraduate students in the United States (about two-thirds were full-time, the other third part-time); the average public institution spent about $16,000 per student. Spending $16,000 on 18 million students would cost about $300 billion annually—about a third as much as the federal government spends annually on defense (National Center for Education Statistics 2012).

13. For an analysis showing that different universities report administrative costs accounting for between 3 and 17 percent of education-related spending, see Belkin and Thurm (2012).

14. Lautzenheiser (2013).

15. Obama (2013c).

16. For example, see Monks (2009).

17. Obama (2013a).

18. Obama (2013a). It is not clear that students would make use of college ratings. A survey of older students considering returning to college found that only a minority considered it important to know a school's graduation or student loan default rates (Public Agenda 2013).

19. Obama (2013a).

20. See, for example, Clarifi (2013).

21. Barnshaw (2013).

22. For one introduction to this literature, see Fine (2006).

REFERENCES

Alexander, Lamar, Tom Coburn, and Richard Burr. 2013. "Playing Politics with Student Debt." *New York Times,* June 5, 25.

Altschuler, Glenn C., and Stuart M. Blumin. 2009. *The GI Bill: A New Deal for Veterans.* New York: Oxford University Press.

American Association of Community Colleges. 2012. *Reclaiming the American Dream: A Report from the 21st-Century Commission on the Future of Community Colleges.* aacc.nche.edu/AboutCC/21stcenturyreport/21stCenturyReport.pdf.

American Council on Education. 2004. "Debt Burden: Repaying Student Debt." ACE Issue Brief. www.acenet.edu/news-room/Documents/IssueBrief-2004-Debt-Burden-Repaying-Student-Debt.pdf.

Apollo Group. 2010. "Higher Education at a Crossroads." Position paper. www.azcentral.com/ic/pdf/1125HigherEd.pdf.

Arum, Richard, and Josipa Roksa. 2011. *Academically Adrift: Limited Learning on College Campuses.* Chicago: University of Chicago Press.

Association of Private Sector Colleges and Universities. 2010. "APSCU's Response to For-Profit College Report by Education Trust." *APSCU Now,* November 24. www.apscunow.org/2010/11/apscus-response-to-for-profit-college.html.

Aud, Susan, William Hussar, Frank Johnson, Grace Kena, Erin Roth, Eileen Manning, Xiaolel Wang, and Jijun Zhang. 2012. *The Condition of Education 2012.* Washington: National Center for Education Statistics. http://nces.ed.gov/pubs2012/2012045.pdf.

Aud, Susan, William Hussar, Grace Kena, Kevin Bianco, Lauren Frohlich, Jana Kemp, and Kim Tahan. 2011. *The Condition of Education 2011*. Washington: National Center for Education Statistics. http://nces.ed.gov/pubs2011/2011033 .pdf.

Avery, Christopher, and Sarah Turner. 2012. "Student Loans: Do College Students Borrow Too Much—or Not Enough?" *Journal of Economic Perspectives* 26 (Winter): 165–92.

Axt, Richard G. 1952. *The Federal Government and Financing Higher Education*. New York: Columbia University Press.

Baker, Peter. 2012. "Obama Calls Passage of Student Loan Legislation a 'No-Brainer.'" *New York Times,* June 21. http://thecaucus.blogs .nytimes.com/2012/06/21/obama-calls-passage-of-student-loan-legislation-a-no-brainer/.

Barnshaw, John. 2013. "Prophets in the Wilderness: Predicting Financial Collapse." In *Making Sense of Social Problems: New Images, New Issues,* edited by Joel Best and Scott R. Harris, 153–71. Boulder, CO: Lynne Rienner.

Barone, Michael. 2010. "Higher Education Bubble Poised to Burst." *Washington Examiner,* September 3. http://washingtonexaminer.com/article/89702.

Bass, Karen. 2013. "The Student Loan Fairness Act." Representative Karen Bass, March 21. http://bass.house.gov/bill/student-loan-fairness-act.

Baum, Sandy, and Kathleen Payea. 2011. "Trends in For-Profit Postsecondary Education: Enrollment, Prices, Student Aid, and Outcomes." College Board Advocacy and Policy Center. http://advocacy.collegeboard.org /sites/default/files/11b_3376_Trends_Brief_4Pass_110414.pdf.

Baum, Sandy, and Saul Schwartz. 2006. *How Much Debt Is Too Much? Defining Benchmarks for Manageable Student Debt.* New York: College Board.

Beaver, William. 2008. "The Student Loan Scandal." *Society* 45 (May/June): 216–21.

Becker, Gary S. 1993. "Clinton's Student-Loan Plan Deserves an 'F.'" *Business Week,* June 14, 18.

Belkin, Douglas, and Scott Thurm. 2012. "Deans List: Hiring Spree Heightens College Bureaucracy—and Tuition." *Wall Street Journal,* December 28. http:// online.wsj.com/article/SB10001424127887323316804578161490716042814.html.

Bennett, Michael J. 1996. *When Dreams Came True: The GI Bill and the Making of Modern America.* Washington: Brassey's.

Bennett, William J., and David Wilezol. 2013. *Is College Worth It? A Former United States Secretary of Education and a Liberal Arts Graduate Expose the Broken Promise of Higher Education.* Nashville, TN: Thomas Nelson.

Berkner, Lutz, and Larry Bobbitt. 2005. "Trends in Undergraduate Borrowing: Federal Student Loans in 1989, 1992–93 and 1995–96." In *Federal Student Loans Revisited,* edited by Lydia N. Vedmas, 69–100. New York: Novinka.

Bernard, Tara Siegel. 2009. "In Grim Job Market, Student Loans Are a Costly Burden." *New York Times,* April 18, B6.

Best, Eric. 2012a. "Debt and the American Dream." *Society* 49 (July/August): 349–52.

———. 2012b. "Are Some Universities Too Big to Fail?" *Society Pages,* June 28. http://thesocietypages.org/specials/phoenix-as-canary/.

Best, Joel. 2013. *Social Problems.* 2d ed. New York: Norton.

Best, S. G. 1962. *From the Indian to the Atom.* Self-published memoir.

Bissonnette, Zac. 2010. *Debt-Free U: How I Paid for an Outstanding College Education without Loans, Scholarships, or Mooching off My Parents.* New York: Portfolio /Penguin.

Blacker, David J. 2012. "The Illegitimacy of Student Debt." *Occupy Student Debt Campaign,* January 23. www.occupystudentdebtcampaign.org/2012/01/the-illegitimacy-of-student-debt/.

Blumenstyk, Goldie. 2011. "For-Profits Scramble as Limits on Federal Student Aid Draw Near." *Chronicle of Higher Education,* April 8, A6, A8.

Blumenstyk, Goldie, and Alex Richards. 2011. "Many For-Profits Are 'Managing' Defaults to Mask Problems, Data Suggest." *Chronicle of Higher Education,* March 18, A6, A8.

Bound, John, and Sarah Turner. 2002. "Going to War and Going to College: Did World War II and the G.I. Bill Increase Educational Attainment for Returning Veterans?" *Journal of Labor Economics* 20: 784–815.

Boushey, Heather. 2005. "Student Debt: Bigger and Bigger." *Center for Economic and Policy Research Briefing Paper.* www.cepr.net/documents/publications /student_debt_2005_09.pdf.

Bozzo, Albie. 1981. "Some Hard Lessons in Reaganomics." *Rolling Stone,* October 1, 62, 65.

Bracey, Gerald W. 2007. "The First Time Everything Changed." *Phi Delta Kappan* 89 (October): 119–36.

Brenton, Myron. 1968. "The Higher Cost of Higher Education." *New York Times Sunday Magazine,* April 21, 32, 76–77, 82–87.

Burd, Stephen. 2004. "Selling Out Higher-Education Policy?" *Chronicle of Higher Education,* July 30, A16–19.

———. 2009. "The Subprime Student Loan Racket." *Washington Monthly,* November/December, 17–22.

Bureau of Labor Statistics. 2010. "Sizing Up the 2007–09 Recession: Comparing Two Key Labor Market Indicators with Earlier Downturns." *Issues in Labor Statistics*, December. www.bls.gov/opub/ils/pdf/opbils88.pdf.

———. 2013. "The Job Market for Recent College Graduates in the United States." *The Editor's Desk, U.S. Department of Labor*, April 5. www.bls.gov /opub/ted/2013/ted_20130405.htm.

Burks, Edward C. 1979. "Congress Weighing Student-Loan Raises." *New York Times*, November 18, NJ1.

Bush, George H. W. 1992a. "Address before a Joint Session of the Congress on the State of the Union." *American Presidency Project*, January 28. www .presidency.ucsb.edu/ws/index.php?pid=20544.

———. 1992b. "Remarks and a Question-and-Answer Session with the American Legion Boys Nation." *American Presidency Project*, July 20. www .presidency.ucsb.edu/ws/?pid=21240.

Bush, George W. 2002. "Remarks at Eden Prairie High School in Eden Prairie." *American Presidency Project*, March 4. www.presidency.ucsb.edu/ws /?pid=63497.

Business Week. 1965. "Battling for the Student Loan Market." July 17, 47–50.

———. 1969. "Why Banks Are Cool to Student Loans." September 20, 142, 144.

———. 1972. "A Sallie Mae to Aid Students." May 6, 26, 28.

———. 1974. "A Rising Fear of Student Bankruptcies." August 31, 56–57.

Butler, Stuart M. 2012. "The Coming Higher-Ed Revolution." *National Affairs* 10: 22–40.

Callan, Patrick M. 2011. "Reframing Access and Opportunity: Public Policy Dimensions." In *The States and Public Higher Education Policy: Affordability, Access, and Accountability*, edited by Donald E. Heller, 2d ed., 87–105. Baltimore, MD: Johns Hopkins University Press.

Carey, Kevin. 2013. "The Federal Parent Rip-Off Loan." *Chronicle of Higher Education*, June 3. http://chronicle.com/article/The-Federal-Parent-Rip-Off/139575/.

Carlsson, Robert J. 1970. "A Federal Program for Student Loans." *American Journal of Economics and Sociology* 29: 263–76.

Carnevale, Anthony P., Stephen J. Rose, and Ban Cheah. 2011. *The College Payoff: Education, Occupations, Lifetime Earnings*. Georgetown University Center on Education and the Workforce, August 5. www9.georgetown.edu/grad /gppi/hpi/cew/pdfs/collegepayoff-complete.pdf.

Carney, John. 2013. "The Student Loan Bubble Is Starting to Burst." *CNBC.com*, September 5. www.cnbc.com/id/101012270.

Carper, Jean. 1975. "Ripping Off the Students." *Nation,* July 19, 39–41.

Carter, Jarrett L. 2013. "Obama Higher Ed Reforms Makes HBCU Perspectives Critical in Policy Development Stages." *Huffington Post,* August 22. www .huffingtonpost.com/jarrett-l-carter/obama-higher-ed-reforms_b_3798232. html.

Carter, Jimmy. 1978. "Bangor, Maine Remarks and a Question-and-Answer Session at a Town Meeting." *American Presidency Project,* February 17. www .presidency.ucsb.edu/ws/?pid=30388.

Changing Times. 1954. "Borrow to Go to College?" February, 31–33.

———. 1956. "Can You Get a College Loan?" February, 39–40.

———. 1958. "Borrow for College, Pay Later." July, 30–31.

———. 1991. "College Loans: The Real Cost of Consolidating." May, 72–73.

Chen, Duke. 2007. "Student Loans in Bankruptcy." *CRS Report for Congress* (Congressional Research Service, July 26). http://assets.opencrs.com/rpts /RS22699/.

Chronicle of Higher Education. 2013. "Major Players in the MOOC Universe." https://chronicle.com/article/Major-Players-in-the-MOOC/138817/.

Chung, Anna S. 2012. "Choice of For-Profit College." *Economics of Education Review* 31: 1084–1101.

Clarifi. 2013. "Student Loan Counseling." Retrieved September 27. http:// clarifi.org/counseling/student-loan-counseling.

Clinton, William J. 1993. "Message to the Congress Transmitting Proposed Legislation on National Service and Student Loan Reform." *American Presidency Project,* May 5. www.presidency.ucsb.edu/ws/index.php?pid= 46525.

———. 1994. "Remarks to the American Council on Education." *American Presidency Project,* February 22. www.presidency.ucsb.edu/ws/index.php?pid= 49681.

———. 1995. "Roundtable Discussion with Students on Student Loans at Southern Illinois University in Carbondale, Illinois." *American Presidency Project,* September 11. www.presidency.ucsb.edu/ws/index.php?pid=51830.

———. 1996. "Remarks at the Princeton University Commencement Ceremony in Princeton, New Jersey." *American Presidency Project,* June 4. www .presidency.ucsb.edu/ws/index.php?pid=52906.

Clowse, Barbara Barksdale. 1981. *Brainpower for the Cold War: The Sputnik Crisis and National Defense Education Act of 1958.* Westport, CT: Greenwood.

Cohn, Jonathan. 1995. "Student Loans: The Wrong Cuts." *Washington Monthly,* October, 42–45.

College Board. 2012a. *Trends in College Pricing, 2012.* College Board Advocacy and Policy Center. http://advocacy.collegeboard.org/sites/default/files /college-pricing-2012-full-report_0.pdf.

———. 2012b. *Trends in Student Aid, 2012.* College Board Advocacy and Policy Center. http://advocacy.collegeboard.org/sites/default/files/student-aid-2012-full-report.pdf.

Collinge, Alan. 2009. *The Student Loan Scam: The Most Oppressive Debt in U.S. History—and How We Can Fight Back.* Boston: Beacon.

Congressional Budget Office. 2013. *The Federal Pell Grant Program: Recent Growth and Policy Options.* http://cbo.gov/sites/default/files/cbofiles/attachments/44448_PellGrants_9–5–13.pdf.

Consumer Financial Protection Bureau. 2012. *Private Student Loans.* Report to the Senate Committee on Banking, Housing, and Urban Affairs, the Senate Committee on Health, Education, Labor, and Pensions, the House of Representatives Committee on Financial Services, and the House of Representatives Committee on Education and the Workforce. July 20.

———. 2013. *Annual Report of the CFPB Student Loan Ombudsman.* http://files .consumerfinance.gov/f/201310_cfpb_student-loan-ombudsman-annual-report.pdf.

Consumer Reports. 1992. "Schools for Scandal," May, 302–6.

Controller General of the United States. 1976. "Examination of Financial Operations for Fiscal Year 1975 Shows Need for Improvements in the Guaranteed Student Loan Program." General Accounting Office, FOD-76-23.

Crain's New York Business. 2006. "Big Bucks for Big Boxes." September 4, 3.

Cruz, Gilbert. 2010. "Student-Loan Reform." *Time,* April 5, 12.

Cunningham, Alisa F., and Gregory S. Kienzi. 2011. *Delinquency: The Untold Story of Student Loan Borrowing.* Washington: Institute for Higher Education Policy. www.asa.org/pdfs/corporate/delinquency_the_untold_story.pdf.

Dealbook. 2007. "Citi Chief on Buyouts: 'We're Still Dancing.'" July 10. http:// dealbook.nytimes.com/2007/07/10/citi-chief-on-buyout-loans-were-still-dancing/.

The Debt Resistor's Operations Manual. 2012. Strike Debt / Occupy Wall Street. strikedebt.org/The-Debt-Resistors-Operations-Manual.pdf.

Delisle, Jason. 2012. "Federal Student Loan Interest Rates: History, Subsidies, and Cost." New American Foundation Issue Brief. http://newamerica.net /sites/newamerica.net/files/policydocs/Interest%20Rates%20Issue%20Brief %20Final_0.pdf.

Delisle, Jason, and Alex Holt. 2012. "Safety Net or Windfall? Examining Change to Income-Based Repayment for Federal Student Loans." *New America Foundation,* October 16. http://newamerica.net/publications/policy /safety_net_or_windfall.

———. 2013. "Free Money for Graduate Students Won't Go Unnoticed." New America Foundation. http://edmoney.newamerica.net/blogposts/2013 /graduate_student_loans_and_income_based_repayment_free_money_ wont_go_unnoticed-79694.

Deming, David J., Claudia Goldin, and Lawrence F. Katz. 2012. "The For-Profit Postsecondary School Sector: Nimble Critters or Agile Predators?" *Journal of Economic Perspectives* 26: 139–64.

Democratic Party. 2000. "Party Platform." *American Presidency Project,* August 14. http://www.presidency.ucsb.edu/ws/index.php?pid=29612.

———. 2004. "Party Platform." *American Presidency Project,* July 26. http:// www.presidency.ucsb.edu/ws/index.php?pid=29613.

Dēmos. 2013. "Dēmos Response to the President's Speech on College Affordability and Student Debt." August 22. http://www.demos.org/press-release /demos-response-presidents-speech-college-affordability-and-student-debt.

Dēmos / Young Invincibles. 2011. *The State of Young America: Economic Barriers to the American Dream—the Databook.* www.demos.org/publication/state-young-america-databook.

Department of Education. 2012a. "First Official Three-Year Student Loan Default Rates Published." Department of Education press release, September 28. www.ed.gov/news/press-releases/first-official-three-year-student-loan-default-rates-published.

———. 2012b. "Five Percent of Career Training Programs Risk Losing Access to Federal Funds." Department of Education press release, June 26. www.ed.gov /news/press-releases/five-percent-career-training-programs-risk-losing-access-federal-funds-35-percen.

———. 2013. "Default Rates Continue to Rise for Federal Student Loans." Department of Education press release, September 30. www.ed.gov/news /press-releases/default-rates-continue-rise-federal-student-loans.

Department of the Treasury. 2012. "The Economics of Higher Education." www.treasury.gov/connect/blog/Documents/20121212_Economics%20of% 20Higher%20Ed_vFINAL.pdf.

Dickinson, Tim. 2009. "Obama's Real Reform." *Rolling Stone,* August 6, 41–43.

Doyle, Denis P., and Terry W. Hartle. 1986. "Student-Aid Muddle." *Atlantic,* February, 30–34.

Draut, Tamara. 2005. *Strapped: Why America's 20- and 30-Somethings Can't Get Ahead.* New York: Anchor.

Dresch, Stephen P. 1980. "Financial and Behavioral Implications of Federal Student Loan Programs and Proposals." In *Subsidies to Higher Education: The Issues,* edited by Howard P. Tuckman and Edward Whalen, 56–92. New York: Praeger.

Du Bois, W. E. Burghardt, and Augustus Granville Dill. 1910. *The College-Bred Negro American.* Atlanta, GA: Atlanta University Press.

Dynarski, Mark. 1994. "Who Defaults on Student Loans? Findings from the National Postsecondary Student Aid Study." *Economics of Education Review* 13: 55–68.

Dynarski, Susan, and Daniel Kreisman. 2013. Loans for Educational Opportunity: Making Borrowing Work for Today's Students. Hamilton Project, Discussion Paper 2013-05 (October). www.hamiltonproject.org/files/downloads_and_links/THP_DynarskiDiscPaper_Final.pdf.

Economic Mobility Project. 2013. "How Much Protection Does a College Degree Afford? The Impact of the Recession on Recent College Graduates." Pew Charitable Trusts. www.pewstates.org/uploadedFiles/PCS_Assets/2013/Pew_college_grads_recession_report.pdf.

Economist. 2006. "An Education in Finance: University Bonds." May 20, 79.

Eden, Max. 2013. "'1 Percent' of the Tuition Problem." *AEIdeas,* September 9. www.aei-ideas.org/2013/09/1-percent-of-the-tuition-problem/.

Edmiston, Kelly D., Lara Brooks, and Steven Shelpelwich. 2013. "Student Loans: Overview and Issues (Update)." *Federal Reserve Bank of Kansas City Research Working Papers.* www.kansascityfed.org/publicat/reswkpap/pdf/rwp%2012–05.pdf.

Egan, Jack. 1987. "Young, Clever, and Filthy Rich." *U.S. News & World Report,* November 30, 48.

Eglin, Joseph J. 1993. "Untangling Student Loans." *Society* 30 (January/February): 52–58.

Eligon, John. 2013. "In Student Housing, Luxuries Overshadow Studying." *New York Times,* June 15, A11.

Elliott, William. 2013. "The Recession's Lasting Effects on a Generation of Scholars." *Ladder,* January 14. http://assets.newamerica.net/blogposts/2013/the_recession_s_lasting_effects_on_a_generation_of_scholars-77118.

Ellmann, Robert. 2009. "Bankruptcy, the Credit Card and American Freedom." *Economic Affairs* 29: 40–44.

Epple, Dennis, Richard Romano, Sinan Sarpça, and Holger Sieg. 2013. "The U.S. Market for Higher Education: A General Equilibrium Analysis of State and Private Colleges and Public Funding Policies." National Bureau of Economic Research Working Paper 19298. www.nber.org/papers/w19298.

Evans, David S., and Richard Schmalensee. 1999. *Paying with Plastic: The Digital Revolution in Buying and Borrowing.* Cambridge, MA: MIT Press.

Fain, Paul. 2012. "Phoenix Reloads." *Inside Higher Ed,* October 26. www .insidehighered.com/news/2012/10/26/university-phoenix-down-not-out.

———. 2013. "Now What?" *Inside Higher Ed,* March 21. www.insidehighered .com/news/2013/03/21/gainful-employments-future-uncertain-after-court ruling.

Fain, Paul, and Scott Jaschik. 2013. "Obama on For-Profits." *Inside Higher Ed,* August26.www.insidehighered.com/news/2013/08/26/obama-speaks-directly-profit-higher-education-noting-concerns-sector.

Federal Student Aid. 2012a. *Annual Report 2012.* www2.ed.gov/about/reports /annual/2012report/fsa-report.pdf.

———. 2012b. "Proprietary School 90/10 Revenue Percentages from Financial Statements" (spreadsheet). U.S. Department of Education. http:// studentaid.ed.gov/about/data-center/school/proprietary.

———. 2013a. "Calculators and Interest Rates." Retrieved July 7. www.direct .ed.gov/calc.html.

———. 2013b. "Closed School Discharge." Retrieved June 9. http://studentaid .ed.gov/repay-loans/forgiveness-cancellation#closed-school.

———. 2013c. "Don't Get Discouraged if You Are in Default on Your Federal Student Loan." Retrieved July 7. http://studentaid.ed.gov/repay-loans /default/get-out.

———. 2013d. "If You Default on Your Federal Student Loan, ..." Retrieved September 23. http://studentaid.ed.gov/repay-loans/default/collections.

Federation for American Immigration Reform. 2012. "Foreign Students." www .fairus.org/issue/foreign-students.

Ferguson, Andrew. 2009. "Need a Student Loan?" *Weekly Standard,* August 3, 8–10.

Fichtenbaum, Rudy, and Hank Reichman. 2013. "Obama's Rankings Won't Solve Crisis in US Academy." *Times Higher Education,* September 12. www .timeshighereducation.co.uk/comment/opinion/obamas-rankings-wont-solve-crisis-in-us-academy/2007156.article.

FinAid. 2013. "Student Loan Advisor—Undergraduate Students." Retrieved July 22. www.finaid.org/calculators/scripts/sloanadvisor.cgi.

Fine, Gary Alan. 2006. "The Containing of Social Problems: Solutions and Unintended Consequences in the Age of Betrayal." *Social Problems* 53: 3–17.

Fiske, Edward B. 1982. "Reagan Record in Education: Mixed Results." *New York Times,* November 14, 1, 38–39.

Flaherty, Colleen. 2013. "Disappointed, Not Surprised." *Inside Higher Ed,* August23.www.insidehighered.com/news/2013/08/23/faculty-advocates-react-obamas-plan-higher-ed.

Flattau, Pamela Elbert, Jerome Bracken, Richard Van Atta, Ayeh Bandeh-Ahmadi, Rodolfo de la Cruz, and Kay Sullivan. 2006. *The National Defense Education Act of 1958: Selected Outcomes.* Science and Technology Policy Institute, Institute of Defense Analysis Document D-3306. www.ida.org /upload/stpi/pdfs/ida-d-3306.pdf.

Flemming, Arthur S. 1960. "The Philosophy and Objectives of the National Defense Education Act." *Annals of the American Academy of Political and Social Science* 327: 132–38.

Fortune. 1984. "Sallie Mae's Fetching Profit Figures." May 28, 196–97.

Fossey, Richard. 1998. "The Dizzying Growth of the Federal Student Loan Program: When Will Vertigo Set In?" In *Condemning Students to Debt,* edited by Richard Fossey and Mark Bateman, 7–18. New York: Teachers College Press.

Foust, Dean. 1993. "Student Loans Ain't Broke, Don't Fix 'Em." *Business Week,* April 5, 74.

———. 1998. "Student Loans Don't Need Clinton's Tinkering." *Business Week,* March 23, 78.

Fraas, Charlotte Jones. 1987. "Guaranteed Student Loan (GSL) Deferments: A Pro/Con Analysis." Congressional Research Service, February 13.

———. 1988. "The Guaranteed Student Loan Program: Status and Issues." *CRS Report for Congress* (Congressional Research Service, November 18).

———. 1989. "The U.S. Department of Education's Student Loan Default Reduction Initiative: Background and Analysis." *CRS Report for Congress* (Congressional Research Service, July 31).

———. 1991a. "Selected Amendments Enacted since 1980 to Control Guaranteed Student Loan Defaults." *CRS Report for Congress* (Congressional Research Service, March 14).

———. 1991b. "Direct Student Loans: A Pro and Con Analysis." *CRS Report for Congress* (Congressional Research Service, September 23).

Frank, Robert H. 2007. *Falling Behind: How Rising Inequality Harms the Middle Class.* Berkeley: University of California Press.

Frederiksen, Norman, and W. B. Schrader. 1951. *Adjustment to College: A Study of 10,000 Veteran and Nonveteran Students in Sixteen American Colleges.* Princeton, NJ: Educational Testing Service.

Frydl, Kathleen J. 2009. *The GI Bill.* New York: Cambridge University Press.

FTI Consulting. 2013. "Innovation Imperative: Enhancing Higher Education Outcomes." Northeastern University, 2nd Annual Innovation Poll, September 17. www.northeastern.edu/innovationsurvey/pdfs/Northeastern_University_Innovation_Imperative_Higher_Ed_Outcomes_Poll_Deck_FINAL_Delivered.pdf.

Galbraith, John Kenneth. 1990. *A Short History of Financial Euphoria.* New York: Penguin.

Gerdes, Lindsey. 2009. "MBA Jobs: For Some, a Waiting Game." *Businessweek,* May 26. www.businessweek.com/bschools/content/may2009/bs20090526_804854.htm.

Gertner, Jon. 2006. "Forgive Us Our Student Debts." *New York Times Magazine,* June 11, E60–66.

Geske, Terry G., and Elchanan Cohn. 1998. "Why Is a High School Diploma No Longer Enough? The Economic and Social Benefits of Higher Education." In *Condemning Students to Debt,* edited by Richard Fossey and Mark Bateman, 19–36. New York: Teachers College Press.

Get Educated.com. 2013. "List of Fake College Degree Accreditation Agencies." Retrieved June 8. www.geteducated.com/diploma-mills-police/college-degree-mills/204-fake-agencies-for-college-accreditation.

Gillen, Andrew. 2013. "In Debt and in the Dark: It's Time for Better Information on Student Loan Defaults." *Education Sector,* July. www.educationsector.org/publications/debt-and-dark-it%E2%80%99s-time-better-information-student-loan-defaults.

Gillen, Andrew, and Richard Vedder. 2008. "The Next Market Bubble: Student Loans?" *Inside Higher Ed,* May 2. www.insidehighered.com/views/2008/05/02/vedder.

Gillon, Steve. 2004. *Boomer Nation: The Largest and Richest Generation Ever and How It Changed America.* New York: Free Press.

Gilpin, Kenneth N. 2002. "Turning a Profit with Higher Education." *New York Times,* October 20, B7.

Gladieux, Lawrence E. 1989. "The Student Loan Quandary: Are There Workable Alternatives?" *Change* 21 (May–June): 35–41.

Gladieux, Lawrence E., and Thomas R. Wolanin. 1976. *Congress and the Colleges.* Lexington, MA: Lexington.

Gobel, Reyna. 2010. *Cliffs Notes® Graduation Debt: How to Manage Student Loans and Live Your Life.* New York: Wiley.

Greenhouse, Steven. 2012. "Jobs Few, Grads Flock to Unpaid Internships." *New York Times,* May 6, A1.

Greenstone, Michael, and Adam Looney. 2011. "How Do Recent College Grads Really Stack Up? Employment and Earnings for Graduates of the Great Recession." *Brookings on Job Numbers,* June 3. www.brookings.edu /blogs/jobs/posts/2011/06/03-jobs-greenstone-looney.

Halperin, David. 2012. "Controversial For-Profit College Industry Using Your Tax Dollars to Support Romney Victory." *Huffington Post,* November 1. www.huffingtonpost.com/davidhalperin/for-profit-colleges-romney_b_ 2058261.html.

Hannaford, Peter. 2010. "Obama's Costly Student Loan Takeover." *Human Events,* April 19, 343.

Hannon, Kerry. 1992. "How You're Getting Stiffed by the Student Loan Mess." *Money,* May, 164–66, 168, 170, 172, 174.

Harris, Seymour E. 1960. "Higher Education on the Cuff." *National Parent-Teacher,* March, 7–10.

———. 1962. *Higher Education: Resources and Finance.* New York: McGraw-Hill.

Hartman, Robert W. 1971. *Credit for College: Public Policy for Student Loans.* New York: McGraw-Hill.

Hassett, Kevin A., and Robert J. Shapiro. 2004. "Annually Adjusted Rates Would Avoid Catastrophe." *Chronicle of Higher Education,* June 18, B12–13.

Havemann, Ernest, and Patricia Salter West. 1952. *They Went to College: The College Graduate in America Today.* New York: Harcourt, Brace.

Hearn, James C., and Janet M. Holdsworth. 2004. "Federal Student Aid: The Shift from Grants to Loans." In *Public Funding of Higher Education: Changing Contexts and New Rationales,* edited by Edward P. St. John and Michael D. Parsons, 40–59. Baltimore, MD: Johns Hopkins University Press.

Heller, Donald E. 2006. "State Support of Higher Education: Past, Present, and Future." In *Privatization and Public Universities,* edited by Douglas M. Priest and Edward P. St. John, 11–37. Bloomington: Indiana University Press.

———. 2011. "Trends in the Affordability of Public Colleges and Universities: The Contradiction of Increasing Prices and Increasing Enrollment." In *The States and Public Higher Education Policy: Affordability, Access, and Accountability,* edited by Donald E. Heller, 2d ed., 13–36. Baltimore, MD: Johns Hopkins University Press.

Hill, Catherine B. 2013. "As Colleges Get Richer, Students Pay More." *Centre Daily.com,* September 9. www.centredaily.com/2013/09/09/3778646/column-as-colleges-get-richer.html, 2013.

Hillman, Nicholas W. 2013. "Reforming Repayment: Using Income-Related Loans to Reduce Default." American Enterprise Institute Conference, June 24. www.aei.org/files/2013/06/21/-kelly-hillmannick-conference_085349110877.pdf.

Hodges, Jane. 1999. "If Education Is Supposed to Be an Investment. . . ." *Fortune,* June 7, 240, 244.

Hyman, Louis. 2012. *Borrow: The American Way of Debt.* New York: Vintage.

Institute for Higher Education Policy. 1995. *College Debt and the American Family.*

Jacobs, Gloria, and Elizabeth Hess. 1981. "The College Loan Crisis: Can You Count on Uncle Sam?" *Ms.,* March, 81–82.

James, Jonathan. 2012. "The College Wage Premium." *Federal Reserve Bank of Cleveland,* August 8. www.clevelandfed.org/research/commentary/2012/2012–10.cfm.

Jet. 1988. "Bad Student Loans May Force Most of 108 Black Colleges to Shut Their Doors." January 11, 22–23.

Johnson, Anne, Tobin Van Ostern, and Abraham White. 2012. *The Student Debt Crisis.* Center for American Progress, October 25. www.americanprogress.org/wp-content/uploads/2012/10/WhiteStudentDebt-5.pdf.

Johnson, Charles S. 1938. *The Negro College Graduate.* Chapel Hill: University of North Carolina Press.

Johnson, Lyndon B. 1965a. "Statement by the President upon Signing the National Vocational Student Loan Insurance Act." *American Presidency Project,* October 22. www.presidency.ucsb.edu/ws/index.php?pid=27327.

———. 1965b. "Remarks at Southwest Texas State College upon Signing the Higher Education Act of 1965." *American Presidency Project,* November 8. www.presidency.ucsb.edu/ws/?pid=27356.

Kamenetz, Anya. 2007. *Generation Debt: How Our Future Was Sold Out for Student Loans, Credit Cards, Bad Jobs, No Benefits, and Tax Cuts for Rich Geezers—and How to Fight Back.* New York: Riverhead Books.

Kelly, Andrew P. 2011. "How For-Profit Colleges Can Save Themselves—and Higher Education." *Atlantic,* September 6. www.theatlantic.com/business/archive/2011/09/how-for-profit-colleges-can-save-themselves-and-higher-education/244595/.

———. 2012a. "Don't Blame For-Profit Colleges for the Higher-Ed Lobbying Epidemic." *Atlantic,* January 5. www.theatlantic.com/business

/archive/2012/01/dont-blame-for-profit-colleges-for-the-higher-ed-lobbying-epidemic/250921/.

———. 2012b. "A Student Debt Cure Worse Than the Disease." *American,* December 18. www.american.com/archive/2012/december/a-student-debt-cure-worse-than-the-disease.

———. 2013a. "How Much Money Does the Government Really Make from Student Loans?" *Atlantic,* April 11. www.theatlantic.com/business/archive /2013/04/how-much-money-does-the-government-really-make-from-student-loans/274912/.

———. 2013b. "Student Loan Interest Rate Drama—It's Back, in a Limited Engagement!" *AEIdeas,* May 13. www.aei-ideas.org/2013/05/student-loan-interest-rate-drama-its-back-in-a-limited-engagement/.

———. 2013c. "3 Questions on Obama's New Higher Education Plan." *AEIdeas,* August 23. www.aei-ideas.org/2013/08/3-questions-on-obamas-new-higher-education-plan/.

Kelly, Andrew P., and Frederick M. Hess. 2013. "Obama's Scattershot Higher-Education Plan." *National Review Online,* August 26. www.nationalreview .com/article/356682/obamas-scattershot-higher-education-plan-andrew-p-kelly-frederick-m-hess.

Kelly, Andrew P., and Daniel K. Lautzenheiser. 2013. "Taking Charge: A State-Level Agenda for Higher Education Reform." American Enterprise Institute. www.aei.org/papers/education/higher-education/innovation2/takingcharge /?utm_source=today&utm_medium=web&utm_campaign=070813.

Kelly, Brian. 2010. "Is College Still Worth It?" *U.S. News & World Report,* September 1, 6, 8, 12.

Kiley, Kevin. 2012. "The Other Debt Crisis." *Inside Higher Ed,* April 10. www .insidehighered.com/news/2012/04/10/public-universities-will-take-more-debt-states-decrease-spending-capital-projects.

———. 2013a. "Crowded Out." *Inside Higher Ed,* April 30. www.insidehighered. com/news/2013/04/30/out-state-enrollment-decreases-minority-low-income-student-enrollment.

———. 2013b. "Price of a Bad Economy." *Inside Higher Ed,* May 7. www. insidehighered.com/news/2013/05/07/nacubo-survey-reports-sixth-consecutive-year-discount-rate-increases.

———. 2013c. "No Such Thing as 'Free Tuition.'" *Inside Higher Ed,* July 9. www.insidehighered.com/news/2013/07/09/oregon-plan-would-shift-tuition-payment-after-graduation.

———. 2013d. "Coming Up Short." *Inside Higher Ed,* July 12. www.insidehighered
.com/news/2013/07/12/loyola-new-orleans-enrollment-shortfall-will-mean-large-
budget-cuts.

Knapp, Laura Greene, and Terry G. Seaks. 1992. "An Analysis of the Probability of Default on Federally Guaranteed Student Loans." *Review of Economics
and Statistics* 74: 404–11.

Koerner, James D. 1970. *The Parsons College Bubble: A Tale of Higher Education in
America.* New York: Basic Books.

Konigsberg, Eric. 1993. "Sallie Maen't." *New Republic,* July 12, 15–16.

Kronstadt, Sylvia. 1973. "Student Loans: How the Government Takes the Work
Out of Fraud." *Washington Monthly,* November, 5–12.

Lareau, Annette. 2011. *Unequal Childhoods: Class, Race, and Family Life.* 2d ed.
Berkeley: University of California Press.

Lautzenheiser, Daniel. 2013. "Getting More Bang Out of College Bucks." *AEI
Education Outlook,* no. 6 (September). www.aei.org/files/2013/09/09/-getting-
more-bang-for-our-college-bucks-2_093111689829.pdf.

Lee, Donghoon. 2013. "Household Debt and Credit: Student Debt." Federal
Reserve Bank of New York, February 28. www.newyorkfed.org/newsevents
/mediaadvisory/2013/Lee022813.pdf.

Leicht, Kevin T., and Scott T. Fitzgerald. 2007. *Postindustrial Peasants: The Illu-
sion of Middle-Class Prosperity.* New York: Worth.

Leonard, Robin, and Deanne Loonin. 2001. *Take Control of Your Student Loan
Debt.* 3d ed. Berkeley, CA: Nolo.

Lichtblau, Eric. 2012. "Romney Offers Praise for a Donor's Business." *New York
Times,* January 14. www.nytimes.com/2012/01/15/us/politics/mitt-romney-
offers-praise-for-a-donors-business.html?pagewanted=all&_r=0.

Lieber, Ron. 2012. "Last Plea on Student Loans: Proving a Hopeless Future." *New
York Times,* August 31. www.nytimes.com/2012/09/01/business/shedding-
student-loans-in-bankruptcy-is-an-uphill-battle.html?pagewanted=all&_
r=0.

Loss, Christopher P. 2012. *Between Citizens and the State: The Politics of American
Higher Education in the 20th Century.* Princeton, NJ: Princeton University Press.

Lowry, Robert C. 2009. "Reauthorization of the Federal Higher Education Act
and Accountability for Student Learning: The Dog That Didn't Bark." *Pub-
lius* 39: 506–26.

Lubasch, Arnold H. 1985. "U.S., in Bid for Repayment of Student Loans, Sues
25." *New York Times,* January 29, B3.

Lynch, Mamie, Jennifer Engle, and José L. Cruz. 2010. *Subprime Opportunity: The Unfulfilled Promise of For-Profit Colleges and Universities.* Washington: Education Trust. www.edtrust.org/sites/edtrust.org/files/publications/files /Subprime_report_1.pdf.

Maeda, Martha. 2009. *How to Wipe Out Your Student Loans and Be Debt Free Fast: Everything You Need to Know Explained Simply.* Ocala, FL: Atlantic Publishing.

Maguire Associates. 2009. "Understanding and Confronting Price Sensitivity." Slide presentation for Enrollment Planners Conference, July 22. www .maguireassoc.com/wp-content/uploads/2010/08/ACT-Enrollment-Planners-Conference-ACT-Enrollment-Planners-Workshop-presentation-Under-standing-Price-Sensitivity-KD-TS-7–22–10.pdf.

Main, Jeremy. 1979. "College Loans at 7%—for Everybody." *Money,* July, 83–86.

Marcus, Jon. 2013. "Why Some Small Colleges Are in Big Trouble." *Boston Globe Magazine,* April 14. www.bostonglobe.com/magazine/2013/04/13/are-small-private-colleges-trouble/ndlYSWVGFAUjYVVWkqnjfK/story.html.

Marklein, Mary Beth. 2012. "Record Number of Foreign Students in U.S." *USA Today,* November 12, 5A.

Martin, Andrew. 2012. "Building a Showcase Campus, Using an I.O.U." *New York Times,* December 14, A1.

Martin, Andrew, and Andrew W. Lehren. 2012. "A Generation Hobbled by College Debt." *New York Times,* May 13, 1, 20–21.

McBride, Bill. 2013. "Mortgage Delinquencies by Loan Type in Q1." *Calculated Risk,* May 11. www.calculatedriskblog.com/2013/05/mortgage-delinquencies-by-loan-type-in.html.

McPherson, Michael S., and Morton Owen Schapiro. 1991a. "Does Student Aid Affect College Enrollment? New Evidence on a Persistent Controversy." *American Economic Review* 81: 309–18.

———. 1991b. *Keeping College Affordable: Government and Educational Opportunity.* Washington: Brookings Institution.

Melville, Yolanda. 2012. "Is College Really Worth It?" *Crisis,* Summer, 40.

Mettler, Suzanne. 2005. *Soldiers to Citizens: The G.I. Bill and the Making of the Greatest Generation.* New York: Oxford University Press.

Mihalic, Joe. 2012. *Destroy Student Debt: A Combat Guide to Freedom.* Amazon Digital Services.

Miles, Barbara, and Dennis Zimmerman. 1997. "Reducing Federal Student Loan Costs: The Options Are Narrowing." *CRS Report for Congress* (Congressional Research Service, February 25).

Mills, C. Wright. 1959. *The Sociological Imagination*. New York: Oxford University Press.

Mitchell, Josh, and Maya Jackson-Randall. 2012. "Student-Loan Debt Tops $1 Trillion." *Wall Street Journal*, March 22, A5.

Mogilyanskaya, Alina. 2012. "3 For-Profit Institutions Lose Student-Aid Eligibility after Failing 90/10 Test Twice." *Chronicle of Higher Education*, September 27. http://chronicle.com/article/3-Institutions-Lose/134696/.

Monks, James. 2009. "Who Are the Part-Time Faculty?" *Academe* 95 (July–August): 33–37.

Moody's Investors Service. 2013. "2013 Outlook for Entire US Higher Education Sector Changed to Negative." January 16. www.moodys.com/research/Moodys-2013-outlook-for-entire-US-Higher-Education-sector-changed--PR_263866.

Morgan Stanley. 2010. Discussion Materials for Meeting regarding Dodd-Frank Act Securitization Provisions. www.sec.gov/comments/df-title-ix/asset-backed-securities/assetbackedsecurities-9.pdf.

Morris, Dick, and Eileen McGann. 2007. *Outrage: How Illegal Immigration, the United Nations, Congressional Ripoffs, Student Loan Overcharges, Tobacco Companies, Trade Protection, and Drug Companies Are Ripping Us Off . . . and What to Do about It*. New York: HarperCollins.

Mumper, Michael. 2003. "The Future of College Access: The Declining Role of Public Higher Education in Promoting Equal Opportunity." *Annals of the American Academy of Political and Social Science* 585: 97–117.

Mumper, Michael, and Melissa L. Freeman. 2011. "The Continuing Paradox of Public College Tuition Inflation." In *The States and Public Higher Education Policy: Affordability, Access, and Accountability*, edited by Donald E. Heller, 2d ed., 37–60. Baltimore, MD: Johns Hopkins University Press.

Nam, Charles B. 1964. "Impact of the 'GI Bills' on the Educational Level of the Male Population." *Social Forces* 43: 26–32.

Nasiripour, Shanien. 2013. "Obama Student Loan Policy Reaping $51 Billion Profit." *Huffington Post*, June 15. www.huffingtonpost.com/2013/05/14/obama-student-loans-policy-profit_n_3276428.html.

National Center for Education Statistics. 2012. *Digest of Education Statistics: 2011*. Washington: U.S. Department of Education. Retrieved September 19, 2012. http://nces.ed.gov/programs/digest/d11/.

National Defense Education Act of 1958. Pub. L. No. 85-864, 72 Stat. 1580, 1580–1605.

National Review. 1971. "Education on the Installment Plan." April 6, 354, 356.

————. 1982. "Student Loans: Theory and Practice." April 30, 469–70.

Nelson, Libby A. 2012a. "How Standardized Should Financial Aid Award Letters Be?" *Inside Higher Ed,* June 6. www.insidehighered.com/news/2012/06/06/how-standardized-should-financial-aid-award-letters-be.

————. 2012b. "Missing the Mark on 'Gainful.'" *Inside Higher Ed,* June 26. www.insidehighered.com/news/2012/06/26/education-department-releases-data-gainful-employment-rule.

————. 2012c. "An Underused Lifeline." *Inside Higher Ed,* October 23. www.insidehighered.com/news/2012/10/23/despite-student-debt-concern-income-based-repayment-lags.

————. 2013a. "Loans Back in the Spotlight." *Inside Higher Ed,* June 3. www.insidehighered.com/news/2013/06/03/student-loan-interest-rate-again-top-political-issue.

————. 2013b. "No Magic Bullet." *Inside Higher Ed,* June 12. www.insidehighered.com/news/2013/06/12/first-year-shopping-sheet-doesnt-make-big-splash.

New Republic. 1971. "Learn Now, Pay Later." February 20, 12–13.

Newsweek. 1958. "Pay Later to Learn." September 29, 87.

————. 1964. "Beg, Borrow, and Bargain." November 30, 67.

————. 1971. "Pay As You Earn." February 15, 69.

————. 1974. "Student Bankrupts." August 26, 89.

————. 1977. "Study Now, Pay Never." March 3, 95.

New York State Higher Education Services Corporation. 2013. "How Much Can You Borrow?" www.hesc.ny.gov/content.nsf/SFC/How_Much_Can_You_Borrow.

New York Times. 2013. "A Federal Prod to Lower College Costs" (editorial). August 23, 26.

Nixon, Richard. 1969. "Statement on the Guaranteed Student Loan Program." *American Presidency Project,* August 14. www.presidency.ucsb.edu/ws/?pid=2203.

————. 1972. "Statement on Signing a Bill Permitting Continuation of the Guaranteed Student Loan Program." *American Presidency Project,* August 19. www.presidency.ucsb.edu/ws/?pid=3532.

Novack, Janet. 1988. "Look, Ma, No Risk." *Forbes,* January 25, 53–54.

Obama, Barack. 2009. "Commencement Address at Arizona State University in Tempe." *American Presidency Project,* May 13. www.presidency.ucsb.edu/ws/?pid=86138.

————. 2012. "Remarks at a Campaign Rally in Madison, Wisconsin." *American Presidency Project,* October 4. www.presidency.ucsb.edu/ws/index.php?pid=102341.

————. 2013a. "Remarks at the University at Buffalo, State University of New York, in Buffalo, New York." *American Presidency Project*, August 22. www .presidency.ucsb.edu/ws/index.php?pid=104020#axzz2fdcr2tvd.

————. 2013b. "Remarks at Lackawanna College in Scranton, Pennsylvania." *American Presidency Project*, August 23. www.presidency.ucsb.edu/ws/index .php?pid=104019#axzz2fdcr2tvd.

————. 2013c. "Remarks at a Town Hall Meeting and a Question-and-Answer Session at Binghamton University, State University of New York, in Binghamton, New York." *American Presidency Project*, August 23. www.presidency .ucsb.edu/ws/index.php?pid=104046#axzz2fdcr2tvd.

Occupy Student Debt Campaign. 2012. "A Statement from the Occupy Student Debt Campaign." www.occupystudentdebtcampaign.org/click-to-read-our-statement-on-student-debt-reform-initiatives/.

Office for Civil Rights. 1991. "Historically Black Colleges and Universities and Higher Education Desegregation." Washington: U.S. Department of Education. www2.ed.gov/about/offices/list/ocr/docs/hq9511.html.

Office of Sallie Mae Oversight. 2006. *Lessons Learned from the Privatization of Sallie Mae.* Department of the Treasury. www.treasury.gov/about /organizational-structure/offices/Documents/SallieMaePrivatizationReport .pdf.

Olson, Keith W. 1974. *The G.I. Bill, the Veterans, and the Colleges.* Lexington: University Press of Kentucky.

Oreopoulos, Philip, Till von Wachter, and Andrew Heisz. 2006. "The Short- and Long-Term Career Effects of Graduating in a Recession: Hysteresis and Heterogeneity in the Market for College Graduates." National Bureau of Economic Research, Working Paper 12159. www.nber.org/papers /w12159.

Organisation for Economic Co-operation and Development. 2012. *Education at a Glance 2012: OECD Indicators.* www.oecd.org/edu/EAG%202012_e-book_ EN_200912.pdf.

Orozco, Viany. 2010. "Student Debt 101: Why College Students Are Burdened by Debt and What to Do about It." *Dēmos Fact Sheet*, March 8. www.demos.org /publication/student-debt-101-why-college-students-are-burdened-debt-and-what-do-about-it.

Payscale.com. 2013a. "2013 College Education ROI Rankings: Does a Degree Always Pay Off?" www.payscale.com/college-education-value-2013.

————. 2013b. "Underemployment in America." www.payscale.com/data-packages/underemployed.

People Weekly. 1985. "For Thousands of Aging Ex-Students Who've Defaulted on College Loans, Uncle Sam Puts Out the Big Chill." February 18, 92–94.

Pérez-Peña, Richard. 2013. "College Enrollment Falls as Economy Recovers." *New York Times*, July 26, A11.

Perkins, John A., and Daniel W. Wood. 1960. "Issues in Federal Aid to Higher Education." In *The Federal Government and Higher Education*, edited by Douglas M. Knight, 140–75. Englewood Cliffs, NJ: Prentice-Hall.

Peters, Jeremy W., and Ashley Parker. 2013. "Unusual Feat in Congress: Student Loan Bill Breezes On." *New York Times*, August 1, 10.

Phillips, Cabell. 1966. "Rise Seen in Student Loans under Johnson Plan." *New York Times*, January 27, 21.

Pope, Loren B. 1958a. "Education Landmark: Federal Aid Bill Is Viewed as a General Stimulant to Schools throughout the U.S." *New York Times*, August 24, 74.

———. 1958b. "Colleges Warned on 'Elite' Concept." *New York Times*, October 10, 64.

Price, Derek V. 2004. *Borrowing Inequality: Race, Class, and Student Loans*. Boulder, CO: Lynne Rienner.

Priest, Douglas M., and Edward P. St. John, eds. 2006. *Privatization and Public Universities*. Bloomington: Indiana University Press.

Project on Student Debt. 2010. "High Hopes, Big Debts." www.ticas.org/files /pub/High_Hopes_Big_Debts_2008.pdf.

———. 2012. "Q&A on the For-Profit College '90–10' Rule." November 9. Retrieved May 26, 2013. http://projectonstudentdebt.org/files/pub/90-10_ Q_and_A_updated_draft_Final.pdf.

Public Agenda. 2013. *Is College Worth It for Me? How Adults without Degrees Think about Going (Back) to School*. November. www.publicagenda.org/files/Is CollegeWorthItForMe_PublicAgenda_2013.pdf.

Quinn, Jane Bryant. 1979. "Where to Get Student Loans." *Newsweek*, May 21, 76.

———. 1982. "The Student-Loan Scare." *Newsweek*, May 24, 68.

Quint, Barbara Gilder. 1979. "Why There's Trouble Ahead If You Don't Repay Your Student Loan." *Glamour*, September, 224.

Quinterno, John. 2012. *The Great Cost Shift: How Higher Education Cuts Undermine the Future Middle Class*. Dēmos. www.demos.org/publication/great-cost-shift-how-higher-education-cuts-undermine-future-middle-class.

Rawe, Julie. 2007. "Student-Loan Shenanigans." *Time*, April 23, 61–62.

Reagan, Ronald. 1984. "Remarks at a Reagan-Bush Rally in Brownsville, Texas." *American Presidency Project*, October 2. www.presidency.ucsb.edu /ws/?pid=40465.

————. 1985. "Remarks at the Annual Meeting of the National Association of Independent Schools." *American Presidency Project*, February 28. www.presidency.ucsb.edu/ws/?pid=38263.

————. 1988. "1988 Legislative and Administrative Message: A Union of Individuals." *American Presidency Project*, January 25. www.presidency.ucsb.edu/ws/index.php?pid=36046.

Republican Party. 2000. "Party Platform." *American Presidency Project*, July 31. www.presidency.ucsb.edu/ws/index.php?pid=25649.

————. 2012. "Party Platform." *American Presidency Project*, August 27. www.presidency.ucsb.edu/ws/index.php?pid=101961.

Reynolds, Glenn Harlan. 2013. *The Higher Education Bubble.* Encounter Broadsides 29.

Rinzler, Carol E. 1985. "Student Loans: Have You Put Off Paying Off?" *Mademoiselle*, December, 108.

Ritzer, George. 1995. *Expressing America: A Critique of the Global Credit Card Society.* Thousand Oaks, CA: Pine Forge.

Rivard, Ry. 2013a. "Ivies Borrow Billions, but Whatever." *Inside Higher Ed*, August 27. www.insidehighered.com/news/2013/08/27/despite-billions-debt-perhaps-little-worry-elite-institutions.

————. 2013b. "Downgrading Elite Colleges." *Inside Higher Ed*, August 30. www.insidehighered.com/news/2013/08/30/prestigious-liberal-arts-colleges-face-ratings-downgrades.

————. 2013c. "Paper (Tuition) Cuts." *Inside Higher Ed*, September 16. www.insidehighered.com/news/2013/09/16/small-private-colleges-steeply-cut-their-sticker-price-will-it-drive-down-college.

————. 2013d. "Micro-Targeting Students." *Inside Higher Ed*, October 24. www.insidehighered.com/news/2013/10/24/political-campaign-style-targeting-comes-student-search#ixzz2ieFPa4XA.

————. 2013e. "Using FAFSA against Students." *Inside Higher Ed*, October 28. www.insidehighered.com/news/2013/10/28/colleges-use-fafsa-information-reject-students-and-potentially-lower-financial-aid.

Roche, Mark William. 2010. *Why Choose the Liberal Arts?* Notre Dame, IN: University of Notre Dame Press.

Ross, Andrew. 2012. "NYU Professor: Are Student Loans Immoral?" *Daily Beast*, September 27. www.thedailybeast.com/articles/2012/09/27/nyu-professor-are-student-loans-immoral.html.

Rothstein, Jesse, and Cecilia Elena Rouse. 2011. "Constrained after College: Student Loans and Early-Career Occupational Choices." *Journal of Public Economics* 95: 149–63.

Rudel, Daniel, and Natasha Yurk. 2013. "Responsibility or Liability? Student Loan Debt and Time Use in College." Unpublished paper presented at the annual meeting of the American Sociological Association, New York.

Russell, L. C. 2010. *Death by Student Loan.* CreateSpace Independent Publishing Platform.

St. John, Edward P. 2003. *Refinancing the College Dream: Access, Equal Opportunity, and Justice for Taxpayers.* Baltimore, MD: Johns Hopkins University Press.

St. John, Edward P., and Ontario S. Wooden. 2006. "Privatization and Federal Funding for Higher Education." In *Privatization and Public Universities,* edited by Douglas M. Priest and Edward P. St. John, 38–64. Bloomington: Indiana University Press.

Sallie Mae. 2013. *How America Pays for College, 2013.* www.salliemae.com/assets /Core/how-America-pays/howamericapays2013.pdf.

Sampson, Zinie Chen. 2012. "College Boards Turn to Business-Style Approaches." *Huffington Post,* June 27. www.huffingtonpost.com/2012/06/27 /college-boards-turn-to-bu_o_n_1631964.html.

Sams, Bill. 2012. "2012 Tipping Point" (video). *EPIC 2020,* May. http://epic2020 .org/.

Saturday Review. 1957. "No Bargain Basement for Higher Education." November 23, 24–25.

Schemo, Diana. 2007. "With Few Limits and High Rates, Private Loans Deepen Student-Debt Crisis." *New York Times,* June 10, 28.

Schenet, Margot A. 1990. "Proprietary Schools: The Regulatory Structure." *CRS Report for Congress* (Congressional Research Service, August 31).

———. 1999. "Federal Student Loans: Program Data and Default Statistics." *CRS Report for Congress* (Congressional Research Service, July 8).

Schneider, Mark. 2008. "The Costs of Failure Factories in American Higher Education." AEI Online, October 30. www.aei.org/article/education /the-costs-of-failure-factories-in-american-higher-education/.

School and Society. 1967. "Loans to College Students." October 28, 373.

Schubarth, Cromwell. 2013. "Disruption Guru Christensen: Why Apple, Tesla, VCs, Academia May Die." *Silicon Valley Business Journal,* February 7. www .bizjournals.com/sanjose/news/2013/02/07/disruption-guru-christensen-why .html?page=all.

Selingo, Jeffrey J. 2013. "A Matter of Ballast." *New York Times,* April 14, ED8.

Shaffer, Leigh S. 2012. "Live Like the Affluent in College, Live Like a Student after Graduation." *About Campus* 17 (March/April): 19–25.

Shear, Michael D., and Tamar Lewin. 2013. "On Bus Tour, Obama Seeks to Shame Colleges into Easing Costs." *New York Times,* August 23, 18.

Short, Doug. 2013. "What Inflation Means to You: Inside the Consumer Price Index." Short.com, April 16. www.advisorperspectives.com/dshort/updates/CPI-Category-Overview.php.

Silver-Greenberg, Jessica. 2009. "A New Deal for Student Loans." *Business Week,* April 27, 21.

Silver-Greenberg, Jessica, and Catherine Rampell. 2013. "Sallie Mae Will Split Old Loans from New." *Dealbook,* May 29. http://dealbook.nytimes.com/2013/05/29/sallie-mae-will-split-old-loans-from-new/.

Simmons, William M., Jr. 1973. "Meet Sallie Mae." *American Education,* October, 27.

Skinner, Rebecca R. 2007. "Institutional Eligibility and the Higher Education Act: Legislative History of the 90/10 Rule and Its Current Status." CRS Report for Congress (Congressional Research Service, November 6).

Smith, Jennifer. 2013. "Crop of New Law Schools Opens Amid a Lawyer Glut." *Wall Street Journal,* January 31. http://online.wsj.com/article/SB10001424127887323926104578276301888284108.html.

Snyder, Thomas D. 1993. *120 Years of American Education: A Statistical Portrait.* Washington: National Center for Education Statistics. http://nces.ed.gov/pubs93/93442.pdf.

Sperling, John. 2000. *Rebel with a Cause: The Entrepreneur Who Created the University of Phoenix and the For-Profit Revolution in Higher Education.* New York: Wiley.

Stainburn, Samantha. 2009. "Promises, Promises." *New York Times,* November 1, ED12.

Stedman, James B. 1975. "Federal Student Loan Programs: 1958–74." *CRS Report for Congress* (Congressional Research Service).

Steinhorn, Leonard. 2006. *The Greater Generation: In Defense of the Baby Boom Legacy.* New York: St. Martin's.

Sternberg, Robert J. 2013. "Giving Employers What They Don't Really Want." *Chronicle of Higher Education,* June 17. http://chronicle.com/article/Giving-Employers-What-They/139877/.

Stockman, David A. 1986. *The Triumph of Politics: How the Reagan Revolution Failed.* New York: Harper & Row.

Stockwell, Anne. 1997. *The Guerilla Guide to Mastering Student Loan Debt.* New York: HarperCollins.

Stoll, Adam. 2001. "The Role the Federal Student Loan Programs Play in Supporting Postsecondary Students." *CRS Report for Congress* (Congressional Research Service, March 12).

Stone, Charley, Carl Van Horn, and Cliff Zukin. 2012. "Chasing the American Dream: Recent College Graduates and the Great Recession." *Worktrends,* John J. Heldrich Center for Workforce Development. www.heldrich.rutgers.edu/sites/default/files/content/Chasing_American_Dream_Report.pdf.

Stratford, Michael. 2013. "Public Hearing on College Ratings." *Inside Higher Ed,* November7.www.insidehighered.com/news/2013/11/07/education-department-kicks-public-hearings-college-ratings-system.

Stratford, Michael, and Paul Fain. 2013. "Agree to Disagree." *Inside Higher Ed,* September10.www.insidehighered.com/news/2013/09/10/gainful-employment-negotiators-face-long-odds-reaching-consensus.

Surowiecki, James. 2007. "Rent-Seekers." *New Yorker,* August 13, 28.

Taibbi, Matt. 2013. "Ripping Off Young America: The College-Loan Scandal." *Rolling Stone,* August 15. www.rollingstone.com/politics/news/ripping-off-young-america-the-college-loan-scandal-20130815.

Taylor, Mark C. 2012. "How Competition Is Killing Higher Education." *Bloomberg.com,* May 17. www.bloomberg.com/news/2012-05-17/competition-is-killing-higher-education-part-1-.html.

Thomas, Elbert D. 1950. "Federal Aid to Higher Education." *Journal of Higher Education* 21: 339–43.

Tierney, Michael L. 1980. "The Impact of Financial Aid on Student Demand for Public/Private Higher Education." *Journal of Higher Education* 51: 527–45.

Time. 1966. "Money for All—Somewhere." October 14, 112, 114.

———. 1971. "Learn Now, Pay Later." February 1, 57.

———. 1981. "Making College More Costly." March 23, 89.

———. 2011. "Is College Worth It?" May 30, 16.

Titus, Marvin A. 2005. "National Center for Education Statistics: Supplemental Table Update, January 2002." In *Federal Student Loans Revisited,* edited by Lydia N. Vedmas, 127–59. New York: Novinka.

Toby, Jackson. 2012. *The Lowering of Higher Education in America: Why Student Loans Should Be Based on Credit Worthiness.* Rev. ed. New Brunswick, NJ: Transaction.

Tolchin, Martin. 1958. "Joe College Due to Major in 'Practical Economics.'" *New York Times,* October 8, 39.

Traub, James. 1997. "Drive-Thru U." *New Yorker,* October 20, 114, 116–18, 120–22.

Tuchman, Gaye. 2011. *Wannabe U: Inside the Corporate University.* Chicago: University of Chicago Press.

Urban, Wayne J. 2010. *More Than Science and Sputnik: The National Defense Education Act of 1958*. Tuscaloosa: University of Alabama Press.

U.S. Census Bureau. 2003. "Education Summary—High School Graduates, and College Enrollment and Degrees: 1900–2001." www.census.gov/statab /hist/HS-21.pdf.

———. 2012a. "Current Population Survey Data on Educational Attainment." www.census.gov/hhes/socdemo/education/data/cps/index.html.

———. 2012b. *2012 Statistical Abstract*. www.census.gov/compendia/statab/.

U.S. Government Accountability Office. 2013. "VA Education Benefits: Student Characteristics and Outcomes Vary across Schools." Report to Congressional Requesters. www.gao.gov/assets/660/656204.pdf.

U.S. House of Representatives. 1965. *Higher Education Act of 1965*. Hearings Held by the Special Subcommittee of Education, Committee on Education and Labor, 89th Cong., 1st sess., February 1–May 1.

———. 1973. *Higher Education Loan Programs*. Hearings Held by the Special Subcommittee of Education, Committee on Education and Labor, 93rd Cong., 1st and 2nd sess., April 3–July 26, 1973; February 5–13, 1974.

———. 1988. *Defaults in the Federal Guaranteed Student Loan Program*. Hearings before the Subcommittee on Postsecondary Education, Committee on Education and Labor, 100th Cong., 2nd sess., June 14, 16.

———. 1995. *Hearing on Federal Student Loan Programs*. Hearing before the Subcommittee on Oversight and Investigations, Committee on Economic and Educational Opportunities, 104th Cong., 1st sess., May 23.

U.S. News & World Report. 1957. "How a College Student Can Get a Loan." August 30, 77.

———. 1977. "Time of Reckoning for Student Deadbeats." July 18, 21.

———. 1987. "A 'Pay Up or Else' Ultimatum from William Bennett." November 16, 16.

U.S. Senate. 1965. *Higher Education Act of 1965*. Hearings Held by the Subcommittee on Education, Committee on Labor and Public Welfare, 89th Cong., 1st sess., March 16–June 11.

———. 1974. *Examination of the Guaranteed Student Loan Program, 1974*. Hearings Held by the Subcommittee on Education, Committee on Labor and Public Welfare, 93rd Cong., 2nd sess., September 15–19.

———. 1975a. *Guaranteed Student Loan Program*. Hearings held by the Subcommittee on Investigations, Committee on Government Operations, 94th Cong., 1st sess., November 14–December 16.

————. 1975b. *Student Loan Programs*. Hearing before a Subcommittee of the Committee on Appropriations, 94th Cong., 1st sess., October 17.

————. 1987. *Problems of Default in the Guaranteed Student Loan Program*. Hearings before the Subcommittee on Education, Arts, and Humanities, Committee on Labor and Human Resources, 100th Cong., 1st sess., December 11, 18.

————. 1990. *Abuses in Federal Student Loan Programs*. Hearings held by the Permanent Subcommittee on Investigations, Committee on Governmental Affairs, 101st Cong., 2d sess., February 20, 26.

————. 2012. *For Profit Higher Education: The Failure to Safeguard the Federal Investment and Ensure Student Success*. Staff report for the Health, Education, Labor and Pensions Committee. www.help.senate.gov/imo/media/for_profit_report/PartI-PartIII-SelectedAppendixes.pdf.

Vedder, Richard. 2013a. "Colleges' Stealth Tax on Family Savings." *Bloomberg.com*, July 7. www.bloomberg.com/news/2013-07-07/colleges-stealth-tax-on-family-savings.html.

————. 2013b. "College Costs Will Keep Rising under Obama Plan." *Bloomberg.com*, August 22. www.bloomberg.com/news/2013-08-22/college-costs-will-keep-rising-under-obama-plan.html.

Wang, Jeff, and Jing J. Xiao. 2009. "Buying Behavior, Social Support and Credit Card Indebtedness of College Students." *International Journal of Consumer Studies* 33: 2–10.

Wang, Marian, Beckie Supiano, and Andrea Fuller. 2012. "The Parent Loan Trap." *Chronicle of Higher Education*, October 4. http://chronicle.com/article/The-Parent-Plus-Trap/134844.

Wang, Penelope. 2008. "Is College Still Worth the Price?" *Money*, September, 86.

Warren, Elizabeth, and Amelia Warren Tyagi. 2003. *The Two-Income Trap: Why Middle-Class Mothers and Fathers Are Going Broke*. New York: Basic.

Weisman, Jonathan, and Shailagh Murray. 2005. "GOP Leaders Agree to $41.6 Billion Spending Cut." *Washington Post*, December 19, A9.

Whitsett, Healey C. 2012. *High Debt, Low Information: A Survey of Student Loan Borrowers*. NERA Economic Consulting, March 21. www.nera.com/nera-files/PUB_Student_Loans_0312.pdf.

Wildavsky, Ben. 2012. "For-Profit Lessons for All." *Inside Higher Ed*, March 1. www.insidehighered.com/views/2012/03/01/essay-what-nonprofit-higher-ed-can-learn-profit-sector.

Williams, Jeffrey J. 2012. "Academic Freedom and Indentured Students." *Academe*, January–February, 1–15.

Wilms, Wellford W., Richard W. Moore, and Roger E. Bolus. 1987. "Whose Fault Is Default? A Study of the Impact of Student Characteristics and Institutional Practices on Guaranteed Student Loan Default Rates in California." *Educational Evaluation and Policy Analysis* 9: 41–54.

Wilson, John T. 1983. *Academic Science, Higher Education, and the Federal Government, 1950–1983.* Chicago: University of Chicago Press.

Wingert, Pat. 2007. "Student-Loan Secrets." *Newsweek,* April 16, 41.

Witkin, Gordon. 1987. "The Bad Business of Student Loans." *U.S. News & World Report,* September 14, 32.

Wood, Peter W. 2011. "The Higher Education Bubble." *Society* 48 (May/June): 208–12.

Yoder, Amos. 1963. "Lessons of the GI Bill." *Phi Delta Kappan* 44: 342–45.

Yoon, Al. 2013. "Investors Say No to Sallie Mae Bond Deal." *Wall Street Journal,* April 25. http://online.wsj.com/article/SB10001424127887323.

Zaback, Katie, Andy Carlson, and Matt Crellin. 2012. "The Economic Benefit of Postsecondary Degrees: A State and National Level Analysis." State Higher Education Executive Officers. www.sheeo.org/sites/default/files/publications/Econ%20Benefit%20of%20Degrees%20Report%20with%20Appendices.pdf.

Zaitchik, Alexander. 2012. "Protesters' New Front: Americans Have Finally Awakened to the Decades-Long Corruption of Higher Education." *Salon.com,* April 23. www.salon.com/2012/04/23/protesters_furious_new_front/.

Zelizer, Vivianna A. 1985. *Pricing the Priceless Child.* New York: Basic Books.

Zumeta, William. 2004. "State Higher Education Financing: Demand Imperatives Meet Structural, Cyclical, and Political Constraints." In *Public Funding of Higher Education: Changing Contexts and New Rationales,* edited by Edward P. St. John and Michael D. Parsons, 79–107. Baltimore, MD: Johns Hopkins University Press.

INDEX